Crossing Boundaries

Crossing Boundaries

Cultural, legal, historical and practice issues in native title

EDITED BY

Sandy Toussaint

MELBOURNE UNIVERSITY PRESS

MELBOURNE UNIVERSITY PRESS
an imprint of Melbourne University Publishing Ltd
PO Box 1167, Carlton, Victoria 3053, Australia
mup-info@unimelb.edu.au
www.mup.com.au

First published 2004

Typeset in 10 point Meridien by
Syarikat Seng Teik Sdn. Bhd., Malaysia
Cover designed by Traffic Design Studios
Printed and bound by CPI Group (UK) Ltd, Croydon, CR0 4YY

National Library of Australia Cataloguing-in-Publication entry

Crossing boundaries: cultural, legal, historical and practice issues in native title.

Bibliography.
Includes index.
ISBN 0 522 85074 X.

1. Native title (Australia). 2. Aboriginal Australians—Land tenure.
I. Toussaint, Sandy.

346.940432

This volume is dedicated to the memory of
Pingarri Bobby Kogolo, a Walmajarri man
committed to the land rights struggle.
A luta continua, *Pingarri.*

Contents

Contributors ix
Acknowledgments xii

Contextualising Native Title, and this Volume 1
Sandy Toussaint

1 Raising the Dead: Reflections on Native Title Process 9
Veronica Strang

2 Anthropology in Native Title Court Cases: 'Mere Pleading, Expert Opinion, or Hearsay'? 24
David Trigger

3 A Short Ride on a Time Machine: Linguistics, Cultural History and Native Title 34
Patrick McConvell

4 Method, Mechanism and Mindset: Collaborative Approaches in Native Title 50
Wendy Asche

5 Beyond Traditional Law: Better Native Title Service Provision 58
Jan Anderson

6 Designing Institutions in the 'Recognition Space' of Native Title 67
David Martin

7 Outsourced Professionals in Native Title Claim Research 77
Julie Finlayson and James Nugent

8 The Evolving Law of Native Title 86
Robert French

9 The Rules for Engagement 97
Fred Chaney

10 Confidentiality and Privilege: Legal Proceedings and Anthropological Research 105
Carolyn Tan

11 Nharnuwangga, Wajarri and Ngarlawangga Consent Determination 121
Philip Vincent

12 Lawyers and Rats: Critical Legal Theory and Native Title 128
David Ritter and Frances Flanagan

13 Reflecting on Past Practice: The Alice Springs Arrernte Claim 142
Mandy Paul

14 Three-legged Elephants: Native Title Histories 152
Neville Green

15 Working as a Barrister on the Miriuwung Gajerrong Native Title Claim 159
Michael Barker QC

16 Working as an Anthropologist on the Miriuwung Gajerrong Native Title Claim 176
Will Christensen

17 Working as a Historian on the Miriuwung Gajerrong Native Title Claim 195
Christine Choo

Afterword 202
Sandy Toussaint and Will Christensen

Notes 207
Bibliography 221
Index 231

Contributors

Jan Anderson is a PhD candidate in anthropology at the University of Western Australia. She has carried out consultant and academic research on land tenure in far north Queensland and Western Australia.

Wendy Asche is an anthropologist who has worked as the Native Title Research Officer at the Northern Land Council since 1996. She assisted in the Miriuwung Gajerrong and Croker Island cases and was a co-author of the anthropologists' report for the Township of Urapunga and St Vidgeon native title applications.

Michael Barker is a Queen's Counsel at the Western Australian Bar. He appeared as Senior Counsel for the Miriuwung Gajerrong native title claimants and on subsequent appeals.

Fred Chaney was involved in the Aboriginal Legal Service in a voluntary capacity in the early 1970s. He was Minister for Aboriginal Affairs from 1978 to 1980. He has been a Member of the National Native Title Tribunal since 1994 and is Co-Chair of Reconciliation Australia Ltd.

Christine Choo is an Honorary Research Fellow at the University of Western Australia, with degrees in social work, Australian studies and a PhD in history. As Historian with the Aboriginal Legal Service, she appeared as expert witness in litigation for native title claims in the Kimberley, Pilbara and Gascoyne districts. She has published widely on race and gender issues.

Will Christensen is the former Director of the John Curtin International Institute at Curtin University where he has been employed as Head of the School of Social Sciences and as Acting Dean of Humanities. Throughout 1999, he worked for the Aboriginal Legal Service as senior anthropologist on the Miriuwung Gajerrong native title claim.

Julie Finlayson is a consultant anthropologist with Anthropos Consulting Services in Canberra, and an independent scholar. She has worked as a senior anthropologist providing facilitation and assistance services to native title claimants in western Queensland, and has extensive experience in the area of consent determinations and the management and governance of Indigenous bodies.

Frances Flanagan is a legal officer at the Yamatji Land and Sea Council, where she is working on a number of claims in both the Yamatji and Pilbara regions. She has written a number of papers on native title, as well as various articles about European history, which have been published in both Australian and international journals.

Robert French has been a judge of the Federal Court of Australia since 1986. From May 1994 to December 1998 he was the inaugural President of the National Native Title Tribunal. He is a science and law graduate from the University of Western Australia, and a Founding Member and Chairman of the Aboriginal Legal Service of Western Australia from 1972 to 1975.

Neville Green is a graduate of the University of Western Australia. He has authored and co-edited a number of books on Aboriginal history and education including *Desert School, The Forrest River Massacres* and *Far from Home: Aboriginal Prisoners of Rottnest Island.*

Patrick McConvell is a Research Fellow in Language and Society at the Australian Institute of Aboriginal and Torres Straits Islander Studies. He has taught linguistics and anthropology for many years at Australian universities, and acted as principal anthropologist on six Northern Territory land claims, and the Girramay native title application for the Central Queensland Land Council.

David Martin is a consultant anthropologist and part-time research fellow at the Centre for Aboriginal Economic Policy Research at the Australian National University. With barrister Christos Mantziaris, he published a plain English guide and book on Prescribed Bodies Corporate as a result of research conducted for the National Native Title Tribunal.

James Nugent is a lawyer who lives and works in Alice Springs.

Mandy Paul is a consultant historian based in Adelaide. She has been involved in historical research for Native Title Representative Bodies since 1995, including four years as native title historian for the Central Land Council in Alice Springs. She is completing a doctorate at La Trobe University on land, race and gender in the history of the pastoral industry in Central Australia.

David Ritter is the Principal Legal Officer of the Yamatji Land and Sea Council, which is the Aboriginal Native Title Representative Body for the Murchison, Gascoyne and Pilbara regions of Western Australia. David is a co-author of the Butterworths Native Title Loose Leaf Service and has written numerous articles and conference papers dealing with the law and history of native title.

Veronica Strang is Professor of Anthropology at the Auckland University of Technology. Formerly the Royal Anthropological Institute 'Urgent Anthropology' Fellow at Goldsmiths University in London, and Senior Research Associate at the Pitt Rivers Museum in Oxford, she is the author of *Uncommon Ground: Cultural Landscapes and Environmental Values,* and continues to provide assistance on land-related matters for the Aboriginal community at Kowanyama.

Carolyn Tan is a lawyer and partner at Dwyer Durack Solicitors in Perth. She is an experienced native title and general litigation lawyer and has represented many Aboriginal groups in Western Australia and elsewhere around Australia in native title claims, future act matters and Aboriginal heritage agreements.

Sandy Toussaint is a senior lecturer in anthropology at the University of Western Australia. She has worked extensively with and for Kimberley Indigenous communities, especially on matters related to land, water and customary law. Publications include *Phyllis Kaberry and Me: Anthropology, History and Aboriginal Australia, Applied Anthropology in Australasia* (co-edited with Jim Taylor), and *A Jury of Whose Peers? An Examination of the Cultural Politics of Juries in Australia* (co-edited with Kate Auty).

David Trigger is a professor of anthropology and Director of the Centre for Anthropological Research at the University of Western Australia. Research interests encompass the significance of land and place for culture and identity. He has carried out more than twenty years of anthropological research on Indigenous systems of land tenure, including resource development negotiation and native title. Publications include *Whitefella Comin': Indigenous Responses to Colonialism in Northern Australia.*

Philip Vincent is a Perth barrister. He has had a considerable involvement in Indigenous legal matters in Western Australia, including as former Principal Legal Officer of the Aboriginal Legal Service in Western Australia. Philip acted as one of the counsel for the applicants in the Nharnnuwangga Wajarri Ngarlawangga application for determination of native title in the Federal Court, and in the negotiations for consent determination of that application.

Acknowledgements

MANY THANKS to the participants in the original conference in 2000, particularly those whose contributions are not obvious here: Greg Acciaioli, Kate Auty, Kim Barber, Jim Birckhead, Simon Davis, Mary Edmunds, Debbie Gittens, Marcia Langton, John Laurence, Dianna Newham, Nicolas Peterson, Peter Sutton, Bob Tonkinson, Michael Walsh and Ted Wilkes. I am grateful to John Henderson for his collegiality as co-convenor of the conference and to Mandy Wilson for helpful assistance on the manuscript draft. Gillian Hutcherson's editorial skills and wise counsel were invaluable with regard to final editing. I would also like to thank an anonymous reviewer for comments on the original manuscript. The Australian Institute of Aboriginal and Torres Strait Islander Studies made available a small grant toward organisation of the 2000 conference, and the Centre for Anthropological Research at the University of Western Australia funded editorial assistance.

Contextualising Native Title, and this Volume

THIS UNIQUE CROSS-DISCIPLINARY volume on legal, cultural, historical and practice issues in native title explores contemporary themes of relations to land, law and representation. Its precedent stems from June 1992 when the High Court found in favour of the Meriam people, custodians of the Island of Mer in the Torres Straits, in what is generally known as the *Mabo* decision.[1]

The *Mabo* decision was significant for many reasons. It recognised that customary laws in land had not been extinguished by the impact of colonisation on the Island of Mer. It established the principles whereby future native title claims might be made. It rejected the legal fiction of *terra nullius* that had underpinned Australia's colonial, moral and legal history for more than two centuries. The High Court's ruling also effectively overturned Blackburn J's 1970 decision in *Milirrpum v Nabalco* (also known as the Gove or Yirrkala case),[2] which had ruled that while Indigenous customary law continued to exist and have meaning for the Yolgnu in Arnhem Land, such law could not at that time be recognised by the Australian legal system.

On the basis of recognising customary laws in land, the High Court introduced a new title into Australia's property laws. While it was not immediately apparent in 1992, this belated recognition of Indigenous land tenure laws also introduced the potential for increasing professional engagement among anthropologists, linguists, historians and lawyers in a way that had not occurred before. The *Aboriginal Land Rights (Northern Territory) Act 1976* (Cwlth) had witnessed the emergence of cross-disciplinary work for claimant groups in the Northern Territory but, as many contributors to this volume show, native title has brought with it a new set of circumstances warranting a rethinking of past and present practices. Issues related to the recording and representation of Indigenous cultural beliefs, practices and laws are paramount here.

Recognition of native title was the first form of land title in Australia that had not emerged from European notions of property ownership. Native title exists only for and can only be claimed by Indigenous peoples. In keeping with the principles enshrined in the *Mabo* decision, the onus is on Indigenous claimants to prove that they have a right to claim native title by showing that an individual or group can demonstrate a continuing connection with the land consistent with Indigenous use (for instance, by continuous possession, residence and/or that rights in land have been conferred by customary laws). Proving, in accordance with legislative requirements, that native title has not been extinguished has been and continues to be one of the most difficult matters facing Aboriginal and Islander claimants, especially those groups most directly affected by colonisation and dispossession.

Some of the principles enshrined in the *Mabo* decision were translated into legislation in 1993 through the creation of the *Native Title Act 1993* (Cwlth) (implemented in January 1994). Unalienated Crown land, some national parks, and reserved Aboriginal land were generally regarded as areas that would most readily engender successful native title claims.

Since its implementation, the Native Title Act has established the National Native Title Tribunal, with a head office in Perth and other offices throughout the country.

The High Court's *Mabo* judgment was unclear whether pastoral leases extinguished native title. In the later *Wik* decision, it found that the granting of a pastoral lease did not necessarily extinguish native title.[3] The High Court judges decreed, however, that where there was a conflict of interest, the pastoral lease would usually take precedence over native title. The *Racial Discrimination Act 1975* (Cwlth) proved valuable with respect to *Wik*, as it had done in the original *Mabo* decision. The High Court ruled that some governmental acts (such as a pastoral lease) that had occurred after the implementation of the Act (on 31 October 1975) may have been invalid resulting in the nature of extinguishment becoming an area of contestation. On the other hand, most past acts of government (public works, freehold title, commercial lease) were defined as having extinguished native title. In the *Miriuwung Gajerrong* case, the High Court determined that pastoral leases could extinguish native title when use of the lands was determined as 'inconsistent' with Indigenous beliefs and practices.[4]

The Native Title Act has continued to evolve since 1993. It has also been amended by a conservative federal government on several occasions, especially in 1998. A document titled 'The 10 Point Plan' outlined the amendments. These have undoubtedly diverged from the principles enshrined in the *Mabo* decision and resulted in difficult consequences for claimant groups, and for those who work with them on the preparation and submission of a claim. For example, one of the amendments now requires Indigenous claimant groups to lodge claims through particular Native Title Representative Bodies rather than through their own local representative group, and claims are more readily directed to the Federal Court.

Native title has become an increasingly significant issue in many people's lives, including with respect to the wider society, media interest and processes of reconciliation, such as that evident in the national group, Australians for Native Title and Reconciliation. Native title has also generated complex areas of historical, legal, cultural, linguistic and methodological debate and interpretation, such as how and why Indigenous cultural beliefs and practices relate to land and continue from the past into the present. Other issues include the basis for the extinguishment of native title, and the cross-cultural reliability of oral and archival evidence. A stark example of a range of issues can be seen in *Yorta Yorta Aboriginal Community v Victoria* in 1998, where Olney J privileged the nineteenth-century writings of squatter and amateur historian Edward Curr to find that native title had been extinguished. That Olney judged Curr's historical material to be more persuasive than Yorta Yorta testimony and the complementary accounts prepared by anthropologists, historians, linguists and legal counsel represents a significant matter for native title claimants and those who work with them on the preparation and submission of claims.[5]

Practitioners and theorists within disciplinary fields such as anthropology and law increasingly appreciate that not only do claimant groups and the legal requirements of the Native Title Act demand individual and professional assistance, but also the professions themselves need to be open to learning more from each other, especially about how they might work more effectively together in a field clearly reliant on productive cross-disciplinary knowledge, expertise and practice.

For this reason, in September 2000 linguist John Henderson and I convened a two-day national conference titled Crossing Boundaries: Anthropology, Linguistics, History and Law in Native Title at the University of Western Australia. Our aim was to create a forum whereby those from disciplinary backgrounds most involved with and experienced in native title could come together to debate, listen, question and learn. Crossing Boundaries drew on ideas, experiences and skills from individuals actually working within a variety of settings, including members of claimant groups, and representatives from the National Native Title Tribunal, land councils, sectors of government and industry, the Australian Institute of Aboriginal and Torres Strait Islander Studies, the Aboriginal and Torres Strait Islander Commission, universities and professional organisations. Independent scholars, practitioners and students were also involved and added their perspectives to the vitality and richness of the forum.

Chapters in this volume reveal the extent to which native title workers need to communicate more cogently and, in some cases, to redefine their practice. How history is interpreted and by whom presents a case in point. While lawyer Fred Chaney cites the need to find a new paradigm by identifying native title as representing a break with the past, anthropologist Veronica Strang shows that representations of a past that continues to have intrinsic meaning in the present is central to Indigenous identity. Included in this is how claimant groups articulate relations to land and water. Under the operation of the Native Title Act it has become apparent that the legal cultures of the state and Indigenous customary laws, and the way that these cultures are represented are not easily reconciled. The constant possibility that Indigenous rights and interests in land will be absorbed by multiple legal relations and requirements has also appeared. David Martin, in a chapter premised on an appreciation that the 1992 *Mabo* decision and the 1993 Native Title Act emerged from a post-colonial legal discourse, is critical of imposed structures that bear little resemblance to Indigenous legal and political frameworks. He foreshadows problems associated with the implications of the 'juridification' of Indigenous relations. Julie Finlayson and James Nugent are also concerned with the imposition of structures (such as Native Title Representative Bodies) that have arisen because of requirements embedded in a Native Title Act dramatically amended in 1998. Legislative requirements rarely mirror Indigenous social and political organisations in Indigenous Australian settings.

Anthropologist David Trigger's view that the state could benefit by incorporating the way in which Indigenous claimants themselves describe cultural and political interests in land also finds some resonance with other contributors. Trigger makes the point that one of anthropology's most urgent tasks is to demonstrate to the courts the reliability and rigour that go into anthropological fieldwork and analysis. Finlayson and Nugent urge anthropologists, linguists and historians to be more prepared for the adversarial circumstances in which native title work generally occurs, a point also addressed by historians Mandy Paul (on the Arrernte claim[6]), and Christine Choo (on the Miriuwung Gajerrong claim).

Lawyer Carolyn Tan takes a slightly different position. Tan describes the need for anthropologists and other expert witnesses to be prepared to meet the demands of court procedures. As someone who works within the legal requirements of the Native Title Act, Tan discusses confidentiality and privilege as legal doctrines. Her chapter ponders the sorts of dilemmas raised by Trigger and others, including the potential for anthropological reports and associated field notes to be subpoenaed. Unlike those anthropologists who work closely with Indigenous groups and are bound by a certain code of ethics and social and cultural etiquette, Tan argues that an examination of the state's 'rules' of evidence should occur as attention to these might be the best way to protect the aspirations of native title claimants. She takes readers through the legal doctrines involved in the protection of knowledge, such as issues of privilege (including a waiver of privilege) and the possibility of litigation. Citing case law and the doctrine of public interest immunity, Tan claims that the law continues to develop and remains in an uncertain state.

That native title law continues to evolve is also discussed by former National Native Title Tribunal President Robert French, who describes it as still 'young enough to accommodate change'. In a chapter that draws attention to the 2002 appeal decisions in the Miriuwung Gajerrong case and Yorta Yorta, French explains that a legal and conceptual shift from a prior emphasis on common law has occurred. He concludes that while these decisions have undoubtedly been discouraging to native title applicants, there is still room for 'negotiation, agreement and positive outcomes'. Lawyers David Ritter and Frances Flanagan take a slightly divergent path, discussing uncertainty as a potential resource for Aboriginal people in mediating and litigating native title matters. Ritter and Flanagan ruminate on the need for lawyers to adopt a critical approach to the application of legal theory and method. Observing that the field of native title is predominantly 'legal', they note that some lawyers misunderstand or fail to acknowledge the instructive cultural role and analyses of historians, anthropologists and others. This point is also raised by Finlayson and Nugent, who stress that most lawyers have little understanding of what anthropologists and linguists actually do.

Philip Vincent, a lawyer with a long history of involvement in the field of Indigenous land claims, discusses the process that led to the Nharnuwangga, Wajarri and Ngarlawangga people's claim in Western Australia.[7] In his view, there is a need for native title interests to be 'balanced'; resolutions should involve pragmatic 'goodwill' from all parties, including among the Indigenous groups and professionals who work on the preparation and presentation of a claim. The example of the Nharnuwangga, Wajarri and Ngarlawangga 'consent determination', presided over by Madgwick J, shows how Indigenous groups, pastoralists and representatives from the mining industry worked together to reconcile a range of co-existent interests. The 'consent determination' approach, however, suggests only tacit acknowledgement of native title and carries with it what some describe as a weakened form of native title rights.

Focusing on the Arrernte claim in Central Australia, historian Mandy Paul draws metaphorically on the expression to 'push back the boundaries of the court' in her discussion on how law and history might work together more productively. Paul explains these disciplines as emerging from different systems of knowledge and maintaining different discursive practices. Critical of lawyers who seek 'positivist' historians to provide concrete chronological time-lines, Paul explores the absences in the written historical record, finding meaning through filtering devices throughout the extant records. Paul also suggests guidelines for a better working relationship among the disciplines, including that all parties should recognise one another's skills, regularly exchange information among themselves and with Indigenous applicants, and prepare joint reports. Historian Neville Green also presents guidelines on how practitioners involved in native title might produce histories that are fully contextualised. Unlike Paul (and sharing some similarities with the concerns of Tan), Green argues for the writing of a history that will meet the stringent demands of the court. Conceptualised this way, the questions of how research is undertaken, and how and by whom evidence is presented in court again arise.

Linguist Patrick McConvell stresses that some native title claims can 'crucially hang' on questions of language. Adopting an approach he calls 'linguistic stratigraphy', McConvell demonstrates how important it is for those involved in cultural research and the preparation of reports with Indigenous claimants to include treatment of language issues, including translation and interpretation, and analysis of linguistic shifts. Concerned to identify the relationships between language, culture and Indigenous affiliations to land and water, McConvell shows that such relationships are not always present in a claim's construction. This absence and a failure to attend to linguistic change over time can result in a lack of sensitivity to Indigenous systems of customary law; they also have the potential to misrepresent a claimant group's land tenure interests.

In the 1998 Miriuwung Gajerrong claim, Lee J found in favour of the applicants with respect to most of their claim in the East Kimberley, a finding that Western Australia appealed.[8] Michael Barker QC, anthropologist Will Christensen and historian Christine Choo present a unique insight into working together on the first stage of the claim through the Aboriginal Legal Service. They provide substantive detail on methods and some of the more complex political native title processes. Barker also highlights the way ambiguous aspects of native title law continue to hamper the work of many professionals engaged in native title research applications. The importance of managing the claim and the benefits and limitations of working across disciplinary boundaries are considered. Each author argues that while primacy should always be given to the evidence of the claimants, the expert witnesses' accounts in the Miriuwung Gajerrong claim clearly strengthened the Indigenous applicants' position.

Will Christensen's reflexive contemplation on methods and politics raises a number of significant practice issues. He highlights three matters that might result in a successful claim: rigorous scholarship, consistent corroboration, and a heavy reliance upon the claimants' direct testimony. Christensen's emphases are not dissimilar to Christine Choo's; she explains how crucial it is for expert witnesses to be prepared for detailed legal interrogation with respect not only to reports prepared on behalf of native title claimants, but also to representative disciplinary methods. As Choo discerns, it was not only her evidence that was put on trial in the Miriuwung Gajerrong claim, but also her discipline. This adversarial nature of native title practice clearly affects not only historians, but also Indigenous claimants. In Strang's analysis, this outcome is one of the most vexatious aspects of native title. As Strang describes in an evocatively titled chapter, 'Raising the Dead', claimants are required to demonstrate the continuation of cultural beliefs and behaviours, some of which necessitate revisiting places associated with the death of loved ones. While claimants often relive emotional stress in a process aimed at restoring legal recognition of their lands, outsiders rarely appreciate the circumstances in which the sorrow is evoked, and the on-site experience does not always result in a successful native title outcome.

Some contributors, such as Paul and Green, make suggestions on how historians might reflect on their own methods as well as engage more critically and confidently with legal colleagues. Anthropologists and linguists such as Christensen, Trigger, McConvell, Martin and Finlayson emphasise the importance of ensuring that complex cultural research in native title continues to be undertaken with adherence to the discipline's aims and integrity, especially the epistemological means whereby Indigenous claimants have the opportunity to represent their own system of land tenure laws. Yet others, such as French, Tan, Chaney and Barker, have formed the view that while the legal requirements of the Native Title Act may not be entirely satisfactory, the legal process surrounding native title has been established, albeit in a state of evolution. Ritter and Flanagan, on the other hand, are concerned to instil a critical, questioning legal process, especially with respect to recognition of Indigenous testimony and the supporting evidence of expert witness accounts. However, as Jan Anderson and Wendy Asche describe from their land council vantage points, questioning the legal process surrounding native title can sometimes be counter-productive.

The contributors to this volume make plain that there is much more room for conversation and action across the disciplines. It is also evident that each discipline needs to undertake some reflection on its own foundations, practices and theories. While some contributors argue for the need to concentrate solely on the rights and aspirations of Indigenous claimants and the expansion of debate on the presentation of cultural evidence in court, others suggest ways in which anthropologists, linguists and historians might work more effectively together and with lawyers on native title claims. Yet others make distinctions between those anthropologists and historians who work for the state, often in opposition to the stated interests of claimant groups and their own professional code of ethics. Matters circumventing objectivity and subjectivity permeate this volume, revealing not only the complex nature of crossing disciplinary boundaries, but also the centrality of native title, and the broader aspects of Indigenous and non-Indigenous relations and reconciliation in Australian cultural life.

Sandy Toussaint

1

Raising the Dead: Reflections on Native Title Process

Veronica Strang

IN 2000, IN THE ABORIGINAL community of Kowanyama in far north Queensland, the traditional owners of the Alice-Mitchell National Park area initiated a meeting with senior members of the Queensland National Parks and Wildlife Service. The Aboriginal group's objective was to affirm their rights as owners and managers of the park and to establish a basis for joint management. The preparation for this meeting and the event itself illustrate some of the issues involved in native title process.

The cultural landscape depicted in the interaction was inevitably heavily influenced by particular political and legal realities. It was constrained, for example, by knowledge about opposition in the National Parks Service (enshrined in its legislative foundations) to the economic use of resources within national park areas, and by a keen awareness of the legal requirements for native title claims. Thus, the reified cultural landscape presented to the 'outsiders', the Queensland National Parks people, was significantly different from the community's usual interactions with country. Such exercises—and their regular repetition throughout the lengthy development of a land claim—raise major questions about the effects on Aboriginal people of engagement with the native title process, and its influence upon their relationship with the land.

Reflecting on engagement

> We feel so small . . . so sad. About our land. We [are] the saddest people in this land, Aboriginal people. It really hurts people inside . . . We all the time listen

> to Government and what they are going to do to us . . . I can feel'm [Government] that chain still round that neck mine. Still round [my] leg like a hobble . . . Today it is still there. Just like a hobbled horse we![1]

Kowanyama is an Aboriginal community on the western coast of the Cape York Peninsula. Since first visiting the area in 1982, I have conducted several long-term ethnographic projects (from 1992 to 1994, and in 2000), which have included assisting the Kunjen people in mapping their traditional[2] country. Much of their land is in the Alice-Mitchell National Park area and to the north of the Alice River. The research also involved recording meetings between members of the community and other interest groups.

Conflicts and negotiations over land are, of course, framed by the problematic relationship between Aboriginal people and the wider Australian society. On the basis of quite straightforward indicators, such as life span, health issues, access to employment, housing conditions and other forms of disadvantage,[3] the Indigenous minority, which is less than 2 per cent of the Australian population, inhabits a position of considerable inequality in social and economic terms. This inequality is similarly expressed in the disempowering position of welfare dependency that characterises many Aboriginal communities. As Bennett asserts: 'Not the least of the negatives affecting Aborigines' place in the economy is the dependence upon welfare that has developed over time . . . such welfare has shaped black-white relations quite dramatically'.[4]

Inevitably, representations of Aboriginality have developed in ways that demonstrate the disparity of this relationship. As Brunt puts it, identity politics is 'politics whose starting point is about recognising the degree to which political activity and effort involves a continuous process of making and remaking ourselves . . . *in relation to others*'.[5] Attwood and Arnold have pointed out (following Foucault) that all such representations are deeply affected by the dominance of European Australians, which enables what they describe as Aboriginalism: 'a mode of discourse which, like Edward Said's "Orientalism" produces authoritative and essentialist "truths" about indigenes'. They go on to explain that: 'Aborigines have lost control over their identity. They are forever being called upon to fulfil what Aboriginalism has defined as the key characteristics of Aboriginality'.[6]

In considering the ways in which Aboriginal groups represent themselves, it is necessary to consider the dominant representational context in which such indigenous artefacts are produced. European-Australian representations of the indigenous 'Other' almost invariably situate Aboriginality in temporal terms, as signifying a pre-modern state of being. As Attwood and Arnold note, this can be evaluated positively (uncorrupted by modernity) or negatively (primitive).[7] Muecke draws attention to three major tropes in

European-Australian representations: the anthropological, the racist and the romantic.[8] These themes are utilised in different ways by different interest groups. For example, in the context of right-wing rural politics, representations of Aboriginality foreground ideas of 'primitiveness' and 'ineradicable weaknesses';[9] in a romantic vision of Aboriginality as a utopian symbol of pre-modernity, the emphasis is on 'ancient wisdom' and 'harmony with the land':

> There was a balance and a rightness to the world ... a knowledge of the environment which appreciated the role of renewal and regrowth ... Aboriginal people knew, loved and respected their land. It was their total raison d'etre. It was their source of spirituality and strength.[10]

Such visions of Aboriginality have been highly popular with the environmental movement, offering relief from an Australian identity heavily committed to 'triumphing over' nature rather than living in balance with it.

Other writers have advanced more psychological analyses, suggesting that Aboriginal people represent, for European-Australians, an answer to the angst of modernity—the sense of spiritual void or what P. Berger called 'homelessness'.[11] Lattas, for example, posits that Aboriginal people are presented as a 'form of redemption from the superficial nothingness which is seen to be invading the modern, western self'. Thus, he argues: 'The primitive provides that sense of historical depth which is perceived to be lacking in the Australian psyche ... In this discourse, Aboriginality becomes part of a quest for national authenticity'.[12] Going further along the pyschoanalytic route, Lattas also points to the idea of Aboriginality as an archetypal 'original' form, which therefore represents a collective unconscious or a pre-intellectual, subjective self. Westerners hope to regain the 'wholeness' lost to modernity by appropriating Aboriginality: 'As the unconscious of humanity, Aboriginal culture allows the white man to escape his own particularity and merge with others in a universal world'.[13] Taking a slightly different tack, Kapferer brings ideas of spiritual essence and uncorrupted morality together, suggesting that 'white Australians have constituted Aboriginal Australians as the conscience of the nation'.[14]

It is evident that all of these representational discourses, whether positive or negative, share the idea of Aboriginality as a prior state of being, a pre-modern ideal of spiritual completeness and secure identity rooted deep in the land. All of these tropes are impressed upon Aboriginal people. In effect, Aboriginal people are surrounded by a hall of distorting mirrors. Most of the images presented to them about themselves are based on the beliefs, hopes and desires of the larger and more powerful society. Their identity is thus colonised, and their choices restricted by deep disapprobation whenever they attempt to offer images of Aboriginality that fail to conform.[15]

Since the 1960s, political activists have challenged the restrictions of European-Australian representations of Aboriginality directly, as Sheridan has noted, by developing an alternative trope, one that emphasises Aboriginal survival and autonomy.[16] Today Aboriginal groups continue to work within the political arena as best they can, highly cogniscent of what Martin calls 'the politics of representation'.[17] Some groups have made astute use of romantic Western visions to occupy the moral high ground in conflicts over land and resources.

In reality, given that European representations of Aboriginal identity are the artefacts of a dominant society, most groups find that escaping them entirely is not possible. The legislation pertaining to Aboriginal issues is largely predicated upon concepts of Aboriginality drawn from their discourses, and this is particularly the case with relation to legislative conflicts over land, and the native title process itself. As Asche notes, in chapter 4 of this volume, and as Langton points out, the legitimacy of native title is 'derived from the authority of the past'; Povinelli comments that the legal criteria for regaining title to land demand precisely the kind of 'authentic' Aboriginality depicted in European-Australian formulations of Aboriginal identity, requiring claimants to demonstrate ancient ties and affective attachment to land[18]—with opponents to their claims arguing that this 'original' order has been 'washed away' in the tides of history. Thus, as observed by Ritchie among others, the effects of legislative engagement are often distortive: 'There is a body of anecdotal evidence that the very inquiries established under legislation which require an investigation of Aboriginal tradition become the catalysts for rapid change and redefinition of specific components of the tradition'.[19]

Even when outcomes are favourable, negotiated settlements often permit only 'traditional' rights of usufruct. This reality emerges, for example, in ongoing conflicts of Aboriginal use of land in the national parks, where opposition to hunting with guns is often accompanied by the comment that hunting with spears would be quite acceptable. In the same way, it is sometimes indicated that 'traditional' humpies might be tolerated in such areas, but not 'modern' forms of temporary or permanent settlement. Such discussions sometimes leave the impression that ochre-painted bodies would also be more welcome than those clad in baseball caps and jeans.

These pressures place severe restrictions upon what can be expressed as Aboriginality without incurring disapproval or hostility: the example of what is acceptable in national parks is just one illustration of the kinds of boundaries that are imposed. More critically, as Povinelli has argued, the meeting of such unrealistic and oversimplified expectations is essentially unattainable for Aboriginal people in the context of a contemporary industrial nation. As she points out, the 'hegemonic domination' of post-colonial societies 'works primarily by inspiring in the Indigenous subject a desire to identify with a lost indeterminable object—indeed to be the melancholic subject of traditions'.[20] Drawing on Freud's work on melancholia and identification with the past, Povinelli considers the emotional and intellectual costs of being required, constantly, to fulfil unrealistic demands: 'To be truly Aboriginal, Aboriginal persons must not just occupy a place in a semiotically determined social space: they must also identify with, desire to communicate (convey in words, practices and feelings), and to some satisfactory degree, lament the loss of the ancient customs that define(d) their difference'.[21] As such, Aboriginal people are directed, through an array of representational tropes, towards a position of mourning, of being the 'melancholic subjects' of a lost past.

The meeting between the Kunjen people and the National Parks officers shows how these pressures can emerge in practice, and how conforming to expectations to mourn 'lost culture' impinges upon people's interactions with their land. There is no real separation between political 'performances' of Aboriginality and continuing interactions with place: relations to land are necessarily permeated by the discourses in which Aboriginal people are engaged. Even the most pragmatic of activities, such as hunting, fishing or gathering, are inevitably coloured by the sociopolitical context in which they take place. Today many Aboriginal interactions with land involve representations to other groups of people: co-managers, tourists, scientists, legal advisors, other land users and of course anthropologists, whose exchange with Aboriginal communities often involves assisting in the construction of particular representational forms.

A meeting in the park

Kowanyama, a former Anglican mission, has been Aboriginal Land via a Deed of Grant in Trust agreement since 1987. The community contains several language groups, commonly described under three major headings: Yir Yoront, Kokobera and Kunjen. These groups have traditional lands extending far beyond the Deed of Grant in Trust area, into neighbouring cattle stations as well as encompassing the Alice-Mitchell National Park. The community recently lodged a large native title claim over these lands, and is now in the process of compiling evidence and constructing its case.

The national park itself became available for claim under the Queensland Aboriginal Land Act of 1991, but that Act requires the land to be leased back to the government immediately, and does not confer even such nominal title until a joint management plan for the area has been 'approved'. These terms are unacceptable to the traditional owners, and the park area is therefore included in their larger native title claim. Meanwhile, the Kunjen families who own land in the park area are involved in negotiations with the Queensland National Parks and Wildlife Service to agree on an interim management plan, with the native title claim providing a useful lever in these discussions. In August 2000, preparations were made for an initial meeting between the Kunjen people and some of the National Parks Service's leading officials.

One of Kowanyama's major strengths is a willingness to seize the initiative and reformulate its relationships with other groups. This is exemplified by the community's lead role in the creation of the Mitchell River Watershed Management Group over a decade ago. This initiative established the community as a major player in the management of the catchment area. The community has been negotiating with the National Parks Service since the mid-1990s but, although generally amicable, this interaction has rarely been on equal terms. The main aim of the August 2000 meeting, therefore, was not to discuss management issues—for example, the thorny questions about Aboriginal hunting, gathering and fishing in national parks, or the controversies about establishing homelands in such areas. Such proposals are strongly opposed by powerful lobby groups in Queensland and effectively prevented by existing legislation. Rather the purpose was to block discussion of the issues and focus instead upon two major goals: improving the National Parks officials' understanding of Aboriginal relations to land, and reconstituting the terms of engagement so that negotiations could take place on a much more equitable basis.

What followed was a representational work of art: a series of events beautifully designed to meet these goals. Prior to the meeting, the community, via its Aboriginal Land and Natural Resources Office, had made a couple of astute moves. First, it had persuaded the new director of the National Parks and Wildlife Service in Queensland, Ian McPhail, to come to a meeting in the national park itself (this was his first visit to the Alice-Mitchell area). His presence ensured the attendance of the regional director from Cairns and other key figures.

Second, a consultant, Viv Sinnamon, who had lived in the community for over twenty years, worked with the Kunjen elders to compile what they called a discussion paper about Aboriginal management of the park 'to begin discussions between the claimants and State of Queensland'.[22] This set out the framework that the traditional owners of the park area wanted to establish for the negotiation, outlined their objectives, and defined the issues in their own terms. It provided a history of the area and the various legal developments from their perspective. Perhaps most importantly, it provided an accessible description of their deep attachment to the land, drawing attention to their long-term ownership and intimate environmental knowledge. It gave a full historical account of their enforced dispossession and described their continued attachment to country and their retention of 'customary' beliefs and practices:

> The boundaries imposed upon the landscape by National Parks, pastoral leases and other kinds of land division have not stopped the people at Kowanyama from expressing their deep association with their country. The spirits of the departed continue to be sent to their home country regardless of what others may consider to be their land.[23]

The discussion paper underlined the much vaunted continuities in Aboriginal culture, but rejected any form of stasis, stressing processes of change and adaptation:

> Now we wear clothes and live a different life but we still have a culture handed down from our ancestors . . . Times have changed but it is clear from the evidence at the [preliminary claim] tribunal hearing that the Alice and Mitchell Rivers claimants do have a culture. It has persisted based upon the traditional knowledge and life ways of their ancestors.[24]

At the same time the document pushed the boundaries of reductive imposed representational forms by presenting a fuller picture, illustrating that the lived reality was much more complex. It described progress towards self-governance in the community and its efforts to be 'heard in local politics'. It considered the 'nuts and bolts' issues of contemporary land management and how that management, while changing, was still predicated on Aboriginal knowledge:

> Management of Aboriginal Country is shifting with the times but has the benefit of hindsight of many thousands of years of intimate knowledge by very close association with place. Times have changed. Issues of tourist numbers and resource management and research are no longer viewed as 'whitefella business'. They have become an important part of 'Aboriginal Management' and looking after country.[25]

Thus, at every turn, the paper attempted to make positive use of existing representational tropes, while in each case expanding or challenging these to assert the community's own beliefs, values and ideas about Aboriginal identity.

The stated purpose of the initial meeting with the Queensland National Parks and Wildlife Service officials was to make a formal presentation of this discussion paper. A few days before the meeting, the traditional owners sat down with their advisers from the Land Office (Viv Sinnamon, Gary Drewien and, in a more low-key role, myself), and considered a program of events for the day, and the messages they wanted to get across. First, they examined the list of National Parks people who were supposed to be arriving, carefully pinpointing the decision-makers to be targeted, and the potential trouble-makers, such as those known to be anti-hunting, who might impede the process of positive engagement.

Much of the discussion centred on how to 'change the ground rules' and the National Parks Service's ingrained perceptions of who was in charge of the park. There was an awareness that many of the National Parks employees would be keen to get on and negotiate practical management issues based on their assumptions that they were the primary managers. The Kunjen people were adamant that their priority was to 'slow them down and steady them up'—in other words, to take hold of the process much more firmly, and make it plain that this was not a matter of fitting into an existing management paradigm, but of creating a new one.

This, it was felt, would be accomplished by several methods: by forging a positive and equal relationship with the key visitors, the decision-makers; by providing them with a clear picture of the relationship between the traditional owners and their land; by blocking the discussion of any management issues for the time being, until a new dynamic was established; and by using the native title claim as a 'background' incentive to these negotiations. It was considered highly important that this crucial first meeting take place 'at home' on the Aboriginal land under discussion, and that the program should be designed and directed by the community in accord with its own priorities and styles of interaction.

A program of activities emerged. The first step would be to give the National Parks representatives a brief welcome in the Land and Natural Resources Office, with local Community Council members and Kunjen elders attending. The 'visitors' (carefully labelled as such) would therefore get a chance to see the well set up office through which the community in Kowanyama manages its land.

Much discussion went into who would then go with whom in which car on the long drive from Kowanyama out to the park itself. The emphasis was on the need for the visitors to be taken to the park by 'the right people'. It was decided that the major owners of the park area would lead the way in a vehicle driven by a senior Aboriginal ranger in the community, taking just the National Parks director and his second-in-command. The order of the following convoy reflected the importance or influence of each visitor and the seniority of the hosts, with the Aboriginal elders in the lead, and any potential National Parks 'troublemakers' way behind in a car by themselves, to prevent them, as one person said, from 'talking about things you don't want to talk about'. It was agreed that children and younger family members would also be encouraged to come along, to demonstrate the large number of people in Kowanyama with a traditional interest in the park area, and the intergenerational nature of that interest.

The journey was divided into two stages: the first stop was to be at a place called Igow, at the junction of the Alice and Mitchell rivers, near the crossing where the Jardine brothers, driving a herd of cattle north to establish the first pastoral station on Cape York in 1864, initiated the famous 'Battle of the Mitchell' in which at least thirty Aboriginal people were killed and many more were injured. As well as drawing attention to the contact history experienced by the Indigenous inhabitants, the site is just outside the national park, which stresses that the area owned by the Kunjen people is unrelated to the recently imposed boundaries of the park itself. It also serves as a reminder that the park is surrounded by Aboriginal land (having the Deed of Grant in Trust land to one side and Aboriginal-owned pastoral leases to the other), and it was felt that this would serve to highlight the logic of Aboriginal management of the relatively small park area.

At Igow, the visitors would be met by the elders most closely connected to this particular site and much of the national park area, and formally welcomed to their country, making the point that this was a visit to Aboriginal land, not the National Parks Service merely accompanying Aboriginal people to a park area. There would be a baptism ceremony—a 'head wetting'—to introduce the visitors to the ancestral land; the story for that place would be sung (in Indigenous language); and a gift would be given to the new National Parks director (an antique bush pannikin or cup made from a syrup tin with a home-made leather handle). This would be followed by a lunch hosted by the traditional owners, and it was decided that this would be done the 'bush way' with no chairs and tables, just a site under a shady tree on the banks of the river, with a billy on an open fire. It was felt that the visitors should also be given as much 'bush food' as possible during the day: damper, wallaby, catfish and, if possible, some freshwater crocodile, maybe cooked on the coals in the 'proper way'.

It was agreed that none of the 'park issues' should be discussed directly, and that this was just a preliminary to that negotiation—a day for 'talking and laughing', as it was described. However, there was a clear intention to lay good foundations for that process through the casual or elliptical discussion of key topics: an account of the Aboriginal history of the area, highlighting the fact that many of the most influential events are quite recent (for example, there are elders still living who lost grandparents in the massacres, or siblings in the removal of children); the drawing of attention to archaeological remains; the description of traditional uses of the local resources and so on. The greatest emphasis was given to the need to express the feeling that people have for the land. As one elder, Alma Wason, put it, 'we talk about our land, our love for our land' so that, as another said, 'they can see them people worried about their country'.

The second stage of the day would be the journey to one of the most important sites in the national park, Emu Lagoon, where there is a major camp site and an old cattle yard. A lot of discussion centred upon where around the lagoon the actual meeting place should be, and what the visitors should be shown. This was particularly sensitive, because the site had been closed for some time due to the death of one of the Kunjen elders, and it was agreed, rather tentatively, that an opening ceremony could be conducted on the day, as this would not only make it possible to hold the rest of the meeting there, but would also serve to teach the visitors about the 'meaning of country'. Following another 'head wetting' for that place, they would be given tea, and some damper baked by the women from that place. The baking would provide an opportunity to tell the visitors about an incident in the early 1900s in which settlers had poisoned the flour used by these women's families. It was decided to show them an important massacre site at the lagoon, and the cemetery that related to this act of genocide, at which several of the grandparents of the elders were buried. It is clear that the aim was not merely to meet with the National Parks employees on Aboriginal terms, but to lead the visitors gently into an engagement with an Indigenous cultural landscape.

On the day of the meeting the events proceeded more or less according to plan. The visitors arrived as a small group and, having been mustered at the land office, were carefully drafted out to various people. They were driven to Igow and, while being fed and watered, were led through an Aboriginal history of the site: how people used to swim the river to get to their country, how one elder's father cured the people given poisoned flour; the way in which people remained on their country by working for the cattle stations. A couple of the elders offered a Christian prayer, and chose to sing a church hymn (in language) to emphasise the oneness of all people.

The visitors were then driven in the carefully designed convoy into the national park where the ritual to open the country took place. The visitors were then 'baptised' at Emu Lagoon, and given some background to the historic sites. They were formally presented with the discussion paper, and there was an informal and very jovial ceremony in which a leading elder 'broke bread' with the National Parks director, sharing the damper cooked for the occasion, along with some jokes about it being poisoned. The proceedings then shifted along the lagoon to the site where a shallow trench marked the graves of the Kunjen people who had been massacred following the spearing of a horse. Here, the visitors were guided around the site, and were able to observe for themselves, the everyday style of the elders' ritual communication with their ancestors.

Apart from this and the solemn and emotive ceremony to open the country (the visitors were invited to follow this procession, but not to participate directly), the tone of the day was at all times welcoming and friendly. The often terrible contact history was related in an indirect rather than accusatory way, and great efforts were made to put the National Parks group at ease, and to construct a positive relationship with them. In the evening, they were driven back to the creek near town where a *cup mari* (sand oven) had been prepared, so that they could eat wallaby, catfish and some yabbies fresh from the creek.

The day appeared to have been a considerable success: by the end of it, the atmosphere had shifted from wary reserve to the most convivial of interactions. The visitors left promising to read the discussion paper with care, and the community felt confident that it would find its way onto the premier's desk within a week. The negotiations were clearly off to a good start, and it seemed that the difficult issues to be debated could now be approached in a fresh way.

Some important questions are raised by the representation that was constructed, and the way in which it necessarily foregrounded particular aspects of Aboriginal identity and relations to land while suppressing others. The difficult political issues surrounding the use of resources in national parks meant that everyday practical or economic interactions within these areas was barely mentioned. Because of a desire to control cultural information about the story places within the context of native title claims and joint management with the National Parks Service, the major ancestral story running through the Emu Lagoon site was referred to only in passing, and little reference was made to the many 'poison places'[26] en route to the lagoon. Instead, the representation focused very heavily on contact history and its harsh effects upon the local population.

The recounting of such events is a delicate matter between groups: too direct a discussion of genocide, maltreatment and dispossession can clearly be counterproductive, stimulating feelings of guilt and thus hostile commentaries about 'black armband history'.[27] However, the audience in this instance was largely sympathetic, and it seemed that the matter-of-fact delivery of the narratives, and the non-accusatory tone, enabled the visitors to gain real insights into the intense feelings that people hold for the land, and this was the primary message they had wanted to get across.

In Kowanyama, the meeting with the National Parks visitors was a singular event, and it would be overstating the case to suggest that it was entirely typical. The recent death of an elder connected with Emu Lagoon clearly coloured the occasion, and no doubt more down-to-earth discussions of everyday issues would follow as the negotiations progressed. However, the representations emphasising a theme of loss and victimhood do occur with regularity in Aboriginal interactions with other groups. It was clearly not considered by any means abnormal in this instance that in the micro-interactions between people, and in the representations about Aboriginal relations to place, most of the day was spent discussing the dead rather than the living. In a variety of ways, for well over a decade, people in Kowanyama have been constructing such representations to other groups in the area, and to the various representative bodies involved in ongoing dialogues about land. In recent years the members of the community have become more and more closely engaged in such interactions, to the extent that these now take up vast amounts of their time and energy. The Kunjen group's negotiations with the National Parks Service and the community's native title claim will probably run for a number of years more, requiring regular repetitions of these kinds of representational performances.

Raising the dead

Peter Whalley, from his experience working with the Queensland Land Council, commented to me that Indigenous culture in Australia readily encompasses the presence of the dead within the landscape. It is clear, in their everyday relationship with the land, that people in Kowanyama draw emotional and spiritual support from the belief that their ancestors and relatives remain with them, held in the land. This integration is nicely demonstrated in the discussion paper itself, in which the dedication reads:

> Three of our family has made the final journey home since the Government gazetted the Alice and Mitchell Rivers National Park for claim, the beginning of talks and our mapping of country. They are with us and watch over us as we begin our talks with the Government. This paper is dedicated to them.

For Aboriginal groups, an acknowledgment of ancestral presence remains integral to interactions with the land, and as anthropologist Marcia Langton pointed out to me 'all interactions with land are sacred' in this respect. Spiritual and social identity emerges from the ancestral forces that are 'held in place' and this stabilising basis for identity—envied by many Westerners in their representations of Aboriginality—appears to provide firm foundations for the construction of identity by contemporary Indigenous Australians.

However, such sustaining linkage with 'ancestral being' is a different matter from the kinds of representations and interactions with land that are required by the native title process, and in the wider political arena. Here, historical narratives increasingly depict instances of trauma, and involve social and psychological identification with the victims of violence and genocide. If such representational forms were rare, then their impact might only be slight. In the reality of modern conflicts over land, however, claims and successful negotiations about access and control are heavily dependent on such imagery. As a result they are now so regularly narrated that there must surely be recursive effects on Aboriginal identity and well-being. In some instances, where people have been moved far away from their own country, and access is impeded (by distance, lack of transport or opposition from those currently in control of the land), these kinds of interactions may even constitute a significant proportion of the opportunities that they have for visiting their own country. For example, Emu Lagoon is nearly five hours drive from Kowanyama, along roads that are extremely rough at best, and completely impassable for much of the year.

Perhaps more critically, such representations, even when counter-balanced by more 'normal' interactions with land, are made intensely powerful by their importance to the larger debates. They have become a central theme in the highly politicised narratives that describe Aboriginality. As Antze and Lambek note:

> We live in a time when memory has entered public discourse to an unprecedented degree. Memory is invoked to heal, to blame, to legitimate. It has become a major idiom in the construction of identity, both individual and collective, and a site of struggle as well as identification. Memory has found a prominent place in politics, both as a source of authority and as a means of attack . . .[28]

Because historical narratives are highly formative of identity, their reflexive influence is likely to be considerable. As Feldman points out:

> The self is always the artifact of prior received and newly constructed narratives. It is engendered through narration and fulfils a syntactical function in the life history . . . in a political culture, the self that narrates speaks from a position of having been narrated and edited by others—by political institutions, by concepts of historical causality, and possibly by violence.[29]

Turner has written extensively about the effects of performance upon the emotions, noting that 'past events remain inert unless the feelings originally bound up with them can be fully revived'.[30] This view is echoed by Schechner, who draws on Ekman's work about emotional responses to narrative performance. The powerfully inculcative effects of ritual performance have also been explored by Myerhoff who considered the role of ceremonies in the creation of collective 'autobiographies' of experience. The work of writers such as Feldman and Antze and Lambek makes it clear that the embodiment of experience, particularly that relating to trauma, is an inescapable part of the narratives of identity. As Bondi says, there is 'a need to resist claims that identity is infinitely fluid and malleable'.[31]

Histories of trauma and violence are thus integrated into the identities of the narrators, physically 'embodied' and embedded in their emotional and mental landscapes. In this way, they are positioned as victims and/or survivors; as inheritors of loss and grief. The negative effects of such identifications are amplified when the perceived perpetrators of the violence deny that such events occurred, or refuse to acknowledge responsibility, leaving many emotional issues unresolved. Increasingly, Indigenous people in Australia are drawing parallels between their lives and those of the survivors of the Jewish Holocaust and other genocides.

At the opening of the 2000 Crossing Boundaries conference on native title, Ted Wilkes, a local Aboriginal spokesperson, referred with pride to his community's survival of 'the holocaust of the last 171 years in this state'. Marcia Langton also drew a comparison between the issues faced by Aboriginal people and survivors of the Jewish Holocaust.[32] There are some useful parallels: like all 'survivors', Aboriginal people are faced with a real dilemma about the extent to which they choose to 'identify with' the victims. Some European refugees—albeit with limited success—have tried to distance themselves from their traumatic histories, adopting 'new identities' and attempting to deny the past. Others regard this as psychologically unhealthy and politically irresponsible, arguing that these narratives must be told 'lest we forget', and that reconciliation—both with 'the other' and with the memories themselves—is only possible through remembering.

'Letting go' of the past and adopting alternative identities is an even less viable option for Aboriginal people in Australia. A culture in which memory and identity are firmly held in the landscape is inevitably highly conservative and does not lend itself to post-modern fluidity. Powerful European-Australian concepts of Aboriginality, as well as Indigenous self-identifications also serve to close many alternative avenues. The social and political dynamics and effects of contact history remain a highly visible part of lived experience, and accounts of the violence and trauma of colonisation are vital elements in the battle to regain title to land. In the political arena, the Australian federal government's persistent refusal to make a symbolic apology for colonial actions is widely perceived as a denial of the past, and this too creates a stubborn obstacle to the 'letting go' that is integral to reconciliation.

Conclusions

Raising the dead is an effective strategy in dialogues about land, and a required focus within the legislative process. The dead impart considerable authority to Indigenous land claims and to the struggle for self-determination. While supportive in many respects, the continual evocation of the presence of the dead must surely weigh heavily upon the living. Many Aboriginal people have little choice but to confront, represent and emphasise repeatedly the harsh social, economic and emotional costs of their recent history. Placed within the context of current social issues in Aboriginal communities, in which untimely deaths and injuries, and the grief that these engender, are experienced all too often, it may be vital to confront the question as to whether a constant repetitive focus upon the most traumatic aspects of experience within the landscape affirms and embodies this sense of loss, and contributes to an identity of 'being a victim'.

Native title legislation is often presented as an empowering process, enabling Aboriginal people to regain their land and with it some kind of social and economic self-sufficiency. The ethnography presented here raises the question as to whether the representations required by the native title process, and by wider political exigencies, are not also disempowering, returning people continually to sites of grief and loss in their cultural landscapes and potentially undermining more sustaining constructions of Aboriginal identity.

2

Anthropology in Native Title Court Cases: 'Mere Pleading, Expert Opinion or Hearsay'?

David Trigger

IN THE CROKER ISLAND case (*Yarmirr v Northern Territory*), heard in 1998, Olney J commented on the anthropologists' report prepared by researchers engaged by the applicants. After referring to its usefulness in 'providing the contextual background against which the oral testimony of the applicants' witnesses can be better understood', Olney commented that: 'Whether or not a particular statement in the report is to be classified as mere pleading, as expert opinion or as hearsay is not always readily apparent'.[1]

Olney's comments were noted in a Western Australian case, *Daniel v Western Australia* (the Ngarluma/Yinjibarndi case), where respondents including the Crown objected to a question put to an expert anthropologist. Michael Robinson's opinion about which Aboriginal group held interests in a certain area (together with other statements by him), was objected to on the grounds that the opinion was based on hearsay evidence, that is on out-of-court statements by claimants who were available to give evidence in the court.[2]

From within the discipline of anthropology, the legal concern with the distinction between an expert opinion and hearsay is not particularly familiar. It is not a distinction given much attention in the training of social scientists, whether anthropologists, historians or linguists. Yet this goes to the heart of the relationship between the conclusions a researcher presents in a court case and the empirical basis for those conclusions. So how do the legal concepts of 'opinion' and 'hearsay' relate to the notions of 'conclusions' and 'data' in anthropology? This question traverses an intellectual border that has practical and theoretical implications for lawyers, anthropologists and other social scientists involved in native title claims.

Before we get to matters of opinion and hearsay, we should first consider Olney's initial suggestion, that some anthropological reportage is 'mere pleading'. What is a pleading in legal terms, and how might it be understood in anthropology? Osborn's *Concise Law Dictionary* indicates that pleadings are statements delivered alternately by parties until the questions of fact and law to be decided in a case have been ascertained. A pleading must state facts and not law, and must not state the evidence by which facts are to be proved. So when Olney refers to the possibility that certain statements in anthropological reportage may be 'mere pleading' I take it he means they may simply state one or more facts to be proved in the claim for native title. An example would presumably be a statement of the kind: 'The applicants have continued to acknowledge Indigenous laws and customs by which they are connected with the land'.

This is something that could be found in an anthropologist's report as well as a lawyer's pleading; but, in the two contexts, the statement arises from different professional bodies of specialist knowledge, and hence the question is whether it is appropriate to call it a pleading when it comes from an anthropologist. The lawyer will make such a pleading as an assertion to be supported by evidence; the anthropologist will give it as an opinion.

While in legal terms this is an opinion asserting a conclusion that is ultimately a matter for the court to decide, from an anthropological perspective it is an opinion that is an interpretation or a conclusion based on examination of a body of information; that is, information about the beliefs and practices of claimants (both at the time of the case and during earlier historical periods). Anthropological reportage surrounding such an opinion is more than a bald statement of the case the claimants intend to present (as in a lawyer's pleading), in that the anthropologist's report usually goes into considerable detail about the evidence likely to be forthcoming from claimant witnesses.

Furthermore, a lawyer prepares a pleading as a statement of a client's case, in the course of acting as an advocate representing the client; a lawyer's pleading thus entails the intention of convincing the court of the truth of the case. However, a researcher prepares a report as an expert who is an independent commentator on the laws and customs of the applicant group; anthropologists do not present their opinions as a form of advocacy, or at least not in the overt manner in which it is appropriate for a lawyer to do so. As I keep reminding my legal colleagues, anthropologists in this sense do not seek or receive 'instructions' from 'clients', but rather they carry out consultations, interviews and observations with those who inform their investigative research.

The Federal Court guidelines for expert witnesses indicate anthropologists and other social scientists ought not operate as advocates for any party and that their paramount duty is to the court rather than to the party retaining the expert. Ken Maddock, among others, has raised doubts about 'whether anthropologists invariably do their jobs with accuracy and objectivity', and has also commented that anthropologists in native title work 'may be tempted to become closet advocates'.[3] Ron Brunton has more bluntly asserted that the political commitment of some anthropologists to support certain Aboriginal interests is not in the closet at all, but is in fact carried out in a manner closer to the legal practice of seeking openly to further one's client's interests.[4]

Among those arguing a counter position, Nicolas Peterson has referred to anthropological 'professionalism, credibility and scholarship' (while acknowledging that Aboriginal people are unlikely to participate in research if it is perceived to be opposed to their interests), Mary Edmunds has pointed out that what is required in native title cases is 'fine-grained ethnographic material' with a commitment to 'absolute accuracy', and I myself have suggested that we would find little evidence of overt bias in the last twenty-five years of anthropologists' work on Aboriginal land and heritage cases in the context of courts, tribunals and inquiries.[5]

Nevertheless, this matter is complicated by the widely accepted proposition in social sciences such as anthropology that social research inevitably entails a degree of subjectivity on the part of the researcher; anthropological or historical studies, whether purely academic or destined from the beginning for an applied or practical purpose, can never be completely objective in the sense of being value free.[6] This is simply to acknowledge the subjectivity involved in interpreting human cultures and the constraints deriving from a researcher's own language and assumptions about the world; it is not to suggest that political neutrality is impossible in the research process, nor that the political commitment of a researcher cannot be suspended in order to apply methods of systematic investigation and thorough testing of possible generalisations and conclusions.[7]

Indeed, if anthropologists could not suspend political judgments, they may as well decline to be involved in court cases regarding native title. Graeme Neate has pointed out that little weight will be given to the evidence of expert witnesses who may be perceived in court to give an impression that they would accept as correct whatever an Indigenous person said (regardless of whether it contradicted other available information).[8] Of course, we would also expect the court to give little weight to evidence from an anthropologist or historian who appeared to pursue actively the interests of other parties responding to claims; allegations of bias or an inappropriate political agenda on the part of a researcher are hardly likely to be confined to those supportive of applicants' cases.

In summary, while individual researchers may vary in the degree to which they appear to adopt neutral positions in presenting the results of research, the overwhelming general expectation in the discipline of anthropology is that for conclusions to be sustainable among scholars, they must arise from reflective studies of all available information. In the case of anthropologists engaged by applicants, this mode of research may well include setting out in reports the basis upon which the applicants' claim is formulated, and, to refer to Olney's phrase, such statements may well be considered at least analogous to a pleading among legal practitioners.[9] However, among anthropologists this reportage will be regarded not as a pleading in any ordinary sense of that term, but as a body of analysis, interpretation and conclusions based on empirical investigations. The closest legal concept to these latter social science notions would seem to be that of expert opinion.

Here we become enmeshed in the legal distinction between reporting an 'opinion', and something else called 'hearsay'—the further aspect of Olney's characterisation of what it is that anthropologists present to the court. What sense do we make of this distinction in anthropology?

Expert opinion

The legal definition of expert opinion given in the *Evidence Act 1995* (Cwlth) (section 79) is that, unlike ordinary opinion evidence (which is not admissible in court), it is based wholly or substantially on specialised study, training and knowledge. From an anthropological perspective, professional opinions are derived from scholarly conclusions, generalisations and interpretations; opinions are based on both knowledge of general theories about human societies, and detailed observations of and conversations with members of one or more particular societies.[10]

By illustrating the legal concept of expert opinion, we can note the concern of Nicholson J in *Daniel v Western Australia* about whether to admit the evidence of an anthropologist when that evidence was based in part on statements from people who were able to be called as witnesses. That is, the judge was considering whether the key data used by anthropologists to inform the development of models and theories, namely talk among people who are the subjects of research, was admissible as part of an expert's opinion. Nicholson J appears to be more comfortable with general propositions from the expert that are descriptive of principles by which a society organises relationships among people and land, than with statements reporting what particular individuals may have said on this subject. To this extent, Nicholson followed Blackburn's discussion of expert evidence from anthropologists in the Gove case of 1970 (*Milirrpum v Nabalco*).[11]

This distinction between opinions and the empirical material on which they are based, may present a difficulty for anthropologists, for whom the task of ethnography outside the courtroom is commonly to describe social action, including people's language and speech in so far as these illustrate how they think and see the world. It would seem the court's notion of an expert opinion is that most appropriately it should comprise the conclusions of the anthropologist without the data; for much of the data or empirical descriptive materials are likely to be regarded in legal terms as hearsay.

What is hearsay?

In an informative discussion of admissibility, hearsay and weight of evidence in Northern Territory statutory land claims, Graeme Neate gives the general rule against hearsay: 'a witness will not be permitted to give evidence in court about what another person said in order to establish that what that other person said was true'. An exception is when an expert gives an opinion based in part on what he or she has heard or read. Neate points out that an anthropologist can give evidence about a 'proposition of anthropology', that is a conclusion that has significance in that field of discourse.[12] The grounds on which opinion evidence from anthropologists is admissible were discussed at some length by Blackburn in the Gove land rights case.[13]

The confusion for an anthropologist may be that Blackburn J commented that the court should actually ask how far an expert's conclusion is based on fact, and weigh the conclusion accordingly; according to the judge, the 'facts' include those established by the methods and terms of the expert's field of knowledge. How then does the anthropologist present an account of the 'facts' informing expert opinions, without those facts being regarded as hearsay, in so far as they are in the form of reporting what the researcher has been told in both informal conversations and more structured interviews?

While I am not aware of any resolution of this question that is as yet satisfying in both legal and anthropological terms, there are some sources that assist us further in understanding the legal perspective. Neate describes two types of expert evidence from an anthropologist, as discussed by Toohey J (in his report on the very first Northern Territory land claim). These are descriptions of the nature of the Aboriginal system of knowledge (involving such concepts as clans, territories, subsections and so on, as rendered in anthropological terminology), and accounts of what particular claimants had told the researcher about the location and features of their country.[14] The first are anthropological models or theories based to a large extent on what claimants have told the researcher. The second are hearsay, but admissible, Toohey said, because the information about particular claimants was relevant, and because the ordinary rules of evidence did not apply in statutory land claim hearings.

A narrower view was taken by Maurice J in the 1988 Warrumungu land claim. He distinguished between two sources that form the basis of anthropological evidence: observed behaviours among the researched community, and talk among them told to or overheard by the anthropologist. Maurice said accounts of observations could be part of an expert's evidence in court, but was not as comfortable with accounts of what the researcher had been told, for this was hearsay. Admitting hearsay as part of an expert's evidence involved, according to Maurice, the risk of denying the court and other parties the opportunity to 'confront and examine the person upon whose out-of-court assertions the proof of important facts may depend'.[15]

This view makes clear that the court regards itself as able to understand the facts of an Aboriginal land or native title claim. While this is probably self-evident from a legal standpoint, anthropologists face a resulting ambiguity about the sense in which the court accepts their standing as experts. Take, for example, a comment from a lawyer representing the state in a recent Western Australian native title case, which would seem to indicate a view that there is nothing particularly special in carrying out ethnographic research on the subject of Aboriginal cultures, or at least that no training in anthropology is required. In the course of arguing about the role of an anthropologist's evidence, the lawyer said to the judge: 'Your honour is the ethnographer at the moment. You will decide what all these people believe, what they assert, what they claim, what their beliefs are, what their myths are, all the rest of it'.[16] Earlier in the day, the same lawyer had suggested to the judge that many of the anthropologist's assertions were not expert opinions, but 'mere fact', ascertained 'not by any accepted research methodology', but by 'the common place technique' of asking claimants questions and recording their answers, or attending a meeting and recording what was said. Indeed, the lawyer opined, 'there is good ground for arguing that a solicitor would be better qualified than an anthropologist to give such evidence'.[17] This suggests that in adversarial trials about native title, some lawyers will not seek to inform themselves at all about the nature of anthropological training and knowledge, but rather simply seek to position expert opinion from anthropologists as marginal or irrelevant to the task facing the court.

Perhaps a more sympathetic interpretation is that the lawyer is unclear about the background knowledge the anthropologist brings to the task of understanding explanations of Aboriginal culture given by the claimants, including those who are witnesses. In suggesting the judge is the 'ethnographer', the lawyer might assume, without knowing much about how ethnographic research is done, that the court will have to make its own interpretations of what emerges from claimant witnesses, as it cannot go beyond this set of data in reaching a decision. On this matter, the challenge for anthropology would seem to be to explain why the relevant 'data' obtained by an anthropologist via ethnographic research over a period of time are likely to be more reliable than some of the evidence presented in adversarial proceedings; a judge cannot be 'an ethnographer' in the court room at all, and ethnography by definition involves lengthy immersion in a social milieu, as well as specialist background knowledge to bring to the task of understanding systems of law and culture that are very different from mainstream Australian society. Cross-cultural understanding is not something lawyers do just as well as anthropologists, an assertion with some potential to be controversial.

Despite such challenges or doubts expressed at times by lawyers, we have now had thirty years of anthropology in Australian tribunals and the courts since the Gove case. It is reasonable to assume that most judges and lawyers, as well as Aboriginal claimant groups and various respondent parties, will continue to seek the services of anthropologists. And the morass of legal discussions about anthropological evidence is not completely without resolution. While Maurice J in the Warrumungu land claim articulated his concerns about hearsay, Neate summarises his general view that it is the proper role of such an expert to give evidence of those 'facts' that are relevant to an opinion; it is just that it is not proper for an expert to become the source of evidence for facts that 'lie beyond the perception of . . . [the expert's] own senses',[18] presumably being facts that can only come from Aboriginal claimants in that they are by definition to be established or proved by them. Maurice allowed hearsay material to the extent that it qualified, explained or provided insight into evidence previously given by claimants.

As yet there are a limited number of native title cases we can draw upon to clarify what the Federal Court will expect from anthropologists as expert witnesses. The rules of evidence now apply in this setting (though they do not in the statutory land claims). We have Olney J's overview comment in the Croker Island case about the anthropological report, that: 'To the extent that it contains assertions of fact in the nature of hearsay, based upon information supplied by informants who later gave evidence, regard must be had to the evidence of the informants rather than to the contents of the report'.[19]

Lee J in the 1998 Miriuwung Gajerrong claim[20] admitted into evidence genealogies prepared by anthropologists, on the basis that they were not only expert opinion, but also evidence of the truth of the statements contained within them. Lee acknowledged that genealogies constitute a record of statements made to the anthropologists, 'the record of which is likely to be reliable, the statements made being appropriate to be admitted in a case of this nature'.[21]

In relation to the Ngarluma/Yinjibarndi case, Nicholson J pointed out that the value of hearsay evidence is that it goes to establishing the foundations of the knowledge of the expert in preparation of the report and expert opinion. His decision was that this is the initial sense in which hearsay evidence should be considered; the court must then determine whether any of it should be excluded. Nicholson found that there is a danger that the use of hearsay evidence might be unfairly prejudicial to a party who has not had the opportunity to cross-examine on it. There would be no proper forensic basis upon which to weigh the hearsay evidence in relation to evidence called in the normal way. Nevertheless, he found that where hearsay evidence is properly reflected in the opinion of an anthropologist and the opinion is admissible, it will be part of the evidence. The test of whether this hearsay (in legal terms) or data (in anthropological terms) is 'properly' reflected in an opinion would seem to be whether it is relevant to the court finding that the expert opinion is based wholly or substantially on specialised anthropological knowledge.[22]

Conclusions

On the basis of the legal discussion of anthropology in land claims and native title court cases, we can clarify several issues perhaps not yet sufficiently considered among anthropologists, historians, linguists and others. While these may appear self-evident, I am not sure they have been reflected upon adequately either by those intending to participate in native title claims as researchers, or by the legal practitioners seeking to call such expert witnesses, let alone by the claimants on whose behalf the social scientists are engaged.

Carrying out research in relation to a native title court case is different from other forms of social science research. As with much applied work, the issues requiring attention are circumscribed quite specifically by the context of legal decisions and procedures. There is a tension here between the necessity for a researcher to fit investigations into this legal context, and at the same time to maintain professional independence such that one's own disciplinary standards and practices are not swamped by the force of the legal process. Ironically, it is the expectation of the court that experts will carry out independent studies according to the norms, theories and methods of their own professions; yet receipt of the results of such research is inevitably subject to legal arguments and cross-examination that are often quite foreign to the experts' disciplines.

When the research involves the likelihood that the anthropologist will be required as an expert witness in court, there are legal rules that need to be understood better within the discipline of applied anthropology, as these affect what is an appropriate and possible role for the researcher. In particular, the body of descriptive ethnographic data that normally goes into a research paper or volume is likely not to be appropriate in a report to be filed with the court. At least, that substantial section of the data that is often in the form of quotations from informants ought only be presented in the report if it is expected that those quoted will subsequently be called as witnesses (or perhaps if the informants have died by the time of trial).

The research anthropologist has to make a judgment about how much of what the courts consider 'factual' material should be in the expert's report. In my view, the standards expected in anthropological discourse require sufficient references to such data to support the conclusions and opinions arrived at by the anthropologist. As with academic writing, such data can be used to illustrate points being made. To the extent that this illustrative factual material reports what people have said in the company of the researcher, it will be regarded as hearsay, but, it is hoped, hearsay that is admissible in that it is relevant to the court finding that the expert opinion is based wholly or substantially on specialised knowledge. There may also be some other factual material in the form of accounts by the researcher of behaviour or social action he or she has observed, and this will presumably attract less legal argument than the quotations or paraphrasings regarded as hearsay.

A related issue is the extent to which anthropologists might support their general propositions or opinions simply by referencing them, that is by referring explicitly to the location of the factual material upon which they are relying, in a fashion parallel to the usual type of references to published literature. Most commonly, references to relied upon data will be to the researcher's own field notes and books, audio tapes, photographs, and so on; they will likely also include unpublished documents a researcher has located in libraries, archives or other storage places.

This type of referencing raises the matter of drawing attention to original research materials, such that they may be subject to court order or subpoena for their production, and that entails the whole issue of confidentiality as understood within anthropology.[23] While this is an issue for a separate discussion, my own view is that it is best to support conclusions and opinions by reference to those primary research materials where this is appropriate in anthropological terms. If this means that field notes and other sources will be available, we ultimately have to comply; though we might foreshadow that the practice of seeking such materials will diminish if it is found they are of limited value for anybody other than the researcher who has authored them. An important point for anthropologists to make in this regard is that their notes and other recordings are not necessarily the complete record upon which they rely in forming conclusions. As Roger Keesing put it some years ago: 'much of what the ethnographer learns never goes into the notebooks; it is in the realm, that for lack of a better term, we can call the "unconscious"—a knowledge of scenes and people and sounds and smells that cannot be captured in the written word'.[24]

Just how we make this point about the nature of 'fieldwork', without diminishing its standing as a reliable disciplinary method in regard to cultural analysis, is but one of the many challenges facing anthropologists in Australian native title cases. For what was not captured in written field notes will commonly emerge in the researcher's reportage, having been recalled from memories of the fieldwork experience.

Generally it would seem the court is most interested in the models or theories developed by anthropologists about a system of Indigenous law. These are the 'propositions' of anthropology discussed by Justice Blackburn, as against information regarding individual people or groups. It is the generalisations arising from the ethnographic detail that are likely to be most crucially of interest to the court.

Finally, in all of this, the different worlds of discourse of law and anthropology are evident. For lawyers, their pleadings are statements that are 'assertions' to be proved or supported by something called 'evidence'; the difficulty is that a social science such as anthropology projects such 'assertions' as conclusions that are already based upon interpretations of action and speech, and that the way one justifies the conclusion is to provide illustrative exemplary material. Our most general challenge in the social sciences therefore lies in better explanation of the nature of research methodologies and theories in anthropology and other disciplines, amidst legal colleagues whose own training is both tantalisingly familiar and frustratingly distant from our own.

3

A Short Ride on a Time Machine: Linguistics, Cultural History and Native Title

Patrick McConvell

THERE ARE AT LEAST three ways in which questions of language can be crucial to native title issues. The first of these is the extent to which the need to prove cultural continuity over a period of two hundred years or more requires demonstration of continuity of language affiliation over that period, what that means and how it can be demonstrated. The second is the extent to which demonstration of the existence of a system of land connection is based on the terminology and expressions used by local people. Hand in hand with this is the extent to which long-term continuity of such terminological/conceptual systems can be proved. The third way is the extent to which the forms and meanings of languages can be used to demonstrate the length of time a language or cultural group has existed in a region. This requires examination using historical linguistics or the combination of historical linguistics and other disciplines such as archaeology.

In order to address these three issues it is necessary first to set the role of linguistic evidence in the context of different approaches to the proof of native title currently being pursued.

'Occupation' and 'regional systems of law' approaches

Native title enquiries are supposed to discover whether specific groups have a continuity in a specific area stretching back to first colonisation by the

British, and whether the customary law of land also exhibits continuity over that period. The 'time machine' of my title comes from the request by a social anthropologist for such a piece of equipment when faced with the challenge of finding out what was going on before white contact and written records in Australia. The bar is being raised ever higher for native title claimants at the beginning of the new century on such matters as these. The issues of just how much detail of previous occupying groups and previous forms of social organisation and customary law should, or could, be provided, which disciplines can provide such details, and with what degree of reliability are matters of immediate concern to all involved in native title.

Many people are now seeking ways to reduce the requirement to detail customary law or its history since white settlement. An alternative way of dealing with the matter is to concentrate only on proving that the particular group occupied the land in question at the declaration of sovereignty and/or first settlement and since then. In these circumstances, lawyers would argue that such occupation of itself implies a form of customary law of possession of land by the group that can be recognised in common law. This method of dealing with native title reduces the need for ethnographic description of both present and previous landholding systems and the changes within them.

In such an 'occupation' approach, evidence needs to be garnered that the 'X' group of people were in occupation of the relevant area around two hundred years ago. However, this assumes that there is a group named 'X' in existence today and that there was an 'X' group two hundred or so years ago and that in fact these are in some sense the same group.

In the great majority of cases the ethnonym X as used in native title claims is a label for a language group, and the name of the language is either the same as or related to the ethnonym. Consequently, the question of the relations between a social group, an ethnonym and a language over time is at the heart of proof of continuity of occupation.

It is doubtful that the question of systems of customary law can be entirely disregarded even by a minimalist occupation approach. The relations between a group, language and group name are part of a system of Indigenous law that is interpreted by local people in terms of concepts and principles flowing from that law. The very existence and persistence of group X over time is derived from the inheritance and assignment of membership rights by a system of customary law.

Evidence about the regional system of customary law will remain important, whether the legal approach emphasises this as the key, or merely holds it in reserve behind an occupation approach. Evidence must be presented about the language and terminology of the customary law of land (and if there has been change) in a region, and clearly linguistics has a role in collecting and analysing such data.

Linguistics is perhaps the most significant, and least acknowledged, way of delving into the cultural history of Australian Indigenous groups over the last few millenniums, and there are many detailed examples of the use of 'linguistic stratigraphy', especially ethnonyms, in relation to native title. Linguistics can also can be used to reconstruct the past by focusing on place-names.[1]

Continuity of language affiliation

The role of linguistic expertise under a minimal occupation approach would focus on the existence of a language group or groups that can be identified as the predecessor of present-day applicants and that occupied the country over which native title rights are being asserted.

In the early colonial period, it was often only a few explorers who sighted Indigenous groups in isolated places. These explorers rarely made contact with these groups and, if they did, found out virtually nothing about them which could determine their identity. In many cases, not even the name that they called themselves was discovered. In the most favourable interactions, the names of a few common objects were elicited and these have been, at least in some cases, enough to identify the language of the people from the language of a group recorded in more detail later.[2] In making this identification we are of course making the assumption (surely warranted in nearly every case but still open to challenge from sceptics) that this was indeed the same group at the two points in history, and not for instance that we are dealing with two different groups that happened to speak a language similar enough to look the same from a small and poorly transcribed sample.

This raises the question of what we mean by two groups at two distinct points in history being the same. Is linguistic continuity sufficient? Is this part of a more general continuity of cultural tradition, which is necessary to qualify the two as being the same? If historical records of the language and language group at or near to first settlement are available, then identification of a language group name in historical records with a present group name, and/or identification of elements of the language then (such as vocabulary lists) with a more recently recorded version of the applicant group's language would be the initial targets of research.[3] Depending on what is said in the early records, this may not be sufficient to show that all the country over which native title is asserted was occupied by the applicants' language group. It may be that there is no record of a language or name for people in part of the area, or that there is a record of people being there and their name is recorded as different from the applicant group's or that elements of the language recorded appear to be different. These are common grounds for objections to parts of native title applications.

Where there is no record of a language or name for the group, oral testimony from members of the group may be called upon to confirm that certain ancestors of theirs did occupy that section of the country and were part of the named language group. Independent evidence from linguistics may be available in the form of place-names in the area. If these are distinctive of the language of the native title group, then there is a good chance that this area was occupied and owned by that language group.

If we rely on the earliest written records for the names of groups, we can often be disappointed. Historical records from the early nineteenth century and even from the late nineteenth century are rarely of the form: 'We encountered some blackfellows camping at Y. They told us that they were called the X and that their country extended from A to B and C to D'. More often they are of the form: 'We encountered some blackfellows camping at Y. We hunted them away'. Or: 'We encountered some blackfellows camping at Y. We asked them where we could find water and they told us by means of hand signs'. On the basis of such testimony the most that can be said is that Aborigines were living at a particular place. Who they were or what the extent of their country was remains unknown. They may even have been visiting the area from some neighbouring area.

Where a group with a different name was apparently resident in part of the claimed country, there are several possible explanations. It may be that this named group was a subgroup of the main named group, perhaps a clan or dialect group, but part of a system of such names that has been partially or completely forgotten. It may be that the people encountered were not permanent occupants of the area but visiting for foraging, ritual or other purposes. One might then expect the name to turn up in accounts of a neighbouring area, but this is not necessarily the case. The name recorded might simply be a vague designation of the people, not their own ethnonym —such epithets as 'people from the south', or simply 'strangers' occur. Regarding names that may be 'loose, ephemeral, or merely descriptive of the behaviour of certain neighbours', Sutton comments that 'it is not advisable for scholars to rely on such terms' in the investigation of land occupation or traditional ownership.[4]

A linguist can help a lot here, for example by tracking down possible meanings of the terms or ethnonyms used. Care needs to be taken, however, since names that originally meant 'southerners' or 'strangers' may, over time, become the ethnonyms used by the group themselves. In fact this seems to be a rather common occurrence. Evidence drawn from the study of time-depth of names ('linguistic stratigraphy') may be needed to distinguish these cases.

Finally, of course it may be that there was indeed a distinct group in occupation that subsequently died out, or was massacred, or moved out, or was absorbed, without leaving a local memory of themselves. The present native title applicant group may have received rights and interests in the land of this group quite legitimately in accordance with the laws of succession in effect in local customary law. As Sutton remarks, 'label extinction [loss of a group name] does not imply group extinction'.[5]

Leaving aside the nature of the social reproduction of the group, the one other obvious characteristic is the name, X. This too may not remain the same but for now I will assume that it does. This question of the identity of a group usually raises the question of language since in the overwhelming majority of cases where group names are used in native title applications, the most important group names are language names. It is assumed that the X are a (or the) group of people who speak, or spoke, the X language. This, though, needs to be qualified.[6]

A model proposed by Alan Rumsey looks at this from a somewhat different perspective: on the one hand, an area of land and a language have a fixed kind of relationship to each other. On the other hand, the human groups tied to such land-language pairs may be more fluid, recruiting some members over time by various means, and shedding others.[7] Over much of Australia, there are numerous Aboriginal beliefs and practices that fit in with this model. For example there is the belief that Dreamings (creator beings) spoke language X while living on or traversing country X but stopped speaking that language in crossing to another group's country. There is the practice that people (primarily X people but including others) should speak X on X country. A further belief is that ancestral spirits resident in the X country should be spoken to in X, so that they are beneficent to the visitors and will not harm them, knowing they are 'countrymen' not strangers.

This perspective has been attractive to followers of the 'occupation' approach as well as to others who wish to reduce reliance on ethnographic data on social organisation and customary law systems over time. If we can assume that the relationship between a language and a stretch of land is fairly fixed then one might reasonably infer from the identification of a language recently or historically with a territory that the relationship has persisted through time. There are problems with the assumptions of that model, however.

Indigenous terminology of customary law

An understanding of customary law is central to the interpretation of native title. A clear understanding of the concepts that make up the framework and practice of customary law depends in turn on understanding the key words that embody the concepts in the local language. Beyond this arguably it would be necessary (even where forms of English are currently used by the group) to study how words are used pragmatically in actual legal discourse and disputation in the Indigenous domain. This is a remarkably under-researched area considering how central the whole issue of the interface between the 'two laws' has been not only in Indigenous affairs but in the entire national life of Australia since the 1970s. Williams's discussion of Yolngu legal concepts and ethnographic description of dispute settlement is a notable exception. The Yolngu themselves are actively seeking recognition of their own legal terminology in furthering negotiations with the state over the interface of the 'two laws'.[8] There is a significant legal anthropology of groups around the world, much of which includes discussion of local terminologies and, in some cases, local discourse structures and processes of inference.[9]

A system of customary law tends to be similar throughout a cultural bloc or regions, and to provide an overarching framework within which disputes between groups can be settled and joint action undertaken. Often the words for the key concepts of the system are the same or, if they are different, the groups residing in the region have an understanding that certain key words in one language are equivalent to key words in other languages.

In some areas there is a widely accepted word for Indigenous law itself. For instance in north-east Arnhem Land it is *rom* and in the Victoria River District among the Gurindji and Ngarinyman it is *yumi*.[10] These words for 'law' obviously do not have connotations of parliamentary institutions and courts in the same way as 'law' or its equivalents in major world languages tend to have. They also encompass a wider field of what some people refer to as 'custom' and 'lore' including proper behaviours between kin, such as avoidance of certain in-laws and siblings, ceremonial and spiritual responsibility and Indigenous knowledge of the environment and its management.

In Gurindji, *yumi* can also be translated as 'rights' and can be used of an individual or family group: for example, *ngayiny yumi* 'it is my right; it is within my rights (to do x)'. The phrase is literally 'my law' and indeed in the domain of Aboriginal English people can say things like 'that's my law' in the sense of 'that's my right'. For this reason I am doubtful of attempts to characterise the discourse of 'rights' in the Western legal framework as alien to the Indigenous framework of customary law. This also illustrates how a different cultural organisation of meaning can persist even after the medium of expression changes from a traditional language to a form of English.

It is essential to understand words and expressions that people use in the course of everyday speech when talking about aspects of their customary law. It may not be possible to elicit such foundational elements by just asking directly about 'the law'. In some cases the words and expressions may have other meanings that appear to be unrelated to the customary law of land, for instance, but when used in context they have an extended or metaphorical meaning that does have such a relation. Spatial metaphors about being 'on top of' the land and the like are very significant in terms of local customary law but may be understood superficially at first encounter, and may exhibit variation between neighbouring languages, which points to a history of change in emphasis.[11]

To take another example from Gurindji, I was not told immediately that the terms *marnaru* and *jawuku* had to with land ownership. I heard them used in speech and when I first enquired I was told that *marnaru* meant 'base or trunk of tree' and *jawuku* 'branch', approximately equivalent to the more common and related words, *marna-marna* and *japi-yapi*, respectively. I then heard them joined together in the compound phrase *marnaru-jawuku*, roughly meaning, I judged at the time, 'related together in a group such that they should not fight each other'. Over the course of time I picked up several other meanings in conversations and narratives related to relationships between kin, and relationships between Dreamings. Eventually it became clear that this relationship 'trunk and branch' was a central metaphor for the relationship between father and child, or 'patrifiliation' as anthropologists term it, in various manifestations, and was a key part of the language used to talk about rights in land.[12]

One of the other key words in Gurindji and nearby languages is *jamarrarn*, which has several related meanings. Again, these are not obvious all at once, but tend to be revealed by close attention to how people use the words in talking about things. Meanings may include: a word or phrase used by a Dreaming which can also be used as a term of address under certain circumstances to a patri-group associated with that Dreaming; a voice quality associated with a Dreaming and inherited from the father; a boundary on a songline where one group takes over from another; and the stretch of country associated with a set of verses of the song sung by a group.

As with *marnaru-jawuku* there is a strong core in this notion that has to do with patrifiliation or patrilineality. The voice quality is something that comes from the father (unlike other aspects, such as the hair and skin, which come from the mother's side), but ultimately from the Dreaming. The 'stretch of country' also comes from the Dreaming, primarily via the father. Can we establish which meaning came first and what the relationship is between these meanings historically? It is extremely unlikely that such an obscure—yet important—word will be found in any earlier vocabularies or traveller's jottings of the region.[13] However, it is possible to trace its development etymologically in the languages of the region.

The word is related to a verb in the Western Ngumpin branch of the Ngumpin-Yapa subgroup of Pama-Nyungan, *jamarrarnu*, which means 'to copy, imitate'. In the Yapa branch (Warlpiri language) the verb refers to the whoop uttered at the end of a verse in ritual songlines. *Jamarrarn* is a noun formed from a verb in an archaic way that is no longer productive. The comparative evidence tends to indicate that the 'copy, imitate' meaning came first and then applied to this specialised sense of 'imitation' of the voice of a Dreaming, with demarcation functions in songs about country. Further back one can recognise that the word was formed from two roots: *jaa*, meaning 'mouth', and a verb, *marrarnu*, which is found in Western Ngumpin in the meaning 'call by name' and 'scold' in different languages, the former probably being the original meaning. It is likely that the meanings of the word related to duplication of a phrase and voice quality were earlier, and those related to boundary developed from the earlier ones. The connection is still very evident since the special *Jamarrarn* words are uttered by the Dreaming at hand-over points in the songlines.

Sutton argues for anthropologists to describe regional systems of law and custom as well as just being occupied with detailing claims of smaller groups in native title research.[14] The people in the Victoria River District consider the separation of their songlines into segments with *Jamarrarn* hand-over points to be a distinctive aspect of their land law as compared to other systems in neighbouring districts. To the outside observer, the differences may not be striking, but it is important to consider how regional people conceive of the distinctiveness of their system of law. By considering the etymology of key terms in such as these systems that are unique to a region, we can get an idea of how such a system developed its uniqueness and of the time-depth of the specific emphases found. For instance, in this case an ethnogenetic belief about inheritance of voice features is bound to a strong segmentation of country by songline stretches.

The time-depth of connection

Linguistic prehistory is in a good position to contribute to reconstruction of the last few hundred or thousand years, which is what native title research is mainly interested in. This linguistic prehistory research can include the working out of a common ancestry of a group of languages, which (together with reconstructions of ancestral environmental vocabulary) may have implications for the location of speakers of these recent ancestor languages. It can also look at reconstructions of cultural vocabulary at various stages of the past and thus shed light on the social and cultural arrangements that may have existed at various periods (and, under favourable circumstances of corroborative evidence from archaeology, be assigned absolute dates). This reconstruction of social and cultural arrangements in the past is perhaps most important in fulfilling the requirement of showing continuity of culture and custom over a period greater than two hundred years.

In native title evidence, there seems no disadvantage in presenting a view, from archaeology, linguistic prehistory or any other scientific discipline, that is based on different methods, alongside Indigenous testimony presenting a traditional view. These differing pieces of evidence gain weight, individually and collectively, by being produced independently by different people using different methods accepted by peers. If they all converge on suggesting a continuous tradition of a people and a law of land in an area, the result can be a strong case.

The technique called 'linguistic stratigraphy' relies on the fact that strata of loanwords and other items within a language can be distinguished by whether or not they have undergone certain changes. This provides a guide to the cultural items adopted at different eras.[15] Since a burst of borrowing usually occurs around early European contact this can provide a benchmark for establishing that some elements predate this era and belong to an earlier stratum. If these earlier elements are associated strongly with a group (for example, its name) or with an element of customary law of land, or place-names on the group's country, then strong inferences can be drawn that these groups and systems were in place for longer than two hundred years.

A view of the relationships between land and language in Australia proposed by Alan Rumsey, already mentioned, emphasises that the association between territories and specific languages persists for long periods. While this may apply in many cases, there are a number of possible problems. Social groups such as clans in Arnhem Land may change their boundaries over two hundred years or less, as was evident in the Gove case, *Milirrpum v Nabalco*, to the disconcertment of the anthropologists appearing for the Indigenous plaintiffs.[16] I have encountered several examples of clan estate boundaries shifting over time in Northern Territory land claims, due to succession arrangements, as have many other ethnographers working on land claims and outside that context.[17] While language group or 'tribal' boundaries may be more fixed, it seems likely that these would be subject to similar pressures over time for the same reasons. There is nothing inherent in the mythological linguistic boundary markers that makes them immune to the usual shifting, negotiation and compromise that occurs when estate groups weaken or die out. This does not imply that language boundaries vary wildly and erratically over time, but some change in their location, constrained by the operation of local customary law, is to be expected over two hundred years. To become committed to a static model is to repeat the mistakes of the plaintiff's case in the Gove case.

Long-term fixed language boundaries are also inconsistent with the general model of language divergence most commonly used in historical linguistics. This model envisages languages differentiating into distinct dialects over time, and eventually into distinct languages, a process represented by a cladistic model—a 'family tree' but with 'daughter' languages having only one parent. Although it is not strictly part of the model itself, this process of divergence is often accompanied by a widening geographical spread of the language. The divergence itself and the expansion of the language territories both imply that languages are not fixed in their association with territory. Differentiation of languages is usually thought of as taking longer than the two hundred to three hundred years we are speaking about here—more in the order of a thousand years. However language spreads, even when it proceeds gradually, may well be noticeable in the two hundred to three hundred-year time frame as shifting language boundaries.

Aside from issues of language and people, the question of how long a language has been in an area is important in itself. Glottochronology is a technique that claims to be able to gauge approximately the time-depth of a common ancestor of a pair of languages that are members of the same family of languages. It takes a standard list of 'basic' vocabulary (usually two hundred words) in two languages, counts the number of words that are common and applies a standard formula. The results are an estimate of the age of the common proto-language. Many linguists have no faith in this technique. Others accept that it can go wrong but still feel that there is a common core of logic in the technique that might allow for its improvement.

Other approaches avoid putting actual years on estimates but use arguments about relative timing. The type of argument developed by Hale for native title purposes has the following structure. A new feature has developed and internally differentiated in a linguo-genetic subgroup of languages. This process of innovation and differentiation of the innovation must (we know from other similar cases elsewhere in the world) take a certain amount of time. Therefore the language group has been in existence for at least long enough for this process to take place.[18] Since generally linguistic change over a period of two hundred to three hundred years is relatively modest, any more substantial change is likely to have taken much longer. Two hundred to three hundred years is as far back as a native title enquiry is expected to go, so a finding of substantial change within the language group invites the inference that it has been differentiating for longer than this period.

One potential objection to Hale's argument is that, if the assumption of a constant rate of change is incorrect, then the last two hundred to three hundred years may have included some periods of accelerated change in which major innovation and differentiation could have occurred over a relatively short period. The argument also does not specifically address the question of location of speakers of the language during the period. While it may be the simplest hypothesis that the languages stayed in place during the period (and that the homeland was within or close to the area) it is logically possible that the differentiation occurred in a different location altogether and the speakers of the language moved into their current location only recently.

In order to negate this alternative hypothesis, which could be damaging to the assertion of rights of occupation by the native title claimants, other types of evidence need to be adduced. Here both positive and negative evidence of borrowing can be particularly useful. If borrowing of elements from neighbouring languages in the present languages under examination can be proved to have been going on for two hundred to three hundred years or more then they must have been contiguous for that length of time. Therefore it is most likely that they have all been in the same present location. Of course the objection could still be raised that they could all have moved together from some other region but the credibility of such hypotheses declines as more unrelated languages are added to the group that supposedly moved.

The complementary negative evidence would be that no recent borrowing has occurred in the languages under examination from distant languages. This would indicate that there is no plausible other location for the languages under examination in the recent past. Of course borrowings from distant sources that have passed into the target language via neighbouring languages would not negate the continuity of the target languages in the location, and such paths can be detected where sufficient information is available about the languages of the region.

Further, borrowings into the languages under examination from sources that today are relatively distant are not necessarily a problem for the hypothesis of continuity of occupation in the recent era. If the location of the languages has changed over time this is unproblematic unless the change occurred over the last two hundred to three hundred years. Establishing that the languages in question were probably spoken at a different location at some more distant period can even be positive for a native title claim, if it also can be shown that the language entered the region where it is currently spoken before two hundred to three hundred years ago.

Place-names

In order to use place-names as a source of evidence in native title, it is necessary to show that they are related to the language of the applicant group spoken in historical times, and that such names have been present in the area for at least two hundred to three hundred years. Evidence of place-names not from the native title group's language is not necessarily negative if they can be shown to be borrowed from another language or if they can be shown to be so old that they do not affect the recent period.

Possible difficulties that may be encountered include situations where the place-names may not be distinctively different from those of neighbouring groups in the first place; and where the native title group replaced all earlier place-names with their own in recent times. This, however, is a quite unlikely occurrence since place-names tend to be conservative. Dual or triple naming practices are known for some areas.[19] This means that a number of groups in an area each had their own name for certain sites, although the sites in question may have only really belonged to one of the groups. Such a situation might more easily lead to a perception, if for instance one group died out, and along with it its place-names, that the alternative name used by a neighbouring group was the original name. This seems to be a relatively rare pattern in Aboriginal Australia, however.

With regard to the time-depth aspect, as with other words in a language, place-names can be assigned to chronological strata depending on whether or not certain changes have affected them. Place-names can also retain archaic elements within them which can guide us in reconstructing the recent history of cultures and social groups and point to the time-depth of particular language groups in the country where the toponyms are found.

One of the types of archaism found in place-names is retention of forms of words as they appeared before recent sound changes.[20] Sometimes such names appear as doublets, that is alternative forms are found, one having undergone the sound change and one not. An example of this is the doublet *Pakarrji/Paarrji*, which is the name of a range of hills in Wanyjirra/Nyininy country south-west of Gurindji. The original form is *Pakarrji*, which has not undergone the process of Lenition mentioned above. The form *Paarrji* has undergone Lenition of the k between the vowels to w, and the subsequent loss of a w between a's forming a long a, which is also a common sound change. People retain a notion of the stem of this word *pakarr* as referring to 'lying down', although neither this form nor the suffix *-ji* is present in the languages of the area today.

A variation on this is where the current form of the root word, as found in general vocabulary, is one that has been borrowed internally within the group of languages from a language that has then undergone changes not undergone by the recipient language. The form in the place-name, however, is the inherited form rather than the modified form with the sound change. This pattern indicates that the place-name was coined before the internal borrowing took place. Since the borrowing is capable of being assigned to a stratum and potentially given a relative date, the place-name can be dated to before that period. Strong inferences can be drawn from this that speakers of the particular language concerned or speakers of the ancestors of that language inhabited the area where the place-name is found at that period, and this can be shown to be over two hundred to three hundred years ago.

The pattern of internal borrowing overlying a general vocabulary form while the place-name root form retains the expected inherited form is found in the Gurindji place-name *Warrijkuny*, which is the name of a large waterhole on the upper Victoria River. This is the site of the contest between the Crocodile and Turtle Dreamings over who is the better diver. This place-name can be broken down into three parts:

Warrij	-ku	-ny
crocodile	DATIVE	NOMINALISER

This can be glossed roughly as '(place) belonging to Crocodile'. The everyday word for crocodile in Gurindji is *warrija*, with a final –a, not *warrij*. The form *warrij* is found in Gurindji's northern neighbour and very closely related Ngumpin-Yapa language, Ngarinyman, as it is a borrowing from non-Pama-Nyungan western Mindi languages.[21] Now, the addition of a final –a to consonant final roots is a typical sound change in Mudburra, but not in Gurindji. We would expect the Gurindji form to be *warrij* and clearly this is what we see in the place-name *Warrijkuny*. However Gurindji has borrowed the Mudburra form *warrija* at some point after that. This is one of a number of Mudburra words, including some affected by a-augmentation, that have been borrowed into Gurindji (and other languages).

The formation of the place-name *Warrijkuny* must precede the borrowing of the word *warrija*. Since this place-name is typical of Gurindji both in root and suffixes, a strong inference can be drawn that Gurindji people were occupying the land and bestowing names on the land of a form reflecting understanding of its mythological significance before the word *warrija* arrived. Absolute dating of the borrowing of *warrija* into Gurindji is not a simple matter. The form was already in use in the 1890s in the general area and this use was recorded but the identity of the people using it is not completely clear from that source.[22] It does tend to indicate that the diffusion of the form *warrija* beyond Mudburra to the Gurindji, among others, was completed by the beginning of the 1900s, and therefore the place-name *Warrijkuny* is older than that.

Another form of archaism in toponyms is grammatical. Some toponyms are unanalysable and have no current meaning, and at least a proportion of these may be so because they are derived from ancient substrate languages whose lexicon and word formation rules are unknown. In most areas many more toponyms are analysable into component morphemes in the present-day language of the area.

In a number of cases the morphemes involved are generally recognisable but the component morphemes and the way of putting them together are distinctly different from the patterns used in everyday speech in the present-day language. In such cases we may suspect that archaic grammar is involved, and evidence from related languages may strengthen this hypothesis. As with sound changes, the fact that grammatical changes have occurred since the time the words were coined is evidence that they are old. Just how old is a more difficult question, but it is not a question that in principle is unanswerable.

In Gurindji and Ngarinyman there are a number of ways in which place-names are constructed by adding suffixes to nouns, coverbs, or sometimes longer phrases. Perhaps the most common way is to add the suffixes LOCATIVE meaning 'at' (-ngka, -la and a number of other variants) followed by *–rni*. The latter suffix has an interesting range of meanings such as 'still' and 'only' in modern Gurindji.[23] Using modern Gurindji as a guide this combination seems to mean 'only at X' or 'still at X'. So the place-name *Mutpurr-a-rni* would supposedly mean something like 'still at the *Mutpurr* tree'.[24]

The locative case suffix in Gurindji has another important grammatical function apart from specifying the place where something is. It also marks a non-finite subordinate clause. Put simply, the locative in this function acts in a similar way to –ing in English: 'I saw him walking along'. The suffix –ing in English is attached to a verb stem such as 'walk'. In Gurindji the locative suffix is occasionally attached to an infinitive form of the verb, but more commonly to a coverb, with the verb omitted; it also attaches to other nouns in the subordinate clause whether subjects or objects.

Sometimes place-names consist of forms of sentences with a noun and a coverb, and in this case the locative suffix is attached to both. For example, the words *karnangka jirrpkularni* can be broken down as

Karn -ngka jirrp -kula –rni
spear LOC stick up LOC STILL
'where the spears are sticking up'

This refers to a Dreaming place with a stand of trees that are the transformed spears of a Dreaming which threw them from about 20 kilometres north. Without the final *–rni* suffix, this is a perfectly normal Gurindji or Ngarinyman non-finite subordinate clause, meaning 'when/if the spears stick up'. The suffix in this case does not mean STILL/ONLY, but is a marker of place-names that derives from some past time when it was more directly meaningful. In other words, it is an archaism.[25]

Nowadays, however, when people want to coin a place-name for a Dreaming, for example when they cannot remember the real name or it is too sacred or death-tabooed, they do not add –LOC –rni , but simply –LOC.

For instance in an area of Gregory National Park the people I was with knew that Turkey Dreaming (*Jantura* 'bustard' in Ngarinyman) had passed through and was associated with a hill. Perhaps to avoid a more sacred name, people referred to this place as *Jantura-la* 'turkey –LOC', as one might call the place 'Turkey dreaming place' in English. People do not coin place-names with –LOC-*rni* in this way.

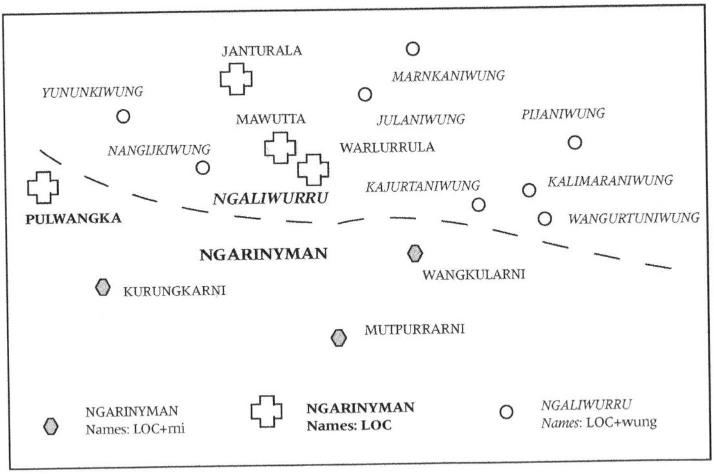

Ngarinyman and Ngaliwurru place-names

When one looks at the distribution of place-name types in the area (as shown in the map) an interesting pattern emerges. If the more complex and parallel -LOC -STILL/ONLY forms in the two languages are plotted, they fall into two clearly distinct zones, with Ngaliwurru names to the north and Ngarinyman names to the south. The line dividing the two zones runs exactly along the line that people of both groups say is the boundary between their countries. This is strong evidence for the long-term continuity of this boundary.

Ngarinyman names with only -LOC as a suffix to some extent are found south of the boundary line, but unexpectedly some are found north of the line, in what is generally identified as Ngaliwurru country, including the name *Janturala*, which has been discussed. This is a newer stratum of names coined during a more recent period, probably by processes similar to that already described, or perhaps by translation from Ngaliwurru. The context of this is the severe decline of the Ngaliwurru language in recent years so that it is now only spoken by a handful of older people. Ngarinyman, on the other hand, while also an endangered language, remains stronger and to some extent has been a lingua franca secondary to Kriol in the region.[26] Hence many people would use Ngarinyman words rather than Ngaliwurru even if they are of Ngaliwurru or other ethnicity, and this is the probable reason for the 'intrusion' of Ngarinyman place-names into Ngaliwurru country. It should not be automatically interpreted as a Ngarinyman take-over of landwhere their language is used to form place-names.

It is essential therefore to distinguish between those features of place-names that belong to older strata, and therefore provide strong evidence for the time-depth relevant to native title, and those that may reflect a contemporary language situation that may not align with traditional language distribution. These latter recent features of place-names are important in themselves since they show an active culture reproducing patterns of naming even if the language has changed. Linguistic as well as anthropological knowledge and research is needed, however, to clarify that these features do not necessarily show that a change of land ownership between groups has taken place.

Conclusions

Linguistics provides a means of understanding what native title applicants or claimants who do not have standard English as their first language want to say about their rights and responsibilities in land, by providing translation of, and commentary on, their statements. This is not just a matter of eliciting superficial statements designed for use in white Australian courts, but ideally should include recording and understanding how words and expressions are used in context in actual conversations and narrations, as is the practice of linguistic anthropologists. In this way some of the basic conceptual schemes of the law and custom of a region can be accessed to provide a broader foundation for native title cases, as has been illustrated here from the Victoria River District.

Linguistics goes further, though, and in my view provides an independent source of evidence. An analysis of current languages can throw light on aspects of the cultural history of peoples, aspects that anthropology in its present configuration, archaeology and history are unable to illuminate. Words and expressions related to land and culture in modern Indigenous languages carry their history within them and that history of words points to the history of their cultures. I have argued that the methods of linguistic prehistory, such as linguistic stratigraphy, can be used to work out the time-depth and significance of land-law concepts, place-names and other items relevant to native title. In this way it is possible to fill in some of the gaps that confront us when we are required to reconstruct the distribution of groups and their systems of law at the time of colonisation.

4

Method Mechanism and Mindset: Collaborative Approaches in Native Title

Wendy Asche

IN 1935, IN THE NORTHERN TERRITORY, Wells J considering a criminal matter before him, adjourned sentencing the prisoners so he could obtain details of the implications of 'tribal law' on the prisoners' actions. Despite the evidence already provided during the trial, Wells J said: 'Here is an occasion where some of these anthropologists may be of use, they always seem to be where they are not wanted, and never where they are wanted'. After due consideration, Wells sentenced the two men to ten years each in prison. The counsel for the defence argued that the Aboriginal people possessed nothing, Europeans having taken their heritage. Wells J replied: 'That is all very well for the subject of an address to a society for the protection of native races but I have no powers to enable me to take notice of it'.[1] I believe we have moved some way since then.

There are commonalities and tensions in the roles of anthropologists, linguists, historians and lawyers. I must admit my bias as an anthropologist who works for a Northern Territory Land Council, but in conducting research for this chapter I have come to have greater sympathy for lawyers.

In the process of research, proofings and hearings for native title applications the relationship between anthropologists, linguists, historians and lawyers necessarily requires good communication and co-ordination. Where tensions arise, these can be classed into the three categories of method, mechanism and mindset.

Method

The method of approach to native title applications follows a regular pattern. Tensions between professionals working on a claim may arise from inadequate communication, often because of exigencies of other work matters, confusion as to who carries responsibility for particular tasks, or personal differences.

Good communication requires time and effort. One of the most crucial stages of an application, the final weeks before submission of documents, is when last-minute amendments are made and people are least able to take the time to sort out those complex issues that require clarification. Often consultants reside interstate and this makes the process of feedback more convoluted. Both land council staff and consultants are invariably involved in other work which may not allow full attention to be given to one particular claim and makes the task of getting all professionals in conference together a logistical challenge.

Different roles are necessary depending on the stage of the claim. There are six branches in the Northern Land Council, and these include anthropology and legal. Each branch has a particular responsibility in relation to native title. For instance, in the early stages of preparation for a native title application the legal branch should investigate the status of the land titles and the legal issues to be addressed, while the anthropology branch assumes responsibility for co-ordination of anthropological, historical, linguistic and archaeological research. There is no independent native title unit so cross-disciplinary teams are composed on a project basis. The branch structure of the organisation can contribute to tensions within the team as staff tend to focus on their own status as professionals rather than as part of a team working towards a successful outcome. Anthropologists may emphasise a theoretical perspective in an application rather than focusing on the applicants' ethnographic reality, for example by fitting the claimants into a neat system of patrifiliation when the fieldwork may indicate a more complex set of relationships. This is not only detrimental to the application as the theoretical system will not be reproduced in evidence, but it also alienates the applicants from involvement and ownership of their claim.

During the early stages of a claim, which may be a period of years while research is continuing, the anthropologists have the greatest contact with the claimants and tend to be the conduit for information relating to the progress of the application. Lawyers and anthropologists need to communicate effectively at this early stage. An example of the problems caused by a lack of communication occurred during a directions hearing for a native title application in 1999. A solicitor for the applicants who was acting in his first claim agreed to the Northern Territory Government's request that personal particulars be provided for all claimants. This included name, date of birth, place of birth and place of residence. Apart from the fact that the date of birth for many older Aboriginal people in the Territory is not known, when the lawyer agreed to this request he was not aware that research was well advanced and to obtain such information from approximately 500 adult applicants was a monumental task. It also set a precedent for such information to be provided by the applicants, which the Northern Land Council argued was unnecessary, intrusive and time-consuming.

Closer to the submission date one or more proofing of documents and Aboriginal evidence occurs when logistics officers are crucial in co-ordinating large-scale meetings.[2] The logistics officers have to satisfy the possibly competing requirements of anthropologists confirming their research and lawyers proofing Aboriginal evidence. At this time too much emphasis on professional boundaries can lose the involvement of claimants. For example, it would be useful if at this point the lawyers spent some time explaining the legal process to both the claimants and the experts. Confusion as to who carries responsibility for particular tasks is most likely to occur as the barrister becomes more involved but until this point management of most aspects of the claim are internal to the Land Council. A high staff turnover does not help in the understanding of roles and responsibilities. Particular tasks such as the physical production and submission of documents may be a shared responsibility because of the exigencies of time. The hearing coalesces with less confusion as by this time the barrister is more familiar with the claimants, land council staff and expert witnesses and has very specific instructions for all involved.

Tensions can also arise in relation to the form of funding for Native Title Representative Bodies as these currently require annual budgets rather than a three- or five-year projection of expenditure. The length of time required for research work by anthropologists, linguists and historians can be estimated from experience of previous comparable claims. However, lawyers often have unforeseen additional expenses as new legal avenues open up or additional parties get involved. Hearings are delayed or extended for various reasons such as interlocutory applications being made and so expenses fall into the next financial year.

The last example of a practical issue that causes tensions among professionals working on a native title application is the choice and availability of particular consultants. Lawyers' and anthropologists' views on consultants may not coincide, as lawyers are used to hiring experts and not researchers. Thus lawyers tend to focus on academic credentials while the anthropologists argue that the ability and availability to do fieldwork associated with the particular area of claim is essential. The Northern Land Council usually engages a combination of researchers and academics in any claim by using academics for peer reviews or as co-authors of the anthropological report.

Mechanism

The mechanism of any native title application is defined by the 1993 Native Title Act and amendments, technicalities and legal processes that both non-lawyers and lawyers often find frustrating and limiting in regard to the admissibility of Aboriginal evidence. However, even before the technical aspects of the law are applied cultural disjunctions are apparent. One aspect that linguists in particular have considered is what Eades terms a 'communicative clash' between Aboriginal English and the legal system. Eades argues that Aboriginal people are at a serious disadvantage in the legal system due to their use of Aboriginal English in an environment of complex legal language. For instance, in Aboriginal English there is no gender distinction in the third person pronoun so 'he' is used to mean either he or she. Obviously misinterpretation is possible in a legal interview. In addition to grammatical differences between Aboriginal English and standard English, pragmatic differences occur. That is, 'language meaning and use are not shared because of socio-cultural differences'. Eades explains that one of the most obvious differences in forms of communication between Aboriginal and non-Aboriginal people is that when 'Aboriginal speakers seek substantial information . . . questions are not used'. A much less direct form of inquiry is made. Eades outlines a number of misinterpretations of Aboriginal responses within the court system of question and answer to elicit evidence, but describes the most serious disadvantage as the feature of 'gratuitous concurrence'.[3] This strategy of Aboriginal agreement with whatever they believe the non-Aboriginal questioner wants has long been recognised by other linguists and anthropologists, such as Strehlow, Elkin and Liberman.[4]

Some practitioners in the legal system have also recognised such disadvantage. For instance the 'Anunga Rules' were suggested by Forster CJ in 1976 as guidelines for use by police in interviewing Aboriginal suspects in the Northern Territory. Among other things they suggest the use of an Aboriginal interpreter and the presence of a 'prisoner's friend during interrogation.[5] Similarly, the *Final Report* of the Royal Commission into Aboriginal Deaths in Custody made recommendations to ensure better communication between those who work with Aboriginal people in the legal system.[6] Lee J also recognised the difficulties of Aboriginal witnesses in court in his judgment in the *Miriuwung Gajerrong* case. He noted that 'a transcript cannot convey nuances of gesture, movement or expression that bear upon an understanding of the evidence received in such circumstances'.[7]

In the native title process, one obvious obstacle is that lawyers and the law focus on individual evidence whereas Aboriginal people often prefer to give evidence as a group. In one native title hearing a number of claimants were allowed to give genealogical evidence as a group, but immediately following this evidence an applicant giving evidence on his own tried to seek confirmation of some of his answers from his relatives sitting behind him. The respondents objected to this and the judge upheld their objection so the witness was admonished and asked to proceed without support. In the context of the previous joint witness evidence this instruction was apparently unfair and inexplicable to the witness.

By contrast the legal process under the *Aboriginal Land Rights (Northern Territory) Act 1976* (Cwlth) demonstrates greater flexibility in land claim evidence as it is a tribunal. Group evidence is allowed. Unfortunately as claims under this Act continue the context of the hearing is becoming more legalistic in that there is increasing cross-examination, more experts are involved and the process is more adversarial. These procedures mean that the claimants lose control of the claim.

Grey J in a recent seminar noted the effect of the 1998 Native Title Act amendments. One of the amendments reinstated the rules of evidence 'unless the court otherwise orders'. These may then be waived at outset or on a case by case basis, so much depends on the attitude of the individual judge. Another procedural amendment has altered the requirement that the National Native Title Tribunal and Federal Court 'must have regard to Indigenous and cultural concerns'. The word 'must' has been amended to 'may' and the words 'but not so as to prejudice other parties' have been added. Now, if restricted women's evidence was given by Aboriginal witnesses, necessitating hiring a female lawyer for some days, the respondents could protest the expense of hiring another lawyer if their lawyer was male. Judges do sometimes exercise their discretion in favour of claimants. For instance, Olney J is experienced in land claims and does not insist on a strict adherence to rules of evidence unless objections are made by respondent parties.

It must also be noted that other disciplines can limit the accessibility of Aboriginal evidence in an academic environment that values literacy above all. Historians, for example, have debated the status of written history over oral history.[8] Although oral history has long been recognised as a way of disclosing the 'hidden histories' of people on the margins, it has been seen by some as unreliable and biased. One criticism is that it is necessarily subjective and revisionist. However, such arguments stem from the assumption that written history is objective. As Roberts points out: 'The assumption that oral sources are in general less reliable than documentary sources remains unproven . . . Any serious historian should automatically be wary with all sources'.[9] A professional historian would necessarily evaluate sources, context and internal consistency of both written and oral history.[10]

Mindset

Mindset is the most difficult and complex of the issues that can create tensions between professionals working on a native title application. Furniss has examined the legal mindset of some Canadian judges. In relation to indigenous land claims, she explored the 1991 British Columbian Supreme Court decision on *Delgamuukw v British Columbia*, also known as the Gitksan and Wet'suwet'en land claim. McEachen J dismissed the claim and the discipline of anthropologists as unscientific and biased. While the decision was overturned on appeal, Furniss argued that McEachen's propositions reflected widespread, conventional beliefs. Legal facts are assembled by multiple epistemologies. These include the frontier myth of the past where North America is seen as an empty unoccupied wilderness; land is free for the taking and resources abundant. Confrontation of opposites occurs between civilisation and wilderness, man and nature, whites and indigenous peoples. The settler struggles in a moral terrain of good and evil to emerge transformed, upholding values of self-reliance, democracy and competition. Indigenous peoples are characterised as a homogeneous group; either hostile and threatening or noble savages to be patronised and protected.

In his decision, Judge McEachen's beliefs were shown in the language he used:

> The total territory is a vast, almost empty area. The Aboriginal life in the territory was nasty, brutish and short. [They] became a conquered people, not by force of arms, for that was not necessary, but by an invading culture and a relentless energy with which they would not, or could not, compete.[11]

Furniss argues anthropologists need to be aware of how unintended cultural meanings are communicated through metaphors and taken for granted representations of indigenous people. Anthropologists do have control over the language in which cultural concepts are communicated and we can not only take care not to reproduce the frontier and other myths in our own discourse but also to ensure that we challenge them. Sometimes, however, cultural stereotypes are deliberately used by anthropologists to win land claims by manipulating the emotions of the judge towards applicants. For instance, the cultural metaphor of Aboriginal people as those who care for their country reverberates with current Western ideals of conservation of the environment.

Historians, linguists and anthropologists may have differences with lawyers about the meaning and associated theories of specific words or concepts that are particular to their own discipline. One example of a concept that illustrates a difference in epistemology between lawyers and anthropologists is 'trade'. In a number of native title applications on the Northern Territory coast, anthropologists identified the trade that had occurred between the ancestors of the applicants and the Macassans during the eighteenth and nineteenth centuries as an important issue.

The lawyers defined trade as a large-scale commercial interchange of commodities between foreign countries, involving significant monetary transactions. Obviously this is a very narrow Eurocentric twentieth-century definition that can be readily challenged by anthropologists. There has been considerable anthropological debate surrounding commerce, trade and exchange but plainly the interaction between Macassans and coastal Aboriginal people can be seen as a form of trade appropriate to the era and density of contact between the two peoples.

Watson's monograph describes *pituri* (indigenous tobacco) trade through Queensland and the Northern Territory. Watson argued that the factor of size and quantity in trade is limited to the absolute density of hunter-gatherers and believed *pituri* functioned as a currency among Aboriginal people in the area. The special quality of *pituri* is that it can be carried easily (behind the ear) and its addictive nature meant there was a form of non-generalised reciprocity characterised by seasonal production and market haggling by individual traders.[12] Watson's example is comparable to the coastal evidence of seasonal production of trepang, pearls and tortoise shell by the Aboriginal people, to be exchanged for tobacco and alcohol from the Macassans.

The lawyers argued that the only comparable case where evidence of trade was accepted for indigenous people in court occurred in Canada where there has been a large-scale indigenous exploitation of fish. Both lawyers and anthropologists were unhappy with the other's lack of understanding of the issue. However, part of the misunderstanding arose from the different perceptions of the roles of the anthropologist in the native title process. Lawyers would see anthropologists as expert witnesses whereas anthropologists in this case would perceive themselves as part of a team of researchers and thus the issue of trade is a concept to be debated and investigated as part of native title.

In a later native title application anthropologists approached the issue of trade with a different strategy. At first the barrister did not accept that trade could be proven but the anthropologists pushed the issue and suggested lines of questioning that elicited evidence of trade.

Similarly, historians have debated approaches with lawyers concerning historical evidence. Paul describes her satisfaction when she convinced lawyers and others in the Alice Springs native title application that history does not always need to be presented chronologically and the perspective of the native title holders would be better articulated in a more complex way.[13]

A more difficult concept is how to explain distortions or absences in the historical record. A potentially damaging historical document for the Miriuwung Gajerrong applicants' case was an oral history report from a now deceased Gajerrong man. The interview recorded the man describing that Gajerrong people had been decimated along the coast and separated from their country by relocation to cattle stations. If the judge had only considered this evidence before him he might have concluded that native title was extinguished in this case. However, Lee J coupled the historical evidence with anthropological evidence that explained how people maintained their connection to country and Aboriginal evidence that showed continuing connection to land arising from an ancestral community.[14]

Conclusions

The Northern Land Council has recognised the value of analysis of historical material to merge anthropological, linguistic and historical perspectives so that native title issues such as occupation can be demonstrated. Barrister Hal Wootten at an Australian Anthropological Society conference in 1995 urged anthropologists to be more assertive in their 'educative role', especially with respect to lawyers. It is always a two-way process where the strongest case in a native title claim can be built from a collaborative effort among all professionals and applicants involved.

5

Beyond Traditional Law: Better Native Title Service Provision

Jan Anderson

NATIVE TITLE LAWYERS and anthropologists are both familiar with the question of whether Brennan J's famous 'tide of history' comment in the High Court's 1992 *Mabo* judgment has washed away Indigenous traditional laws, customs and rights in land. If native title is to be recognised, Indigenous traditional law must have been preserved. Interestingly, however, the tide of history has not washed away some of the traditional laws, customs and practices of lawyers and anthropologists, and the native title process might be better off if it had. As someone who has attempted to straddle the divide between the native title legal process and academic anthropology by participating simultaneously in both, it is my belief that anthropologists and lawyers have to encourage new understandings of each others' professions to improve the native title process.

Two areas in which relations between anthropologists and lawyers are currently strained, and where changes need to be made in order to improve the current native title situation, are in contractual research agreements designed by lawyers to ensure a high quality research product, and legal privilege and limits on the distribution of information about Indigenous traditional land tenure. Both are problematic because they are often derived from traditional legal thought, rather than cross-disciplinary communication and consensus. Native title service providers can work together to provide more creative, shared solutions to these problems, bringing better results both for parties to native title claims and service providers involved in those claims.

The contractual relationship

The Federal Court's *Guidelines for Expert Witnesses* states that anthropologists and other researchers are expected to provide independent comment, and to ensure that proceedings are well informed. Their paramount duty is to the court. They are not advocates for the clients who retain them. Regardless of whether or not this is ever entirely possible, it is those researchers who appear most independent who gain credence with land claim judges, and who can best aid the progress of native title cases.[1]

Currently, some contractual relationships between lawyers and researchers can make this independence particularly vulnerable to challenge. Where bias of this nature is found to exist in court, it can topple the professional credibility of the expert witness, and consequently damage the credibility of the Indigenous evidence on trial. Palmer, Macdonald and McIntyre have argued that any contract makes the expert witness a party with the client to a greater or lesser extent, though they accept that there is no consensus among anthropologists on this issue.[2] It does appear that some contracts are more at odds with researcher independence than others.

For example, in order to protect the interests of their clients, lawyers may encourage anthropologists and other practitioners to enter into research agreements that indicate that their working drafts and reports will be subject to legal scrutiny and approval, and can be modified or suppressed if a lawyer ultimately decides they do not promote the interests of the clients. One research agreement offered to me stated that the matter of whether my research results prejudiced the interests of my 'informant community' could ultimately have been determined by a Native Title Representative Body. This contract was perhaps less worrying than other standard contracts I am aware of, where anthropologists have been asked by lawyers to declare that they will promote the interests of claimants.

Is this the best way to ensure the production of well-founded and rigorously researched anthropological materials concerning Indigenous clients? Anthropologists themselves currently provide little formal guidance on this matter for one another, or for lawyers and other potential client representatives. The Australian Anthropological Society's code of ethics gives little assistance on this issue, and can even cause some confusion. For example, Section 6 of the code requires that:

> Members should respect the role of corporate bodies operating on behalf of those studied and should include them where relevant in the negotiation of field research agreements.

> Members should keep such relevant bodies informed of their activities in the field and, where no breach of confidentiality or agreements with those studied should be incurred, supply them with copies of research results.
> Members should *respect the confidences* of such bodies.

However, section 4.11 says that:

> Members *should not enter into agreements* with sponsors, gatekeepers, those studied or other entities which *entail essentially political direction of anthropological research,* or which confer on those entities powers of political censorship over results *as distinct from reasonable protection of privacy and confidentiality.*[3]

What do these statements mean? Where does one draw the line between political censorship and reasonable protection of privacy and confidentiality? How does one best respect the role and confidences of corporate bodies, particularly if they are in conflict with the role and confidences of one's research subjects, or in conflict with the role and expectations of oneself as an anthropologist?

Even if the Society's ethical standpoint was less confusing, it currently has no solid mechanism for verifying that its professional members enter contracts that are ethically and professionally sound, and that promote excellence in the conduct of research. At present, anthropologists are relatively powerless to collectively review restrictive contracts pressed upon them by others.[4]

Palmer, Macdonald and McIntyre believe that consultant anthropologists should welcome constructive feedback and comment on their reports, and point out that this is common practice. However, they also argue that:

> it is essential that the integrity of the professional anthropologist's work be maintained. Consideration may be given to the inclusion of a clause whereby the parties acknowledge the independence of the consultant and agree that the consultant's findings will not be altered or modified subsequently unless it is agreed between the parties in writing.[5]

Asserting this independence can be difficult when individual anthropologists find themselves alone in deciding whether or not their contracts contravene written or tacit ethical standards.[6] Palmer, Macdonald and McIntyre point out that for those of us with no knowledge of contract law, the contracts we are presented with 'are typically long, complex and sometimes incomprehensible documents with many clauses which are, to the uninitiated, unintelligible'.[7] Responding to these contracts individually, we might be pressured into accepting them even if we are not quite sure what they mean, and do not feel comfortable with them.

Ultimately, we have no specialist professional anthropological body for anthropologists, native title lawyers or parties to native title claims to consult on matters concerning high quality anthropological research. It is not surprising that individual native title lawyers try to protect their Indigenous clients from what might be poor or contentious anthropological research, by attempting to establish their own legally oriented controls over the production and utilisation of anthropological work.

Client legal privilege

Another contentious issue between lawyers and anthropologists is the use of legal privilege on communications between anthropologists and parties to native title claims (Trigger and Tan also discuss this, in chapters 2 and 10 respectively, in this volume). While legal privilege may work well in protecting the confidentiality of trial-oriented conversations between lawyers and their clients, it creates a variety of uncomfortable issues for the discipline of anthropology on the whole, as a profession that was not purpose built for litigation and court proceedings.

A serious concern for anthropologists is the possibility that court systems are not always obliged to respect the confidentiality of Indigenous groups. Under ordinary anthropological research conditions, this confidentiality has generally been respected,[8] meaning that private and sensitive communications between Indigenous individuals and ethnographers could be recorded in personal field notes, but normally never appear elsewhere. However, researchers' field notes have been subpoenaed during land claims under the Native Title Act, as well as claims under the Aboriginal Land Rights (Northern Territory) Act and the Queensland Aboriginal Land Act.[9] Two recent Federal Court judgments, namely *Daniel v Western Australia* (in 1999), and *Clarrie Smith v Western Australia* (in 2000), show that regardless of whether legal privilege attaches to materials prepared for the court, sensitive material recorded in these field notes and observations may eventually be used to cross-examine Indigenous witnesses.

Nowadays, whether or not legal privilege is sought, it appears that anthropologists' field notes, recordings and reports may all be made available to counsel for parties opposing native title. The question of whether or not this information could successfully be protected from exposure in court, if it is subject to legal privilege, is discussed by Tan in this volume. Can it be protected, and can we be certain of it?

Following the *Daniel v Western Australia* judgment, Blowes and Trigger argued that 'In the light of the recent judgment . . . it is unlikely that any understanding as to confidentiality will be respected'. Even in the case of consultants hired specifically to collect materials for native title litigation, they advise that 'all records created in relation to the research effort are likely to become available for inspection by all parties and by the court'. Hence, they argue that it is the responsibility of lawyers to direct anthropologists with clarity and caution as to the basic extent of information that must be collected by researchers to satisfy native title case requirements, and as to how various recorded forms of communication between individuals involved in the claims process may be used in court.[10]

It was suggested at the Crossing Boundaries conference in 2000 that the best way to protect Indigenous confidentiality was to restrict the recording of information on contemporary land tenure systems to court oriented research, because this research was uniquely placed to attract legal privilege. However, in light of recent court findings, a new question arises. Is Indigenous privacy protected by restricting the distribution of traditional land tenure information to a court system which itself has the unusual and unpredictable power of being able to dismiss people's claims to confidentiality?

Alternatively, do native title service providers have a responsibility to ensure that the court's capacity to override the privacy of Indigenous groups is made transparent to both Indigenous groups and the researchers they may work with? Does the way in which information is gathered need to be modified in order to make it more suitable for court conditions? If so, how quickly can methodological changes like this be made if anthropologists across Australia are not able to avail themselves of the experiences of other professionals carrying out research into traditional Indigenous land tenure systems?

Already native title consultants are being advised to pay special attention to the way in which they record information, in preparation for court scrutiny of primary research documents.[11] On the basis of this understanding, for example, anthropologist Peter Sutton argues that consultant anthropologists should adopt a more stringent and transparent style of note taking, to prepare for the possibility that all of the information they collect will be exposed to discovery in court. As he sees it, 'one should have nothing to hide and transparency of the ethnographic/anthropological process is a must'.[12] Blowes and Trigger have argued similarly that anthropologists should be prepared to have primary research materials discovered and utilised in court:

> Appropriately detached professionalism is called for in all aspects of the involvement of the researcher, not just in relation to the final report and performance in the witness box, but also in relation to the creation of field notes and any other documents. The expert should make transparent his or her independent consideration of the broad range of material that will typically be available.[13]

The question remains as to why researchers could not apply these techniques to research for purposes other than litigation, in consultation with Indigenous groups, legal representatives and Native Title Representative Bodies.

For anthropologists, this issue of privileged information is setting in place another problem with long-term and widespread consequences. In particular, restricting non-court oriented research has a direct effect on the number of qualified and experienced anthropologists available for use by Indigenous groups and others in native title claims. There is currently a shortage of experienced graduate anthropologists who can provide service in Australian native title claims. As Michael Barker QC argues from a lawyer's point of view, the ideal anthropologist for a native title case is one who has built up a close rapport with members of the Indigenous claimant group, and has a relatively well-developed understanding of their traditions, customs, laws and social networks.[14] Ironically (from an anthropologist's point of view), the most common medium through which anthropologists have traditionally experienced relatively long-term contact with Indigenous groups has been academic field research, an activity now restricted by native title legal issues.

High professional standards in anthropological research are promoted through open debate and discussion. However, we have reached a situation in Australia where contemporary Indigenous land ownership systems from specific regions may be discussed by researchers in the courtroom, but not in the lecture hall, the heritage centre, the popular monograph or the conference, because this information is being made subject to restrictions articulated by legal practitioners. Indigenous people's own non-court oriented research into their local history and heritage, because it is intended for purposes other than native title claims, can be made subject to the same conditions. In the long term, as Trigger, Robinson and Gladstone point out, 'without the continued exchange of information, and the associated patterns of debate within the anthropology profession, the very skills and research perspectives being contractually sought by client groups will dissipate over time and ultimately risk losing the capacity to fulfill the needs of clients'.[15]

It can be easy to forget that a substantial amount of the ethnographic research that goes to court in native title cases today is not, and never has been, subject to legal privilege. In fact, works that cannot attract client legal privilege are fundamental to anthropology's contribution to the native title process in Australia, and the contribution of many other research disciplines. Without access to them, the face of the claims process would look very different. Consultant anthropologists regularly use the non-court oriented works of their independent colleagues in order to cross-check, substantiate and compare the results of their own contemporary research. Also, many eminent Australian anthropologists (whose consultant services are often in demand) have published academic research that is not only commonly available in public libraries and museums across Australia, but now also appears in court. One such anthropologist is Jeremy Beckett, whose academic works were used in the *Mabo* case.

If current non-court oriented research can also be successfully utilised in the native title claims process, the benefits would appear to outweigh the potential negatives. In an era when time, resources, funds and consultants are all in desperately short supply, universities, Indigenous research centres and other research institutions still represent an under-utilised resource for Native Title Representative Bodies and other Indigenous groups. Also, where academic debate is enabled to proceed, researchers' collective knowledge and understanding of the variety of contemporary Indigenous land ownership systems continues to grow, and methods of describing the nature, transmission and development of different cultural phenomena improve. Further, constructive criticism through independent peer review can help to ensure that evidence is well founded and presented. Finally, as Rigsby points out, academics and/or academic backgrounds can be well regarded in court, because court emphasis is placed on independence from fee-paying client control.[16]

Both anthropologists and lawyers are expected to play some part in making sure that court judges are able to make well-informed decisions by providing them with clear and accurate evidence about contemporary Indigenous rights in land. As mentioned earlier, however, lawyers and Native Title Representative Bodies currently have no formal safeguards to ensure that their clients and the courts will be provided with suitable, high quality ethnographic research. Currently, anthropologists in their role as academics probably appear even less manageable and more unpredictable to lawyers than anthropologists in their role as consultants, given the lack of mechanisms available to ensure that academics meet stringent professional standards. Can this be changed?

Professional bodies and codes of conduct

In seeking to ensure quality native title service provision, can anthropologists, lawyers and parties to native title claims come to new arrangements that rely less on written contractual obligation or the restriction of land tenure information to the court system, and more on consensus between different groups as independent entities? This should be a possibility. However, if researchers are asking lawyers to relinquish some control in their relationships with anthropologists and other parties involved in native title claims, anthropologists will also need to accept a greater level of responsibility for their actions.

If lawyers and parties to native title claims are being asked to trust anthropologists with more professional independence, surely it is up to researchers themselves to collectively ensure that their services are accountable and reliable. Tonkinson points out that, currently, an unprecedented demand for consultant anthropologists in Australia 'has led to underqualified and inexperienced researchers entering these fields', and that without remedial action, this situation could prove damaging to both clients and other members of the discipline. Relevant professional bodies, such as the Australian Anthropological Society, already have difficulty monitoring standards of research and censuring unprofessional behaviour because they are not equipped with the resources to do this.[17] As the recent past President of the Society pointed out to me, ensuring standards is not possible when a profession is not legally required to allow only registered members to practice. In other words, there is currently no safety net for claimants and lawyers seeking anthropological services.

Within the anthropological profession, strong cases have been made for the establishment of professional associations to guide the conduct of practitioners, and to offer both them and their clients support, advice and, potentially, legal protection.[18] Though academic codes of ethics and conduct have existed for some time in anthropology, there is a growing concern that these are inadequate to cover both consultants and academics, given the different conditions under which these groups work. Beckett argues that consultants need a strong, recognisable and enforceable code of ethics and conduct that will serve to protect both practitioners and the clients they work with. Fegan asserts that professional conduct would need to be carefully scrutinised in order to ensure compliance: 'The only body that could do so would be a consultant's professional association, which does not yet exist'.[19]

Such a body could also assist people involved in native title claims to negotiate sound, workable research contracts to protect both practitioners and the clients among whom they carry out research. Further, membership of this body and compliance with its codes could provide qualified, professional consultants with formal recognition, and also provide potential clients with the security of knowledge that the service they are retaining will be subject to strict professional scrutiny and rules of accountability.[20] Fegan claims that academics, rather than being left on their own, would also need to show that they were members of a professional organisation like this as a requirement for permission to undertake outside employment. This argument is an important one, given the academic background of the discipline, and given that many of its practitioners are still associated with universities and the like. I would like to take the argument one step further and suggest that anthropologists who are paid by research institutions to carry out applied work should be members of a professional body. Perhaps in the case of students, they should at the very least have a firm supervisory arrangement with a member of a professional body who has access to its advice and resources.

Currently, the numbers of applied anthropologists are still relatively small compared to those employed in research institutions. Little academic training is offered on issues associated with the practice of applied anthropology.[21] A professional body could liaise with Indigenous representative groups, practising native title service providers from various backgrounds, and the Australian Anthropological Society to help ensure that the style and content of academic training offered was more appropriate for people intending to work in this area.

Conclusions

It would appear that we are well overdue for a formalisation of roles and relationships between independent practitioners in the native title claims process, as well as between practitioners and the clients they serve, so that we can find more of a sense of direction and build new understandings. Based on their experiences in native title, lawyers Ritter and Garnett write that:

> there is plenty of anecdotal evidence of interdisciplinary tension . . . [However] there is much to be gained from a multi-disciplinary approach to native title practice. This multi-disciplinary approach can also assist to keep the objectives of the process in sight and to provide opportunities to consider alternative, creative (often non-legal) outcomes and processes.[22]

In the future, a professional body for applied researchers should help negotiate cross-disciplinary solutions with legal practitioners as they arise, paving the way for more successful relations between individuals involved in the claims process and, in turn, for more co-ordinated and productive native title service provision on the whole.

6

Designing Institutions in the 'Recognition Space' of Native Title

David F. Martin

FOLLOWING THE 1992 *Mabo* decision, the common law has approached native title as a system of communal rights that may, on occasion, support individual rights.[1] However, it has provided little guidance as to how individual native title holders could exercise those communal rights, or how they could exercise individual or subgroup rights. The *Native Title Act 1993* (Cwlth) and the regulations made under it provided the basic framework for the resolution of this legal and organisational problem. This legislation prescribed a regime for the management and holding of the title that relies on corporations that act as either the agents or the trustees of the native title group. These corporations are called Prescribed Bodies Corporate. Once these corporations are placed upon the Native Title Register, they are called Registered Native Title Bodies Corporate. Here I focus on the concept of 'native title recognition space' and consider whether corporations might provide appropriate institutional vehicles for Indigenous self-determination.[2]

Recognition space

Native title in each instance takes its form and its content from the manner in which the Australian legal system recognises a selected set of relations ordered by the relevant system of traditional law and custom. The native title resulting from each determination can therefore be considered to lie in a 'recognition space', between the particular Indigenous system of traditional law and custom, and the general Australian legal system. This recognition space can be presented through the visual device of two intersecting circles, one representing the Australian legal system and the other the system of traditional law and custom.[3] The use of the 'recognition space' device is restricted here to the description of particular, essentially legal, phenomena. It is only one dimension of the complex zone of social, cultural, political and economic interaction between Indigenous and non-Indigenous societies.

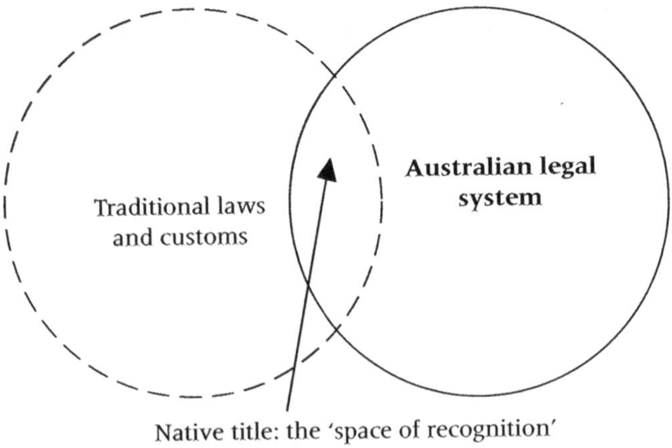

Figure 1: The 'recognition space' of native title

It is of fundamental importance to differentiate between native title on the one hand and, on the other, the particular system of connections an Indigenous group may have to its traditional country. The character of the connections to country of a particular Indigenous group, which are established through and structured by traditional law and custom, may not necessarily be appropriately described in terms of 'rights and interests'. The principles that inform the relations among the members of the group, and between that group and its land and waters, are potentially quite different. For example, the work of Myers offers a rich and complex alternative to descriptions of Aboriginal relations to country couched in terms of the language of 'rights' and 'interests'.[4]

These relations, and the system of traditional law and custom through which they are ordered, are the subject of the recognition process. They are translated through the concept of native title in order to take effect as rights and interests that can be incorporated into the categories of Australian property law, though they are not identical to these categories. The particular system of Indigenous relations to the country is the subject of the recognition process, but it is not the result of it. The result is native title, which following *Mabo* we understand as being comprised of native title rights and interests. This translation process is illustrated in the accompanying diagram.

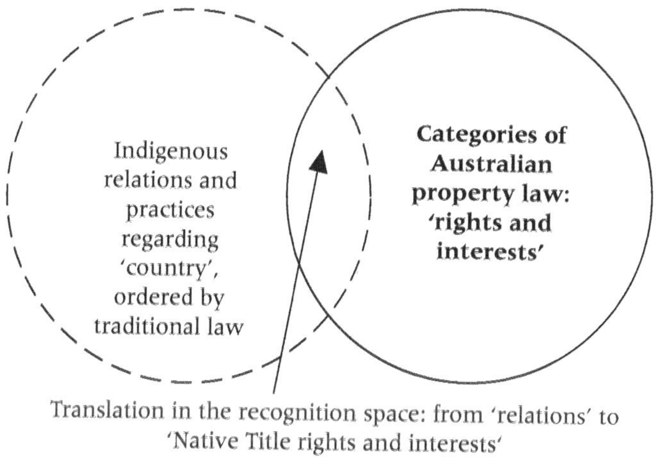

Figure 2: Terminology used to describe native title rights and interests

A distinction between the relations, which are the subject of the recognition process, and the legal rights and interests, which are the result of the recognition of these relations by the Australian legal system, has been distorted by both the legal and the anthropological thinking on native title. The legal distortions have been produced by careless usage—slipping unremarked from native title to the Indigenous system itself—and also by an underlying systemic preference for the recognition of relations that are easily understood in terms of Australian property law concepts.[5] The anthropological distortions arise from social anthropology's intellectual roots and from its particular history in Australia, which have led to widespread utilisation of the language of rights and interests to describe complex systems of Indigenous relations to country.[6]

This distinction between an Indigenous system of relations and the native title through which it is recognised is of great significance. For example, the fundamental role of a Prescribed Body Corporate under the Native Title Act is the management of the group's native title: that is, the management of the rights and interests recognised by the court. Its role (in the first instance at least) is not the regulation of relations within the group, or between the group and their traditional country. This has important implications for how Prescribed Bodies Corporate are to be conceptualised, and for their design.

Management of native title

The Native Title Act establishes a framework for the holding and management of native title. It requires the use of corporations that stand in a relationship of either 'trust' or 'agency' to the members of the native title group. Regulations made under the Act specify the characteristics and functions of the native title corporations and lay down procedures to be followed by the Prescribed Body Corporate in decisions relating to native title matters.

Three core elements of the management regime established under the Native Title Act can be identified. First, the Prescribed Body Corporate Regulations mandate incorporation under the *Aboriginal Councils and Associations Act 1976* (Cwlth). Second, the corporation must act as either the agent for the members of the native title group, who will thus hold the native title directly, or as the trustee for the group, in which case the corporation holds the native title and the members of the native title group are the beneficiaries of the trust. Third, the regulations have adopted procedures to be followed by the corporation in managing the native title that are based on the 'consent and consultation' procedures of the *Aboriginal Land Rights (Northern Territory) Act 1976* (Cwlth). These procedures were introduced to ensure that the corporation conducts dealings in the native title with the informed consent of the members of the native title group.

There are therefore three—potentially conflicting—sets of legal relations between the corporation holding or managing the native title and the members of the native title group: those deriving from the various corporate law relationships between the corporation and those members of the native title group who are actually members of the corporation; those deriving from the statutory trust or agency relationship between the corporation and members of the native title group; and those arising from the statutory 'consent and consultation' requirements set out in the regulations.

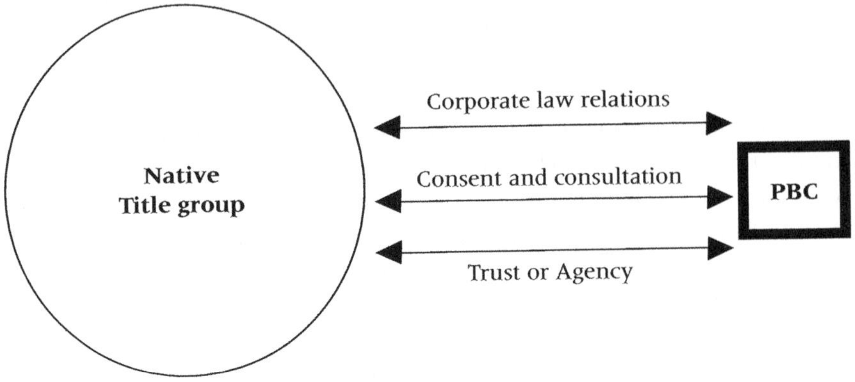

Figure 3: Multiple legal relationships between the corporation and the group

A multiplicity of legal relations between the corporation and the group creates a quite unnecessarily complex and potentially unstable management regime for native title groups.[7] The fact that under the current scheme it is mandatory for native title to be managed by means of corporations, and that these are established under the Aboriginal Councils and Associations Act, introduces some problems. This Act establishes an associational form of corporation, which is controlled directly by a membership of 'natural' persons. The Act places particular emphasis on control of the association through the general meeting. In the context of native title corporations, the use of the Act's associational model introduces six main problems.[8]

The first is the assumption that the membership of a corporation can be made to be congruent with the membership of the native title group. There is a host of reasons, both technical and sociocultural, why this cannot in general be the case; a bounded and prescriptive list of the individuals who have been accepted as corporate members in accordance with procedures set out in the constitution can only ever approximate, at best, the composition of characteristically fluid and permeable Indigenous groupings.

The second problem lies in the reliance of the associational corporation on a governance model that has emerged from historical and cultural circumstances quite distinct from those of Australian Indigenous societies. Members and officers of Indigenous corporations bring values to bear on their participation in corporations that may differ from, or even conflict with, those required under law. For example, directors of the corporation have a fiduciary duty towards the corporation as a whole, not towards particular members or groups of members. It is the corporation that owes duties to the native title group members, under the statutory trust or agency relationship. Directors who infringe this fiduciary duty may be subject to severe penalties. Yet, this legal schema, which interposes the corporation between the directors and the members of the group in the establishment of legal duties and obligations, potentially conflicts with widespread features of Indigenous societies. Here, individuals are typically embedded within systems of social relations that give primacy to allegiances based on kinship and the representation of particular interests. The pressure to discharge obligations to particular constituencies may well cut across legal abstractions such as duties to the corporation as a whole.

The third problem is caused by the insertion of corporate law rights and obligations generated by the associational corporation into an existing organisational culture, in which Indigenous organisations have come to play fundamental roles in the ongoing struggles over identity, legitimacy and authority within Indigenous societies. In particular, Indigenous corporations are frequently characterised by a highly competitive politics of representation, in which groupings such as those based on 'families' compete for control of the corporation through control of the general meeting and nomination or election of their representatives onto the board. Many corporations are consequently highly unstable, with alternative factions gaining control of the board, and thus of the resources of the corporation.[9]

A fourth problem is created by the establishment of a set of parallel and potentially conflicting legal relations between the native title group and the native title corporation, expressed through the statutory relationship of trust or agency and the consent and consultation provisions. The result is that these latter two relationships, which go to the heart of native title management, may be compromised by or conflated with, the corporate law relationships between the corporation and its members.

A fifth problem lies in the difficulty in establishing organisational structures under the Aboriginal Councils and Associations Act that reflect relevant categories or groupings under law and custom within the broader native title group. While attempts have been made at establishing quasi-classes of membership by some Act associations, the administration of the Act has hitherto emphasised majoritarian principles drawn from the dominant society, in which decisions of the corporation are reached through an undifferentiated majority vote at general meetings. However, it should be noted that problems will inevitably be created by attempts to assimilate the structures and operations of corporations to those of the Indigenous non-corporate domain. The main advantage of being able to establish distinct membership classes within an Indigenous corporation arguably lies in the enhanced capacity of the corporation to appease the competitive politics of representation, rather than the capacity of membership classes to mirror Indigenous structures and political processes per se.

A sixth problem is created by the assumption that the corporation is the product of voluntary association. However, membership of the native title group (as opposed to membership of the corporation) is not, in general, voluntary. It results from a number of attributes, such as descent, which are not matters of individual volition. Nor have native title corporations emerged from a surge of enthusiasm for incorporation from within the Indigenous polity. They have emerged from the requirements of the native title legislation, and the political demands within the resource and land management sectors for certainty in dealings with native title.

Self-determination

The native title management regime mandates the use of corporations acting as either trustee or agent for the members of the native title group. The use of corporations as such to hold or manage the title is probably unavoidable in the Australian context; it is in part a response to the problem confronted by the general land and resource management regime in dealing with a form of property interest that is communal rather than individual in nature.

A major concern of Parliament, both in the passage of the original Native Title Act and in subsequent amendments, was what was termed 'certainty' for resource and other land-based industries. Despite this, it is arguable that major uncertainties and instabilities have been introduced into the native title management regime by the use of the Aboriginal Councils and Associations Act with its associational model of the corporation as the vehicle through which native title protection and management are to be implemented.

To return briefly to the discussion of native title with which this discussion began, it was argued that it is important conceptually to separate native title, the product of the recognition process, from the Indigenous relations that are its subject. A distinction was also made between the particular recognition space of native title—an essentially legal construct—and the complex, multidimensional and ever-changing zone of mutual interaction between Indigenous societies and the general Australian society.

An important question is raised here for native title groups and their advisers, legal and otherwise. Should Prescribed Bodies Corporate be seen as vehicles for the wider goals of the native title group, such as self-determination, perhaps a degree of political autonomy, and economic advancement? Or should they be limited to their statutory role of native title management? The case for the latter is persuasive.

First, the statutory role of the Prescribed Body Corporate is to manage the native title of the group, that is to manage the rights and interests that lie in the recognition space between the two systems of law. It is not its role to manage the system of relations under law and custom between the group and its country, or among the members of the group. The statutory native title management regime has not been established by Parliament for the benefit of Indigenous people or to advance their wider social, economic and political goals, but rather to integrate the management of native title into the general land and resource management system.

Second, and related to the first point, the Prescribed Body Corporate is, by definition, a corporation whose characteristics are prescribed through statute. There is limited flexibility available under the current regime for its design to take account of the particular circumstances, aspirations and structural features of a native title group. For example, despite the capacity for the rules of Aboriginal Councils and Associations Act corporations to reflect

Aboriginal custom where appropriate, the Act and its administration have proved highly inflexible in terms of enabling basic features of Indigenous society, such as internal differentiation within groups on the basis of families or language groups, to be reflected in the structures or the procedures of the corporation. Paradoxically, such features can be more easily accommodated under the general corporations law.

Third, the Act corporations and Prescribed Bodies Corporate have been placed under a uniquely interventionist and restrictive regulatory regime. Given that, currently at least, there is no possibility for incorporating corporations under an alternative statute, it is arguably strategically far preferable for native title groups wishing to incorporate to achieve their other, wider, goals to consider doing so through corporations set up under alternative legislation, such as the corporations law.

Fourth, the Act, despite its common use by Indigenous groups for a wide range of purposes, in fact offers a very inadequate vehicle for Indigenous groups to achieve these wider goals, particularly those relating to commercial enterprises. At the very least, the management of the native title should be structurally separated from the management of other assets and from the means for the achievement of other, wider goals of the group.

In the absence of treaties or other such formal political instruments for achieving wider Indigenous political and other goals, it is probably inevitable in the Australian context that various corporate forms must be used by Indigenous people to achieve such goals. However, corporations are subject to a range of regulatory and other forms of scrutiny that may be inimical to true Indigenous self-determination. Furthermore, while the Act may provide an unduly inflexible incorporation and regulatory regime, all incorporation statutes are based upon sets of values and practices that have their origins within the dominant legal, political and economic system. The more attempts are made to reflect the complexities and subtleties of the values and practices operating within the Indigenous realm in corporate structures and practices—for example, regarding such matters as authority and decision-making structures and the various forms of Indigenous groupings and subgroupings—the greater the risk that the formal corporate structures and processes over time will supplant the informal Indigenous forms, a process known as the 'juridification' of Indigenous relations.[10]

There are, therefore, from this perspective, compelling arguments for establishing Indigenous corporations that leave as much social and political process as possible within the informal Indigenous realm, and do not attempt to codify it within formal corporate governance mechanisms. The focus in such corporations would be on developing procedures to ensure effective and accountable relationships between the corporation and the relevant

Indigenous group, and corporate governance would serve only to maintain a viable corporate entity as the interface between the group and the wider world. Indigenous self-determination through corporations then may best be served by developing structures that present the minimum profile to the stormy political and regulatory seas in which they must sail.

Conclusions

The central focus of the native title management regime should be on the relationship between the corporation and the members of the native title group. This is currently established through the consent and consultation provisions as required under the regulations, and the statutory trust or agency relationship between the corporation and the members of the group. The corporation should exist only to be the legal bearer of these statutory obligations and functions.

As an aside, there are arguments that the current consent and consultation provisions, virtually 'cut and pasted' from the Northern Territory's Land Rights Act, 'overdetermine' the legal relationship between the group and the corporation, which can be established appropriately through the terms of the statutory trust or agency.

The current scheme unwittingly focuses attention on corporate governance, by using an associational model that implicitly assumes that the membership of the corporation is congruent with the membership of the native title group. By using this model, experience with other Indigenous corporations strongly suggests that politicking, competition and conflict within the native title group will inevitably be brought into the governance of the corporation, thus adversely affecting the viability of the Prescribed Body Corporate and its capacity to protect and manage the native title. Equally, use of the associational model carries with it the risk that the corporation itself will be seen (by both members of the group and by others) as in essence identical to the group, and that corporate governance roles and procedures will replace those operating within the informal Indigenous domain—one form of the process of 'juridification'.

The regime under the Native Title Act contrasts unfavourably with that under the Northern Territory Land Rights Act tripartite scheme, in which there is a passive land trust (essentially removed from politicking because it transparently has no authority), professional and well-resourced Land Councils, and 'traditional Aboriginal owners' and others affected by potential dealings in Aboriginal land. The traditional owners and the Land Councils are linked through the informed consent provisions; dealings in Aboriginal lands cannot proceed without the informed consent of the relevant Aboriginal people, ascertained by the relevant Land Council, which has the relevant resources and expertise to undertake the task, and which instructs the Land Trust to act accordingly.[11] The scheme under the Native Title Act essentially collapses the functions of the Land Trusts and the Land Councils into the one body in each case, a Prescribed Body Corporate that is in all likelihood poorly resourced, without appropriate expertise, and may also be riven with factional politicking.

7

Outsourced Professionals in Native Title Claim Research

Julie Finlayson and James Nugent

THE REGION OF WEST QUEENSLAND is comprised of two areas: the Greater Mt Isa region and an area serviced by the Carpentaria Land Council Aboriginal Corporation. Previously, the Native Title Representative Body operated from a head office in Burketown, but maintained regional offices in Doomadgee, Mornington Island and Normanton.

Native title claimants requiring assistance and facilitator services in the Mt Isa region and as far south as Birdsville had no recognised Native Title Representative Body in the region. This was in part caused by the difficulty in reaching a consensual position among the diverse native title claimant communities on proposals to constitute a 'representative' organisation, especially when this was interpreted under the Native Title Act of 1993 to require representatives of the regional claimant groups to hold representative positions on the governing committee or board. Needless to say, consultation and research on proposals for a Native Title Representative Body have been progressively promoted in the region since the introduction of the Act.

In November 1998, the continuing absence of a service provider led to the introduction of the Greater Mt Isa region Claims Coordination Service as an interim measure. The Service operated with one staff member, a legal practitioner, who was joined in 2000 by a senior anthropologist.

The Greater Mt Isa service area is extensive, being roughly equivalent to the size of Victoria. It includes the highly prospective Mount Isa-Carpentaria Mineral Province. According to the Queensland Government, major mining or infrastructure projects worth some $2500 million (not including the $900 million Century Zinc project located in the Carpentaria Land Council region) have commenced in this province in the four years of 1996–2000 and the expected export revenue from metallic mineral production in the region over the next twenty years is estimated at $30 billion. Among these projects are at least four recent start-up mines with costs of between $145 million and $650 million, as well as several major pipeline and power-line projects and numerous smaller scale developments.

At the commencement of the Claims Coordination Service there were sixteen native title claims lodged in the region, most of which overlapped to some extent and many of which were lodged by factions of a single group of native title holders. Considerable time has been spent mediating these differences with the Kalkadoon people, who in 1998 had six overlapping claims, and who are the region's major group numerically. The Kalkadoon now operate under the auspice of a single steering group known as the Nadji Guningala Committee and are progressing two complementary non-overlapping claims. These claims are also the focus of a vast amount of future act work given the prospectivity of the area, evidenced by some 200 mining tenements that affect Kalkadoon interests currently in the backlog created by the Queensland Government. Not surprisingly, the Kalkadoon have one lawyer dedicated to the future acts aspects of the claim and another lawyer working on the claim progression.

The current dynamic of lodged native title claims reveals nine contemporary 'tribal' groups who seek representation and at present eight groups have claims that have passed the registration test. One group is undertaking research with a view to lodging a claim in the near future. Most of the claims are broad acre 'boundary' claims, which seek to include the entirety of a group's country, while at least two groups have opted to lodge smaller 'strategic' claims, which focus either on development works or areas of particular significance to the claimants.

Anthropological perspectives

The professional tasks required of the anthropological position in the Claims Coordination Service focus primarily on the management and oversight of outsourced anthropological (and legal) work funded by the Service and undertaken in the region. Particular attention is paid to protecting the clients' best interests, namely, the quality of the anthropological research and scholarship, and the protection and strategic management of claimants' intellectual property rights. While general protocols for management and quality control of professional expertise had been implemented, there was a need for standardisation in the conduct of particular anthropological matters.

One of these is the conduct of peer review provided by the anthropologist. All claims in the Greater Mt Isa region are currently outsourced, so it is not surprising that significant variation occurs not only in the quality of consultants' work, but also in the range of experience and expertise they bring to their work. It is also the case that in the current native title landscape there are not enough experienced researchers for all the work that is available. Consequently, claimants and funding bodies need assurance that research undertaken on their behalf is of a high standard and that accountability mechanisms are in place to monitor the quality of the consultant's service.

Peer review is one method of providing accountability. There are at least three obvious reasons for implementing such a process. The first reason has already been raised: consultants varying widely in their experience and expertise with native title research. Second, preparing evidence for native title claims differs markedly from the preparation of evidentiary material required of land claim research for the *Aboriginal Land Rights (Northern Territory) Act 1976* (Cwlth). Third, consultancy research is generally pegged to a legislative framework and criteria, and should not be approached as if the exercise imposed requirements akin to writing ethnography for an academic audience. Native title must directly address issues of evidence as required by the legislation (a point examined by other contributors to this volume). A fourth reason to implement peer review is that it potentially ensures evidence presented for a claim is credible, appropriate and conforms to the requirements of the amended Native Title Act. While it is clear that such a process benefits both claimants and researcher, the process must, nevertheless, be carefully managed.

Our experience is that views differ among the contracted professionals as to the extent of the overseeing role of the Claims Coordination Service. There is a need to appreciate that while a process such as peer review must be strategically managed because of legal concerns, some form of quality control or accountability must be a standard requirement of the terms and conditions of employment. There is also a notion in some quarters that anthropology has little to offer claim research other than the expertise to develop genealogies. On this view, it has been suggested that the lawyer to whom the anthropologist is contracted is entitled to provide peer review.

In Queensland, the State Government has outlined specific content and format requirements of anthropological research presented for mediation. Connection reports have become a mandatory condition of the state's willingness to join mediation.[1] Notwithstanding such a condition, the presentation of a connection report immediately raises questions of the level and extent of material facts to be exposed to government as a non-claimant —and opposing party—to the claim. The question of the content of connection reports goes to the heart of claim management, and involves issues of the strategic management and presentation of such research. At present, the principal research activity undertaken by consultant anthropologists in the Greater Mt Isa region is preparation of a connection report. Some cultural heritage protection work and area clearances are also commissioned, but these are usually triggered by mineral exploration.

For Native Title Representative Bodies and similar services there is increasing concern about peer review and its relationship to legal professional privilege. The Claims Coordination Service ensures that all consultant anthropologists are engaged through a solicitor to attract legal professional privilege to their research. However, while the legal sensitivities of peer review may be evident to some anthropologists and their solicitors, no general awareness can be assumed.

The conduct of peer review must be a clearly understood and carefully managed process in circumstances where the research is potentially the subject of litigation. While many consultant anthropologists are likely to be familiar with peer review as a common academic process, in the context of their employment as expert, serious consideration must be made to protect both the evidence of the expert and of the witnesses. For this reason, all communication reviewing research materials and connection reports should be via the legal representative. Emails and written documents are treated with the same status.

Blowes and Trigger have explained the detail of why protection of evidence is important and how it can be achieved. They claim that:

> If communications have not been carried out via the conduit of legal representatives, the entire set of communications involved in the review process may be made available if sought be a respondent party to a claim. Once made available to another party in the discovery processes, peer review communications may be used to cross-examine the expert, and be provided to other experts engaged by particular parties ... For the legal representative, the primary objective may be to ensure that the standing or authority of the expert engaged by his or her clients is not seen to be undermined by peer criticism. Yet a researcher used to normal peer review will commonly wonder why an open discussion of different expert interpretations should be so dangerous for those seeking his or her services.[2]

There is a possible alternative, but it involves collaboration, communication and supervision between experts. Blowes and Trigger suggest that client privilege could be extended to an expert's report if peer review was sought through the legal representatives engaging the consultant anthropologist and the review was considered akin to a 'second opinion'. In their view, 'Such a process would not strictly be a "peer review" but rather the provision of assistance to the legal representatives of the claimants in assessing the potential expert evidence'.[3] The main issue here is to ensure that any peer review of evidentiary arguments must be conducted differently from the way in which peer review is commonly applied in academic situations. Further, there is the matter of protecting the integrity of evidence by implementing the kind of review process that involves critical commentary, yet does not impinge on the evidence in a substantive way.

A second matter requiring standardisation is in the area of contracts. In general it is possible to develop a standard form contract for anthropological research. It should specify employment terms and conditions, while defining the tasks involved, and provide protection across a number of matters (such as intellectual property rights, copyright, fees, professional insurance and so forth) for both parties.[4]

Liability also needs to be addressed, especially following the 1998 South Australian Hindmarsh Island Bridge dispute. It is now imperative that consultant anthropologists take out professional indemnity insurance. The various Hindmarsh Island inquiries and litigation have focused on the professional conduct of the researcher involved. The lesson from this case is clear: an experience of this kind could happen to any consultant.[5] Moreover, the risks exposed by the Hindmarsh Island case are endemic to the nature of much consultancy work. Accountability requirements must now be a critical consideration for all consultants and Native Title Representative Bodies.

Within the 1998 amendments to the Native Title Act, the accountability mantel rests on Native Title Representative Bodies to a greater extent than it has previously. In particular, corporations established under the Aboriginal Councils and Associations Act 1976 must now operate in line with the Commonwealth Authorities and Companies Act 1997. The Native Title Act provides that the directors, executive officers and former executive officers of representative bodies are now subject to the Commonwealth Authorities and Companies Act.[6] For the Native Title Representative Bodies' own protection this will necessitate codes of conduct for directors and executive officers. But there is also the matter of the circumstances under which a 'business judgment' is made in an Native Title Representative Body and whereby a decision is reached through reliance on a professional adviser or expert, in the reasonable belief that the matter is within the realm of the person's professional or expert competence. Anthropologists both in-house and those acting as consultants will need to be mindful of this liability.

Professional and methodological issues

The professional differences and tensions often experienced in anthropological and legal teamwork arise from fundamentally different visions held by these professions in regard to their enterprise, methodology and modes of operating. In addition, there is the question of professional respect based on an understanding of what each discipline offers in the research process and the capacity to work to the mutual advantage of the client.

Three key points of methodological difference are evident. First, the adversarial nature of much legal practice and performance is not common to an anthropological method that requires a good deal of active listening and quiet reflection on what is said by claimants and the context in which it is said. Second, the legal method rests on the articulation of a set of instructions from the client (or clients) to initiate action. By contrast, the anthropologist's understanding of the meaning of social action is often derived through participation and specific observation in conjunction with a broad knowledge of the ethnographic literature. Third, the anthropologist is often exploring a holistic understanding of a specific research question. Again, this differs from the pattern of legal representatives seeking instructions relating to particular goals and outcomes possible under the terms of legislation as an outcome of conversations held. In the native title field, this method of operation assumes that many forms of conversation between client and solicitor carry the same value, without necessarily recognising or distinguishing between political agitation and instruction.

In the native title arena basic misunderstandings seem to arise too readily between professionals. For example, some solicitors are sceptical of the methodological approach used to gather anthropological evidence and why the allied question of identifying the client should be problematic. For anthropologists, identifying the client is often part of a larger question of how the native title holding group is identified and constituted, and whether there is a wider community of interested parties whose rights and interests also need consideration. In part, these explorations are necessary to establish who holds the necessary political authority for decision-making and for group representation. Thus, what seems a simple question for one professional may be an open-ended one for another.

The question of the client's identity within a particular social group provides another dilemma. In practice, anthropologists may work with more than one group of people on a common inquiry given the necessity to explore the extent of individuals' cross-cutting alliances and kinship affiliations. For the legal practitioners such behaviour is problematic. Their view of who constitutes a client is more strictly defined.

Legal perspectives

That a lawyer was asked to undertake the Claims Coordination Service role in the Greater Mt Isa region in the absence of a Native Title Representative

Body is largely (one imagines) a function of the overtly (and overly) legalistic and combative native title framework. A symptom of this condition is the tenacious grasp that many of the lawyers operating in the region had on the plethora of lodged claims.

Initially, the Claims Coordination Service involved the crisis management of funds that had already been allocated by the regional Aboriginal and Torres Strait Islander Commission office to some claimant groups (and to competing factions within claimant groups) together with discussions with Aboriginal people in the region to determine claim needs. As there was no local body capable of receiving and accounting for native title allocated funds, a conduit for funding and an administrative system to handle the moneys had to be created. To keep matters interesting the solutions had to be politically neutral, pose no threat to existing contenders for Native Title Representative Body status and be kept distinct from the regional Aboriginal and Torres Strait Islander office that had borne the brunt of claimant requests for assistance.

The 1998 Native Title Act amendments, which substantially increased the workload of claimant service providers, came into affect at the same time that the Claim Coordination Service commenced. Within four months the Minister for Aboriginal Affairs had amended the boundaries for Native Title Representative Bodies, combining the Greater Mt Isa region with the Gulf region, serviced by the Carpentaria Land Council.

The Claims Coordination Service has no capacity to undertake the actual services for claimants but operates to manage the finances, oversee quality of work and co-ordinate services between various groups, such as in overlap mediation. Long-term planning is difficult as the Service is temporary; agreements for its provision are only for six-month periods. With the appointment of the Carpentaria Land Council as the north-west Queensland Native Title Representative Body, the Service should have been winding up but a funding dispute meant that the Service has persisted, at least for the short term. Professional advisers are suggested to claimants and matters of importance are discussed with the advisers. The legal role within the service extends to financial control, as well as the management of consultant lawyers and occasionally the mediation of disputes between lawyers and consultant anthropologists.

In general, these disputes have arisen where there has been a failure to communicate between the professionals involved at an early stage of the process. This in turn has precipitated later misunderstandings. There are a number of factors that contribute to this breakdown between professionals whose stock in trade, one way or another, is meant to be communication.

The first of these factors is the tyranny of distance. No consultants working in the Greater Mt Isa region live within 500 kilometres of the region and the service does not have a well-resourced central meeting facility. The Claims Coordination Service shares a converted butcher shop with its accountants who provide the shop front for the service. This makes it more difficult for the lawyers and anthropologists to spend time developing and discussing their respective functions and work methods when they are undertaking claims work. Telephones and emails are wonderful tools but for complex multidimensional tasks that are so dependant on both legal and anthropological input, such as claim preparation, there is no substitute for time spent face to face discussing what each party requires of the other and expects the other to deliver.

Most lawyers working for claimants in the region prior to the introduction of the Claims Coordination Service came from litigation backgrounds —not from Aboriginal land rights organisations—and had little if any native title experience. Few lawyers have any idea what anthropologists actually do. Lawyers are told that anthropologists are the relevant experts and so they request funds to get an expert report. In much the same way that a worker's compensation case will require the lawyer to send the client to a medical expert to ascertain the degree of injury the client is suffering, there seems to be a presumption that the anthropologist needs no particular briefing and that a report will duly be delivered indicating the degree of native title that the claimant group is suffering.

Ideally such inexperienced practitioners should be removed from the system until such time as they have educated themselves to a sufficient level, but the current demand for services precludes this. Instead, a greater level of discussion must be encouraged between professionals before they commence fieldwork or attend claimant meetings so that each is aware of what it is they are required to do.

The tensions that arise between professionals working in the multidisciplinary field of native title are not new constructions; there is mythological evidence and explanations for these occurrences. The *Jukurrpa*, or Dreaming, that informs contemporary professional antipathy transpires in the distant times before native title was a feature on the legal landscape. That landscape became inhabited by the mythic ancestral lawyer and anthropologist, beings who dabbled in the now largely forgotten art of land rights in that legendary territory known only as 'Northern'.

The ancestral battlefield was called Warrumungu and among the many battles fought was the struggle to protect those most sacred of objects—the anthropological field notes (an issue that still lives with us today[7]). A pitched battle was fought (in court) by the ancestral professionals and the sacred materials were found to be protected by the magic of lawyers (legal professional privilege). But there was a great gnashing of teeth as the ancestral anthropologists argued that the battle should be rejoined, for the law must recognise that there is anthropological magic too with which to protect the sacred material, not merely that of the lawyers.

The ancestral lawyers were unmoved, however. 'Since the sacred material was safe', they said, 'why should we go into battle again? Our magic is strong enough ... and who knows if you mob really have any magic worth fighting for?'[8] The ancestral anthropologists were not impressed. Ever since these times, placing a lawyer and an anthropologist in close proximity has generally led to a gnashing of teeth somewhere along the line. The Mt Isa Claims Coordination Service has provided no empirical evidence that would contradict the essential truth of the *Jukurrpa*.

Conclusions

At one level the Claims Coordination Service provides an interesting collaborative model in that it is undertaken jointly by an anthropologist and a lawyer. While there is a clearly defined separation of roles, the most valuable aspect of the collaboration is the ability to discuss the issues that arise with an experienced professional who has a quite different set of filters and viewpoints. A balanced solution can be derived that takes into account many more possibilities than might be the case individually or even in discussion with other similarly minded specialists.

Greater discussion is required at the outset to define the roles of the professional parties and the outputs required from each. Neither lawyers nor anthropologists should assume that they have absolute control of native title proceedings. Ostensibly, as other contributors to this volume observe, this belongs to the claimants. While lawyers have the carriage of the legal proceedings, there is a need to acknowledge the greater client contact and knowledge of the claimant group that anthropologists have and for all professionals involved to understand the roles that each performs and to contribute their skills to achieving claimant goals.

8

The Evolving Law of Native Title

Robert French

THE IDENTIFICATION OF Indigenous groups, their rules of definition and membership, their traditions and customs, their relationship to land and waters and the land and waters to which they relate, may be described and interpreted by anthropologists and other experts. But those things constitute the objects of consideration by the common law and statute law of native title. That law sets up the rules, lawyer made, or, to be more precise, judge made, which are the rules for recognition, by the non-Indigenous law, of the Indigenous relationship to country. Certain benefits attach to that recognition. They include common-law protections for that which is recognised. And beyond the common-law protections there are those conferred by the statute law, such as the right to negotiate and the entitlement to compensation for the loss of that which is recognised. The rules of recognition found in the common law of native title are qualified and limited. They are but a poor reflection of the full cultural, historical and human realities that are their object. While ambulatory in nature they are confined and reductionist. Nevertheless, along with the requirements of the Native Title Act, they largely define the terms of the debate in which the lawyers who participate in native title litigation, their clients and their expert witnesses must engage if recognition, for what it is worth, is to be invoked. This will have its own distorting effect upon the presentation and representation of Indigenous culture, as Veronica Strang suggests, in chapter 1 in this volume, when she refers to a 'reified cultural landscape presented to the "outsiders" . . . significantly different from the community's usual interactions with country'.

This does not mean that the common-law rules of recognition are to be regarded as immutable or all-powerful. The courts that make such rules can, within bounds, change or refine them. But the time for such change is earlier in their development rather than later when they have become elaborated and settled. Judge-made law is the product of decisions about individual cases. Its development is generally incremental, underpinned by slow growing policy. It involves the refinement and elaboration of rules as new circumstances for their application arise. It allows also for the construction of emergent principles that generalise existing rules or otherwise subsume them in higher orders of classification. As always, there is the ill-defined border, beyond which the adoption of new rules or the abolition of the old will be seen to trespass into the realm of the elected law-makers and thus lack constitutional legitimacy.

The *Mabo* decision itself was close to that border. As Gummow J said of that case in *Wik Peoples v Queensland*: 'To the extent that the common law is to be understood as the ultimate constitutional foundation in Australia, there was a perceptible shift in that foundation away from what had been understood at federation'.[1] That seismic shift established certain basic rules of recognition. They have been and are still being developed but that is through the traditional processes of the common law. As Lee J said in 1995 in the Full Federal Court decision in the Queensland *Waanyi* case:

> Exegesis of the operation of the common law in respect of native title will take place in the judgments of Australian courts which consider and apply *Mabo* (No 2). There will be an incremental development of the law according to the particular facts of each case as those cases are brought to the courts for decision.[2]

There is a power imbalance here. The common law is made and changed by judges who also interpret and apply the Act. Although judges of the Federal Court at first instance and on appeal may influence that process, the ultimate arbiters of the common law and the interpretation of the Act are the justices of the High Court. They in turn must yield to the changes the Parliament itself may, within constitutional limits, introduce by statute law.

Recognition of native title

Judges are significantly dependent upon the quality of the material and the arguments put before them. The extent to which the rules of the common law of native title and the interpretation and application of the Native Title

Act become better adapted to their subject matter will depend in no small measure upon the skills of the professionals involved in the court processes. This is more evident in the proof of the positive recognition of native title than in the area of extinguishment. Even in that latter area, what is really under consideration is not the operation of laws that annihilate or nullify Indigenous relationships to country, as the metaphor of extinguishment might suggest. Rather, what the courts are concerned with there are rules limiting or excluding recognition in certain circumstances, which generally involve the application of other rules of the common law or statute that are inconsistent with the recognition of native title.

It is instructive against this background briefly to consider the things the common law and the statute law require to be demonstrated to establish the necessary conditions for the recognition of native title. The basic ground rules of the common law were laid out in *Mabo*. To demonstrate the existence of native title it was necessary to show that the Aboriginal or Torres Strait Islander group said to hold the native title had a continuing connection with the land in question and had rights and interests in that land under Aboriginal or Torres Strait Islander traditional law and custom, as the case may be;[3] and continued to observe laws and customs that defined its ownership of rights and interests in the land.[4]

An early post-*Mabo* formulation of what was necessary to establish native title was offered by Mason CJ in *Coe v Commonwealth*. His Honour was sitting as a single judge in the High Court's original jurisdiction dealing with the viability of a statement of claim asserting Wiradjuri ownership to large parts of New South Wales. He said that the conditions that must be established by an applicant claiming native title included that the title had not been extinguished by inconsistent Crown grant—and that it had not been extinguished by the Aboriginal occupier ceasing to have a requisite physical connection with the land in question.[5]

Mason CJ relied upon a passage from the judgment of Brennan J in *Mabo* where his Honour had said:

> native title to an area of land which a clan or group is entitled to enjoy under the laws and customs of an Indigenous people is extinguished if the clan or group by ceasing to acknowledge those laws, and (so far as practicable) observe those customs, loses its connection with the land or on the death of the last of the members of the group or clan.[6]

Mabo was a case, however, in which the relevant community had a physical connection with the land in question. The question of whether physical connection was a necessary condition of recognition was not in issue. The Full Court of the Federal Court, reflecting broader concepts of

Indigenous connection with country, in *Western Australia v Ward* (the *Miriuwung Gajerrong* or *Ward* case),[7] had a different approach, albeit justified by reference to prior authority. Beaumont and von Doussa JJ in their joint judgment said:

> The evidence as to the relationship of the applicants and their ancestors to the determination area accords with evidence which has frequently been given in other cases, about the nature of the relationship of Aboriginal peoples with their lands. That relationship has been described as a 'religious relationship' (Milirrupum v Nabalco Pty Ltd at 167) and as 'primarily a spiritual affair' (R v Toohey; Ex parte Meneling Station Pty Ltd at 358).[8]

Their Honours also held that actual physical presence upon the land in pursuit of traditional rights to live and forage there, and for the performance of traditional ceremonies and customs, would provide clear evidence of the maintenance of a connection with the land. However, the spiritual connection and the discharge of responsibility for the land could be maintained, even where physical presence had ceased for reasons beyond the control of the people.

The High Court, on appeal from the Full Federal Court in *Ward*, held that the nature of the connection with land or waters necessary to establish native title was governed by Indigenous law and custom. It expressed no view on whether a spiritual connection to the land would suffice. But physical presence was not necessary. On the other hand occupation of itself was not sufficient for a finding of native title. It was necessary to identify the rights and interests that exist under traditional laws and customs.[9] The definition of native title in section 223 of the Native Title Act requires, so it was held, consideration of whether, by the traditional laws acknowledged and the traditional customs observed by the people concerned, those people have a connection with the land or waters. That requires identification of the content of the traditional laws and customs and the characterisation of the effects as constituting a connection. Absence of evidence of recent use would not necessarily negate the existence of that connection.[10]

The Full Court of the Federal Court in *Ward* had also discussed the rules by which the group asserting native title could be defined. The state had proposed what the court described as 'a narrow and exclusive test of biological descent'. The state relied upon observations of Brennan J in *Mabo* and contended that a strict patrilineal descent test should have been applied, which would have had the consequence that a number of applicants would not have established ancestral connection with the native title holders at the time of colonisation. The Full Court however did not read Brennan J as mandating 'strict biological descent'. Their Honours interpreted him thus:

> we understand Brennan J to be expressing a requirement that there be an identifiable community with an entitlement to the present enjoyment of native title rights in relation to land arising from the adherence to traditionally based law and customs. A substantial degree of ancestral connection between the original native title holders and the present community would be necessary to enable a group to be identified as one acknowledging and observing the traditional laws and customs under which the native title rights were possessed at sovereignty.[11]

In any event, their Honours did not see any requirement for biological descent as limited to patrilineal descent. They expressed rather a broad view:

> The identity of those presently entitled to enjoy native title rights, is to be ascertained by reference to the traditional laws and customs as currently acknowledged and observed. The evidence in this case is to the effect that under the traditional laws and customs, a whole range of relationships may lead to membership of the community, including 'father's country', 'father's mother's country', 'mother's country', 'mother's mother's country, 'regent's country', the country of a spouse, and spiritual conception or birth within the area.[12]

While some element of biological descent still appears to be necessary, the range of links between the native title holders and those holding native title at the time of sovereignty is to be defined by reference to traditional laws and customs. These are to be acknowledged and observed by the communities in the determination area at sovereignty and as currently acknowledged and observed by those recognised among themselves as the present members of the native title community. Nothing in the High Court decision in *Ward* appears to undercut this aspect of their Honours' reasoning in the Full Federal Court.

The majority in the Full Court elaborated the nature of connection necessary to establish native title by holding that it was not necessary for every member of the native title group to have a full array of rights over the whole of the area under claim. Their Honours said: 'It follows from what we have earlier said that it is not necessary for each of the named applicants who bring the proceedings in a representative capacity to establish that they possess rights and interests uniformly over the entire determination area'.[13] So the trial judge was found to have been correct in holding that the Miriuwung and Gajerrong communities, having at one time acknowledged and recognised separate territories, in more recent times had become regarded (among themselves) as a composite community with shared interests.

The development of the rules for recognition, which make up what could be called the positive common law of native title, depends upon their ambulatory character and the preparedness of the court to apply them across a variety of circumstances and of traditional laws and customs by which native title groups and their relationship to country are defined.[14] However the High Court in its decision in *Ward* has emphasised the importance of the statutory definition of native title in section 223(1) of the Native Title Act. Although that definition is drawn from words used by Brennan J in *Mabo* those words have become the words of a statute. Moreover they are treated as requiring native title to be analysed as a bundle of rights the separate components of which could be extinguished separately. The approach adopted, tied as it is to the words of the Act, is less flexible than the common-law approach. It is questionable whether the Parliament intended the Act to freeze the concept of native title in statutory amber rather than to provide a vessel for its ongoing development.

The Full Court had rejected a finding by the trial judge that native title rights recognised by the common law extended to a right to prevent misuse of cultural knowledge. The majority judgment did not think this was a right in relation to land of a kind that could be recognised. The High Court agreed with that view.[15]

An example of importance in which the ambulatory approach to the identification of native title rights and interests may operate is that of succession to country. In my decision as President of the National Native Title Tribunal in 1995 in the *Waanyi* case, I observed:

> The applicants' case on native title would, no doubt, face considerable obstacles, not least the characterisation of their connection with the land as traditional. But that characterisation and their possible succession to the land after the Injilarija depends upon factual exploration of the social structure that encompasses both groups as part of a cultural block and the question whether, if some such structure exists, it can be said to embody traditional laws and customs regulating succession to the land that would be recognised by the common law.[16]

There was a contention in that case that the original occupants of the land subject to the Waanyi claim were Injilarija who had died out and that the Waanyi had merely moved in to occupy vacant space. The High Court later reversed the decision in this case on grounds relating to the proper approach to the acceptance function under the Act as it stood prior to 1998. The conclusion as to the possibility of the succession of the Waanyi to the Injilarija in accordance with laws and customs defined within a cultural block was based upon evidence submitted by anthropologist David Trigger.

In December 1999, with the decision of the Full Court of the Federal Court in *Commonwealth v Yarmirr*,[17] the common law took a further important step, with the aid of the Native Title Act in extending recognition to native title in offshore waters. This was against a contention by the Commonwealth itself that no native title existed in waters outside the limits of the Northern Territory for the reason that the common law of Australia did not, of its own force, apply outside those limits. The common law, it was said, stopped at the low water mark of the mainland and offshore islands. This proposition was rejected in the Full Court but interestingly in part by reference to the provisions of the Native Title Act. Because the Act applies under section 6 to the coastal sea of Australia and to any waters over which Australia asserts sovereign rights, it sidestepped argument about the territorial limits of the common law. Beaumont and von Doussa JJ in *Yarmirr* agreed with Olney J at first instance that section 6 of the Native Title Act, coupled with the recognition of native title accorded by section 10, supports the proposition that the legislative intent was to provide a statutory basis for recognition offshore.[18] Thus the Act itself was invoked to support the application of common-law rules of recognition for native title in offshore waters. The High Court upheld the decision of the Full Federal Court.[19]

Notions of 'tradition'

The judgment of the Full Federal Court in *Yarmirr* contained some important reflections on the dating of traditional laws and customs that are the subject of recognition. While the date of acquisition of sovereignty by the Crown remains central to the determination of native title, from a practical point of view, the particular date is of no importance. *Mabo* had recognised that the laws and customs of Indigenous people may undergo change subsequent to the acquisition of sovereignty and the means of enjoyment of native title rights and interests can change with the times, such as to permit the hunting of estuarine crocodiles with the use of an outboard motor as in the *Yanner* case.[20] The fundamental requirement identified by the court is not that the rights and interests were acknowledged and observed at any particular date, but that they follow from the acknowledgment of traditional laws and the observance of traditional customs. The word 'traditional' here is used in the dictionary sense of that which is 'handed down by tradition', 'tradition' being 'the handing down of statements, beliefs, legends, customs and so on from generation to generation, especially by word of mouth or practice'. So it was said:

> In most cases where the date of acquisition of sovereignty was coincidental with, or preceded, first European contact in a particular area, there will be no reason to doubt that the rights and interests of the Indigenous inhabitants, so long as they reflect the laws acknowledged and customs observed, were rights and interests possessed under traditional laws and customs.[21]

Since the Crossing Boundaries conference in 2000, the High Court in the *Yorta Yorta* decision upheld a finding that the Yorta Yorta people had failed to prove the maintenance of their connection with the land under claim from settlement to the present day in accordance with their traditional laws and customs from the time of annexation.[22] The original occupants of the land had ceased to observe their traditional laws and customs by 1881. This was a consequence of European settlement and the suppression of the languages and tribal customs. Evidence of past occupation was insufficient to show the required acknowledgment and observance of traditional laws and customs. The trial judge had concluded that 'the tide of history has washed away any real acknowledgment of their traditional laws and any real observance of their traditional customs'.

The High Court held that the native title rights and interests referred to in the Native Title Act are those that have their origin in laws and customs predating annexation by the British Crown. It is only the normative rules of the Aboriginal and Torres Strait Islander societies that existed before the assumption of sovereignty by the Crown that are traditional laws and customs. The normative system under which the relevant rights and interests are enjoyed must have had a continuing existence since sovereignty. Once the system has ceased to exist, later attempts to revive adherence to it will not resurrect the traditional laws and customs that form part of the definition of native title under the Act. The Court did recognise that change to and adaptation of traditional laws and customs will not necessarily be fatal to a native title claim. What is necessary is the continuity of acknowledgment and observance of traditional laws and customs substantially uninterrupted since sovereignty. It is not clear how these approaches would affect succession of the kind discussed in the *Waanyi* case. It may be that succession, as in that case, could be accommodated under an overarching system of traditional law and custom attributable to a cultural block including the successor group.

Extinguishment

The other side of the recognition of native title at common law is reflected in the concept of extinguishment. This is in essence a rule of limitation or qualification of the recognition that may be afforded native title at common law. In *Mabo* Brennan J used the term 'extinguish' as a label for the consequence of acts of the Crown wholly or partially inconsistent with the continuing right to enjoy native title. His Honour also used it in what I think is a quite different sense when he said:

> native title to an area of land which a clan or group is entitled to enjoy under the laws and customs of an Indigenous people is extinguished if the clan or group by ceasing to acknowledge those laws, and (so far as practicable) observe those customs, loses its connection with the land or on the death of the last of the members of the group or clan.[23]

The use of extinguishment in these two senses risks confusing two quite different concepts. One is that of extinguishment as a limit on common-law recognition, which does not and cannot of itself affect the relationship between a native title group and its country. The other concerns the loss of that relationship, which means there is no subject matter for recognition by the common law.

The notion of extinguishment as a limit on what the common law can do is affected by the nature of the metaphor the word imports. It is too easy to think of common-law extinguishment as something that annihilates Aboriginal culture. But as Toohey J said in the *Wik* case, native title rights affected by inconsistent grants are 'unenforceable at law and, in that sense, extinguished'.[24] There is the risk, by the use of this metaphor, of conceptual confusion. Indeed it may be an impediment to the development of a coherent theory of extinguishment, which is best regarded as a mutable rule of recognition or non-recognition. So, in *Fejo v Northern Territory*, the High Court held that native title is extinguished by a grant in fee simple and is not revived if the land reverts to the Crown. In explaining the common law underpinning this proposition, their Honours said: 'The underlying existence of the traditional laws and customs is a necessary prerequisite for native title but their existence is not a sufficient basis for recognising native title'.[25]

In dealing with the issue of revival of native title it was said:

> The rights created by the exercise of sovereign power being inconsistent with native title, the rights and interests that together make up that native title were necessarily at an end. There can be no question, then, of those rights springing forth again when the land came to be held again by the Crown. Their recognition has been overtaken by the exercise of 'the power to create and to extinguish private rights and interests in land within the Sovereign's territory'.[26]

So expressed, not without some ambivalence, the rule seems to be one about recognition rather than any direct operation upon the traditional laws and customs of the people. The joint judgment in the High Court in *Ward*, consistently with that approach, treated extinguishment as 'the withdrawal of recognition by the common law'.[27]

The Native Title Act itself tries to give permanence to extinguishment by its definition of the word in section 237A, which provides:

> The word 'extinguish' in relation to native title means permanently extinguish the native title. To avoid any doubt, this means that after the extinguishment the native title rights and interests cannot revive, even if the act that caused the extinguishment ceases to have effect.

This definition only applies to extinguishment for which the Act provides. But extinguishment recognised by the common law is mutable and whether derived from common law or imposed by statute it can be reversed by statute law. Paradoxically, the Native Title Act itself demonstrates the revocability of the concept in sections 47, 47A and 47B. These provide that under certain circumstances prior extinguishment of native title is to be disregarded for all purposes under the Act. Those circumstances relate to pastoral leases held by native title claimants and reserves and vacant Crown land covered by claimant applications.

In the *Ward* case the Full Federal Court held in 2000 that in Western Australia the grant of pastoral leases and certain mining leases extinguished native title. It also held that the Ord River Project considered as a whole was operationally inconsistent with the subsistence of native title rights and interests and that it extinguished them.

In 2002 the High Court considered the effect of the historic grant of pastoral leases. It referred to the history of Western Australia land law. In the light of that history pastoral leases were seen as a 'precarious interest' for limited purpose and 'not to be understood as rendering unlawful what was previously a lawful use of the land by native title holders'. So, like the pastoral leases in *Wik*, those granted in Western Australia did not necessarily extinguish native title even though they extinguished any right to control access to the land. The High Court also held that the Full Court had erred in taking a global approach to the Ord River Project in determining that it extinguished native title rights and interests. The High Court made clear that what was required was an analysis of the legal effect of the various grants that had been made under a variety of laws for the purpose of establishing the project. The actual administrative management of the project did not of itself involve operational inconsistency giving rise to extinguishment of native title. The High Court further found, contrary to the view of the majority in the Full Court of the Federal Court, that the grant of mining leases was not necessarily inconsistent with the continued existence of all native title rights and interests. The grant of exclusive possession under a mining lease was directed to prevent others from carrying out mining and related activities on the relevant land. In three areas, the effect of pastoral leases, mineral leases and the Ord River Project, the outcome in the High Court was favourable to the native title applicants. However, the finding in the joint judgment, that the vesting of Crown reserves under section 33 of the Western Australian Land Act, and in particular the creation of national parks by that process extinguishes native title, has a major impact in respect of areas where coexisting native title rights might be thought to have survived.

The law of native title continues to be elaborated by the courts, teased out and discussed by commentators and applied in negotiations between parties to claims. The law has developed substantially in recent times.

Having regard to the massive resource burden imposed by native title litigation, it is to be hoped that there will be an increasing incidence of negotiated outcomes on pending applications.

Conclusions

I have not endeavoured here to cover the full contemporary content of the law of native title as it stands at the moment. I have tried to advance the proposition that the common-law rules and the rules or processes by which they change, together with the Native Title Act, form the universe of discourse within which Indigenous people seeking recognition under the common law, their lawyers, anthropologists, historians, linguists and others must operate. That is not to say that the special knowledge and insights of all cannot effectively be brought to bear within that framework. Much of it is ambulatory and capable of operation across a variety of facts and circumstances. While recent decisions of the High Court, particularly in *Ward* and *Yorta Yorta,* have been discouraging to native title applicants there is still much room for negotiation, agreement and positive outcomes which will require the resources of a number of different disciplines.

9

The Rules for Engagement

Fred Chaney

THE LEGAL RECOGNITION of native title has given rise to issues and processes that provide challenges to anthropologists, linguists, historians and lawyers. Those issues not only cross the boundaries of these areas of expertise, but also involve the whole community. It is the community that is required to absorb and act on a new paradigm for the relationship between Aboriginal and non-Aboriginal Australia with respect to dealings in land. For the first time since colonisation, rights intrinsic to Aboriginal people have an impact on fundamental questions relating to land management. The recognition by the common law of rights and interests arising from the traditional laws and customs of Aboriginal people is a far cry from the broader aspects of Australia's post-colonial history, and challenges the mindset of all but that minority which has seen recognition of Australia's first nations and their interests in land as both just and practicable.[1]

In 1992 the High Court of Australia decided, in *Mabo*, that 'the common law of Australia recognises a form of native title which, in the cases where it has not been extinguished, reflects the entitlements of the indigenous inhabitants, in accordance with their laws and customs, to their traditional lands'.[2] That decision made it clear that the landmass of Australia was not *terra nullius* when the Crown assumed sovereignty. Rather, Indigenous people held rights and interests in land that could be recognised and protected by the law of Australia.

Because native title exists already—and, unlike statutory land rights, is not granted by the Crown—there were various questions facing Indigenous people, governments and others with interests in land. For example:

- Where does native title exist?
- Who holds native title in relation to an area of land or water?
- What are the native title rights and interests in relation to each area?
- How are native title rights to be protected?
- What is the relationship between native title rights and interests and any other rights and interests in relation to each area?
- How can new interests be created in relation to areas where native title exists?

These are national issues with significant practical consequences. After *Mabo*, there were various options for dealing with them. One option was to allow Indigenous people to assert their rights and, where it was necessary to prove those rights, to require Indigenous people to seek a judicial declaration that they hold native title. Another option was to create a more informal way of allowing Indigenous people to assert their native title rights and allow others whose interests might be affected by those rights to negotiate with them about whether and how the native title should be recognised.

The latter approach was adopted in the Commonwealth's Native Title Act 1993, the preamble to which states:

> A special procedure needs to be available for the just and proper ascertainment of native title rights and interests which will ensure that, if possible, this is done by conciliation and, if not, in a manner that has due regard to their unique character.
>
> Governments should, where appropriate, facilitate negotiation on a regional basis between the parties concerned in relation to:
>
> (a) claims to land, or aspirations in relation to land, by Aboriginal peoples and Torres Strait Islanders; and
>
> (b) proposals for the use of such land for economic purposes.

It is the Native Title Act that provides the framework within which the parties asserting and contesting native title engage. The National Native Title Tribunal is an administrative body established in accordance with the main objects of the Act, to provide assistance or undertake mediation in matters relating to native title and with power to make determinations about whether certain future acts can be done and whether certain agreements concerning native title are to be covered by the Act. The powers and functions, membership and administration of the Tribunal are governed by the Act and by regulations made under the Act.

The Act confers various specific functions on the Tribunal including in relation to Federal Court proceedings arising from native title determination applications and compensation applications. When the Court refers proceedings to the Tribunal for mediation, the Tribunal holds conferences of the parties.[3] The Act sets out how mediation conferences are to be conducted, who may attend or participate in conferences, the circumstances in which questions of fact or law may be referred to the Court, and the way in which reports about the mediation are to be made to the Court.[4]

The Tribunal must pursue the objective of carrying out its functions in a fair, just, economical, informal and prompt way. In carrying out its functions, the Tribunal may take account of the cultural and customary concerns of Aboriginal peoples and Torres Strait Islanders, but not so as to prejudice unduly any party to any proceedings that may be involved. The Tribunal is not bound by technicalities, legal forms or rules of evidence. The Tribunal may sit at any place in Australia or in any other place to which the Act extends.[5]

According to the Native Title Act, the statutory scheme for the resolution of native title claimant applications provides that:

- claimant applications are to be filed in the Federal Court;
- applications are sent to the Registrar of the Tribunal who undertakes various administrative procedures (including applying the registration test to each application and notifying the relevant persons, bodies and the public about each application);
- the Federal Court decides who should be parties to the proceedings and whether each application should be referred to the Tribunal for mediation;
- the Tribunal carries out the mediation of each matter referred to it and reports to the Federal Court on the progress of mediation;
- where native title exists, the Federal Court makes an appropriate determination of native title, either in or consistent with the terms agreed by the parties or as decided by the Court after a trial.

The various steps taken in relation to a native title application are summarised in the accompanying table.

Generally speaking, the Federal Court refers every claimant application to the Tribunal for mediation, including the ascertaining of agreed facts, as soon as practicable after the end of the notification period for the application.[6] In addition, the Court may, at any time in a proceeding, refer the whole or part of the proceeding to the Tribunal for mediation if the Court considers that the parties will be able to reach agreement on (or on facts relevant to) any of the matters set out in section 86A(1).

Steps taken in relation to a native title application

Main steps in native title applications	*Responsible agency*		*Relevant section of the Native Title Act*
	Federal Court	*National Native Title Tribunal or equivalent state or territory body*	
Filing	Application filed and checked for compliance with procedural requirements		61 61A 62
Referral #1	Application referred to Tribunal or equivalent body		63
Notification #1		State or Territory Government and Native Title Representative Bodies provided with a copy of application	66(2) 66(22A)
Registration		New registration test applied to native title application	190B 190C
Notification #2		Native title application advertised and other potential parties notified	66(3)
Parties	Applications for party status assessed and determined		84 (84A)
Referral #2	Native title application referred to Tribunal or equivalent body for mediation		86B
Mediation		Mediation conducted	136A
Agreement		Mediated agreement referred to Federal Court	136G(1)
Agreed determination	Court considers if appropriate to make determination of native title		81 87 94A

No agreement		Tribunal makes mediation report to Federal Court	86E 136G(3)
Contested determination	Court decides whether to make a determination of native title (Court may refer matter back to Tribunal or equivalent body for further mediation)		81 94A 86B(5)

The statutory framework is imbued with the idea that matters will be settled by agreement. Furthermore, all state governments have expressed the desire to settle native title claims by agreement. But it is important to understand that the agreements sought by the states and put forward for the sanction of the court are not agreements made at large. So far at least they are not political settlements based on an assessment of what might be a desirable outcome balancing Aboriginal and non-Aboriginal interests and aiming at the social and economic integration of the disparate communities.

Of direct relevance to all specialists engaged in native title work is that the process is rigorous and not just a well-meaning search for an acceptable outcome. An examination of the rules of engagement in two states illustrates the point. In Western Australia, the State Government has issued general guidelines for native title determinations and agreements. They provide that the government will consider negotiation of native title claims where:

(i) the native title claimants provide satisfactory evidence of their ancestry and their continuous traditional connection (the evidence is to be incorporated into what is referred to as a 'connection report');
(ii) there are no overlapping claims other than those which reflect shared native title rights and interests;
(iii) the native title claim excludes exclusive tenures granted by the Crown;
(iv) native title rights and interests claimed over non-exclusive tenures are consistent with other parties' rights and interests; and
(v) the native title claimants acknowledge that any native title rights and interests are subject to State laws of general application.[7]

Each native title claim is assessed on its merits to determine if there is scope for a consent determination of native title.

A need for extreme care and rigour in the preparation of connection reports is emphasised by the following provisions in the guidelines:

> The negotiation process, including draft agreements, acknowledgements, proposals and the like, will be without prejudice, i.e., they will not be used or referred to in litigation or made public . . . However, claimants should be aware

> that, if the application goes to trial, the State does not undertake to continue to preserve the confidentiality of the connection report in the event that evidence at the trial is inconsistent with the connection report. That is to say, claimants and their experts should ensure that statements in the connection report are made with the same care as would statements in court.

In the balance of the document the state sets out in some detail the information it requires, with respect to the native title applicant group. For example, it requires genealogies for all people holding native title; information on the traditional system of land tenure; the continuous connection between the applicant group and the claimed land; the asserted rights and interests; and a comprehensive bibliography. Whether all the detail required is necessary to establish that native title exists, and, if so, in what form, is a matter for expert judgment and views will differ. Nevertheless, these are the preconditions to engagement with the state and no doubt represent its view of what is required.

The approach of the Queensland Government is substantially similar in content although there are significant differences in the role assumed by the state in establishing the conditions for recognition of native title. In terms of rigorous assessment of what rights might be legally recognised there is no difference.

The 1999 *Guide to Compiling a Connection Report* issued by the State of Queensland describes the approach in that state in some detail. As expressed by Queensland Premier Beattie in the preface to the guide:

> our whole approach was built on a determined policy shift away from litigation towards negotiated agreements between native title claimants and other land users . . .
>
> An important starting point for negotiated and mediated agreements between native title claimants and the State of Queensland is the compilation and presentation of a Connection Report, aimed at establishing that applicant groups are the traditional owners of the land or waters claimed.
>
> The Queensland Government is acutely aware that these reports, which are often critical in determining whether native title claims are recognised or rejected, represent a significant burden on claimant groups and representative bodies. Their compilation can be difficult, time-consuming and expensive.[8]

The guide also states:

> Connection Reports (also known as anthropological reports, historical reports, claimants' statements) are presented to the Queensland Government as part of the mediation process carried out under the Commonwealth *Native Title Act 1993*. The Connection Reports are presented at an early stage in the mediation process with the purpose of determining whether the Applicant group is the holder of native title over the particular areas of land or water being claimed.[9]

The guide lists the three essential elements of a connection report as being:

1. evidence that the applicants are in fact the traditional owners of the land and waters claimed;
2. evidence of a continuity of connection; and
3. evidence of existence of traditional law and custom which gives rise to the claim and of continued holding of the native title rights and interests by the group in accordance with those laws and customs.[10]

Recognising that the compilation of connection reports can be a very costly exercise, in both time and money, for applicant groups and their representative bodies, the Queensland Government is keen to make sure that those undertaking the required research should be given a clear understanding of what the State of Queensland expects so the reports can be compiled and produced as inexpensively and succinctly as possible.

In Queensland as in Western Australia the state must be satisfied, in the context of evolving and sometimes uncertain law, that native title can be proven to exist. The difference between Western Australia and Queensland is that Queensland's Native Title Services Unit, within the Department of Premier and Cabinet, includes a Historical and Anthropological Unit. This is described in the guide at the outset as:

> a multidisciplinary team with specialists who have expertise in history, anthropology, archaeology and linguistics. They are available to assist native title applicants find their way through the maze of records to locate material that provides support for their native title claims.

This unit has responsibility for assessing the connection reports that the native title applicants provide to the state to establish that they are the traditional owners of the area claimed and that they have had a continuing connection to the land or sea under claim. These reports are critical in the mediation of native title claims before the National Native Title Tribunal, and in other negotiations.

> Although these specialists do not do the actual compiling of the reports, they can assist with source analysis, and by acting as 'signposts' in finding references to documents that may be in the libraries and archives to which they have easy access in Brisbane. Assistance can also be provided in locating references to material that may be located in other national libraries or archives.[11]

The guide also reveals the value of legal critique. After comments on three important Federal Court decisions on native title claims that dealt with the issue of connection, the Yorta Yorta, Croker Island and Miriuwung Gajerrong claims,[12] it was observed that: 'All 3 of these decisions are currently on appeal and it is important to recognise that everyone is operating in largely uncharted waters until legal finality is established in each case'.[13]

This comment confirms the contestability of propositions of law that determine what facts have to be ascertained in any particular case.

Conclusions

Given the legal (and potential political and constitutional) implications of native title it is not surprising that its assessment is seen as a matter to be addressed critically and rigorously. It is this that makes the work of all those involved challenging and difficult because they and their work will be challenged and often contested as the search for legal finality continues.

The mediation process requires skills of a high order from lawyers, anthropologists, historians and linguists. Those skills cannot be deployed successfully in isolation from each other. The overt team approach adopted by the Queensland Government is a reminder of what is required. Anthropological work needs to be relevant to what must be proved to establish common-law recognition of native title. Lawyers need to be brought to an understanding of the complex and shifting bodies of Aboriginal law and custom that accommodate the massive effects of settlement and economic development.

10

Confidentiality and Privilege: Legal Proceedings and Anthropological Research

Carolyn Tan

In cases of native title we have seen the phenomenon of anthropologists being issued with subpoenas to provide access to their notebooks, videos, tape recordings, and so on, which contain the record of comments made by Aboriginal informants and also any personal observations. Such records may have been made in the context of heritage surveys, research for native title claims or other research. While the cases have concerned anthropologists, the issues could apply equally to historians, linguists and others who might be recording information from native title claimants.

In the course of conducting research with a particular community, there may be a lot of things said and recorded that may not have been checked or explored fully or may have simply been misunderstood or taken out of context. Such material is not intended to find its way into a final report nor is it to be the basis for conclusions to be drawn in such a report. The spectre of these comments being publicised in court and put to Aboriginal witnesses in cross-examination is naturally horrifying for researchers who like to make detailed notes.

In addition, there is the issue of confidentiality and duties owed to Aboriginal people who have shared their knowledge. The code of ethics of the Australian Anthropological Society and the Anthropological Society of Western Australia, for instance, includes such principles as:

(i) Where a conflict of views or interests arises, the views and interests of those studied should be placed first;

(ii) Any voluntary revelation of personal identities or of confidential information should be solely by agreement with those whose identities or knowledge have been recorded by the anthropologist.[1]

In this regard there is a clause that says that members should explain to those studied that, despite every effort anthropologists may make to preserve the anonymity or privacy of individuals or the confidential status of information, there may arise legal contexts where these efforts fail.[2] The code also says:

(iii) Members should not knowingly or avoidably allow information gained on a basis of trust and cooperation of those studied to be used against their legitimate interests by hostile third parties.[3]

While these leave open the possibility that anthropologists could be subpoenaed and forced by court processes to reveal the information to hostile third parties, it is clear that this would be contradictory to the spirit in which such research is conducted.

The arrangement between the informants and the anthropologists could be such that in addition to ethical issues, there may even in some circumstances be a legal duty of confidentiality and a breach of that duty may give the informants rights to bring injunction applications against the anthropologist to prevent information from being revealed in circumstances outside a Court hearing. In the case of *Foster v Mountford* in 1976 in the Northern Territory, the Supreme Court granted an injunction to stop the publication of a book that described Aboriginal cultural and religious secret ceremonies, disclosed in confidence some years before.[4]

This raises the question of what, if anything, can be protected from disclosure and when. The usual situation when disclosure can be avoided is when the communication is privileged.

As a lawyer who acts mainly for native title claim groups, my instinctive approach is to seek to prevent potentially adverse material from being disclosed. While this seems to be in the spirit of the code of ethics referred to earlier, this may not always accord with the ways of researching or communicating that some consultant anthropologists may be used to and also may not accord with the notion of consultants being completely independent and objective. Mine is just one point of view and it is necessary for all professionals involved to work together with the clients to find the appropriate balance in each case.

Disclosure of documents and information

There are three main occasions in legal proceedings where disclosure of confidential information is likely to be required. These are in discovery of documents; in subpoenas to produce documents, usually at trial; and in questions asked of a witness in the course of the trial. Discovery is a process in legal proceedings where each party is required to provide to the other parties a list of all relevant documents that each party has in its 'possession, custody or control' and to then allow inspection of the relevant documents except those that are exempt from this requirement due to privilege or other reasons. General discovery is not common in native title cases. However, it is a standard process in most civil litigation so it could well come up in cases to do with heritage protection litigation in civil courts, such as injunctions to stop the destruction of sites.

Private documents or recordings belonging to anthropologists often do not have to be considered for discovery because they are not in the 'possession, custody or control' of the parties to the litigation, for example Aboriginal parties, as long as those parties or their lawyers do not have a copy of them. While discovery of documents belonging to third parties is allowed in some instances, this still tends to be the exception rather than the rule.

Discovery and production of documents can be objected to on grounds such as privilege and, if this is disputed, the court can determine whether the objection is valid. If the court finds that the document has to be produced, then it can order this and it will be a contempt of court to refuse.

A party, such as the state, can organise for subpoenas to be issued to people, including third parties, such as consultant anthropologists or other experts, to bring documents to court or to give evidence in court. These are usually issued for the first or a later day of the trial but there is scope for this to be done before the main trial commences. A party seeking to challenge a subpoena can apply for it to be set aside or for other orders limiting disclosure. A failure to comply with a valid subpoena can be a contempt of court as well.

Expert or other witnesses can be asked questions in the course of a trial which will require them to reveal confidential information told to them. The general rule is that relevant questions must be answered, unless there is a good ground, such as privilege, to object and, again, it is a contempt of court otherwise.

Withholding information and documents

The general rule is that parties to the litigation should be entitled to have access to relevant documents. Mere confidentiality is not enough to withhold disclosure. There is no general rule that documents should not be discovered or subpoenaed just because they are confidential or because the person asked to produce them is under a duty of confidentiality. For instance, it is common for a court in commercial cases to require confidential business information and trade secrets to be provided if they are relevant to the case, but disclosure can be limited by orders as to who can see the documents and the number of copies that can be made. In those circumstances there is often a requirement at least to provide the information to the court as well as to the lawyers and experts for the other parties.

The major ways in which a party can object to documents or information being produced is through the documents being subject to what the law recognises as 'privilege'. There are two main categories of such privilege. The first of these is legal professional privilege, otherwise known as client legal privilege, and the other is public interest privilege or public interest immunity. There are some other exceptions to the general rule, such as the privilege against self-incrimination, but these are not relevant here.

Client legal privilege is a principle that protects two main kinds of communications: confidential communications between lawyer and client or their agents for the purpose of legal advice; and confidential communications between lawyer and client or their agents or with third parties for the purposes of or in anticipation of litigation.

Client legal privilege belongs to the client. If the client, such as the native title claimant group, through its lawyers, chooses to reveal the information or allow it to be revealed, then the consultant expert cannot prevent this, even if this is against the spirit in which the information was obtained. Naturally this assumes that the legal representatives of the claim group have the authority of their clients to agree to disclosure.

The privilege applies when the dominant purpose of the communications was one of the purposes set out above, that is for legal advice or for litigation. This is now the position at common law and the Commonwealth Evidence Act has a similar provision in section 118 for evidence submitted at trial in the Federal Court. Previously the High Court had said that the privilege only applied if the legal advice or litigation was the sole purpose of the communication.

The protection is for communications and legal advice or reasoning and documents or recordings that record those communications, advice or reasoning. If there is a mere description of something or a video or audio recording of matters or events that are publicly observable, then there have been cases that suggest these are not covered by client legal privilege. This would be different if the document or recording was selective as to what was recorded in a way that would reveal what the legal advice or reasoning was.

The rationale of this rule is to encourage full and frank disclosures between lawyers and their clients, without having to fear subsequent disclosure of such information.[5] This has been said to represent a balance found by the courts between the competing public interest in making access to all information available for a fair trial on the one hand, and protecting full communications with lawyers on the other.

There is no general corresponding rule in Western Australia protecting confidential communications between clients and professionals other than lawyers, such as anthropologists, from disclosure in the courts. For instance, the Media, Entertainment and Arts Alliance's Code of Ethics for journalists forbids members from revealing sources of information given in confidence. However, there have been quite a few cases where a journalist's refusal to reveal the source of information on the basis of ethical duty to maintain the confidentiality of such sources has been held to be contempt of court. In some cases journalists have been given short-term imprisonment or fines.[6]

Another example is that in Western Australia members of clergy also have no general right to refuse to reveal confessions to the courts even though this would require a breach of religious obligations. The Commonwealth Evidence Act has enacted a privilege for religious confessions that applies in the Federal Court (section 127), but this deals with a specific and limited situation of such confessions. One may well query the inconsistency between the protection of confidential communications with lawyers and other professions. However, that is the position of the law in Western Australia and many other states.

As a general principle, where anthropologists are obtaining information from native title claimants for the dominant purpose of gathering evidence for a native title claim, this should be privileged. By contrast where communications are made during heritage surveys, which are being carried out with no view to legal advice being obtained and where litigation is not contemplated, these would obviously not be subject to client legal privilege.

Waiver of privilege

Client legal privilege can be waived or lost if some information is used that would be unfair to use without also requiring otherwise privileged information to be revealed. One of the leading cases dealing with the question of waiver of privilege at common law is *Attorney-General v Maurice*, part of the Warrumungu land claim.[7] This case concerned a claim book that had been circulated previously and that referred to source materials. The High Court said that the question of whether privilege to the source materials was waived depended on whether it would be unfair or misleading to allow a party to refer to or use the material and yet assert that the material was privileged and not to be given to the other parties. The High Court said that if the claim book had gone into evidence (as anthropological reports do) then the other party would have been entitled to test its accuracy and weight and that could hardly be done unless it knew what sources it was based on. However, in the case itself, the claim book was not put into evidence and there were just references to it in the opening of the case and some questions put to two of the witnesses. It was not used to establish the truth of any particular proposition and it was found not to be a case where the disclosure of the document would give a partial or misleading picture. The source materials for the claim book therefore remained privileged.

The Commonwealth Evidence Act, in sections 122 and 126, also sets out cases where client legal privilege can be lost so that the evidence can be led in the Federal Court. These include situations where the substance of the evidence has already been knowingly and voluntarily disclosed to another person; a document is used to revive a witness's memory; and the information is necessary to enable a proper understanding of another piece of evidence.

One illustration of the principle is where a consultant's report, which draws conclusions and opinions based on communications from the members of the claim group, is put into evidence. It is generally accepted, as reflected in the Warrumungu case, that in order to enable the other parties and the court to fairly test and judge the expert evidence, it is necessary to have access to and to be able to question the expert witness on the source material.

This is reflected in the *Guidelines for Expert Witnesses in Proceedings in the Federal Court of Australia*. These provide that the expert's report must attach or summarise all instructions, facts, matters and assumptions on which the report proceeds and the documents and other materials the expert has been instructed to consider. The waiver principle also extends to other communications or opinions that form the basis of the expert report.

In the case of *Towney v Minister for Land and Water Conservation*,[8] which concerned the native title claim over Peak Hill in New South Wales, subpoenas were issued to various anthropologists by the Minister. In the course of the proceedings, the claimants had been ordered to file expert reports that they would be relying on. The claimants filed two reports by anthropologist Dr Gaynor Macdonald, one being an interim report and the other a final anthropological report. The final report acknowledged the contribution of other anthropologists, including Dr Peter Sutton, who was said to have reviewed drafts of the report and made extensive comments.

The documents in question included reports by Peter Sutton prepared for the case; correspondence and draft reports sent between the anthropologists; and notes of meetings between anthropologists. Subpoenas were issued for these and the Minister's lawyers wanted to inspect them.

It was accepted that client legal privilege applied as the correspondence, meetings and draft reports were all for the purpose of the native title litigation. However, the question was whether the privilege was waived by the filing of the interim and final anthropological reports on the basis that the documents in question were, in the terms of section 126 of the Commonwealth Evidence Act, reasonably necessary to enable the proper understanding of the final and interim anthropological reports.

The court observed that the law did not go as far as to say that just because a source document is referred to in the report the source document must be reasonably necessary for a proper understanding of the report. This was too wide. It depended on the purpose for which the source document had been referred to and whether it could be divided up into different parts. A mere reference was not enough. In the case in question, however, there were references in Gaynor Macdonald's final report to Peter Sutton's concepts of 'absolute continuities' and 'underlying continuities' and Sackville J decided it was necessary to look at the whole of Peter Sutton's report to understand this analysis fully. He came to a similar conclusion in relation to the comments and correspondence of Peter Sutton about the draft reports.[9]

Sackville J did note that this did not mean that client legal privilege would be lost in all cases where someone commented on a draft of an expert report and that each case would depend on its own circumstances. In the *Towney* case the reports and comments had to be disclosed because it appeared that Sutton had played an extensive role in the preparation of what constituted the final report and it was necessary to understand how much of the analysis was Macdonald's and how much was Sutton's.

By contrast, other items subpoenaed in the case were records in tape and document form of a claimant meeting at which there had been discussions about mining developments, the native title claim generally and other matters. These were not referred to in the reports nor were they a source for anything in the reports and therefore the privilege was not lost and the documents did not have to be disclosed.

The first leading Western Australian case on this issue was *Daniel v Western Australia*,[10] delivered October 1999 during the course of the hearing into the Ngarluma/Yinjibarndi claim in Western Australia. The State of Western Australia had issued subpoenas to Michael Robinson, a consultant anthropologist, who had prepared an anthropological report that had been filed but not yet tendered in evidence.[11] At the time the subpoena was issued, the Crown could have used the documentation in cross-examination of the native title claimant witnesses. The subpoena sought production to the court and to the state and other respondents of all notes, books, video, audio tapes and other documents in his possession, custody or control that 'contained or recorded interviews, conversations or correspondence or observations of members of the native title claim groups'. The state relied on the fact that in the report filed by Robinson he had made reference to a number of quotes and statements made by various members of the native title claim group.

The solicitors for the claimants claimed legal professional privilege over these documents. The field notes fell into four main categories with regard to the issue of privilege. First were the records of communications with the lawyers for the claimants. These were held to be privileged because they recorded legal advice. Second were the communications of the claim group members to Robinson for the purpose of heritage surveys and work program clearances. Robinson's evidence was that the reason why he recorded these communications and the reason why the information was given to him was so he could provide it to solicitors to enable them to advise on a third party future act development. It was held that, in so far as this was the case, they would be privileged. The third category comprised communications from members of the claim group to Robinson concerning genealogical and other information relevant to the claim. The reason for the communications was for Robinson to prepare a report for the litigation. The court accepted these were subject to privilege. The fourth category comprised observations by Robinson. It was held that these were not communications made to anyone to which privilege attached.

There were other documents also in issue. Heritage survey reports were to be provided to developers and were not for legal advice or litigation so no privilege could attach. Another argument would have been that these reports once given to the third party developer would have amounted to a waiver of privilege anyway. A video recording of an inspection of a particular area was made just for use in the proceedings but it was simply recording and observing the behaviour of a member of the claim group and was not a communication or document of communication. The court held that simply recording a fact observed attracted no privilege as it was not a communication. A video in which applicants were explaining the significance of a site amounted to an actual communication and recording for legal proceedings, and therefore it was said that it could be privileged but the court was going to inspect it to see if it was just recording events that occurred in public and that were not confidential. There were also audiotapes taken during heritage surveys for the purposes of those surveys. These were held not to be privileged because they were not clearly taken for the purposes of legal advice. There were other documents such as drawings, loose bits of paper and annotated maps and there was no evidence that these were communications from clients to Robinson rather than Robinson's own observations and ideas. On this basis, it was not established that they were given for the dominant purpose of the litigation or communications. The copies of witness proofs or statements were clearly prepared for the purpose of litigation and were privileged.

The case was decided at the time when the prevailing view was the sole purpose test, meaning that the test was to determine whether the communications were made for the sole purpose of the legal advice or litigation. This has since been modified by the High Court to a dominant purpose test but probably would not have made much difference to the result.

The court then considered the question of waiver of privilege in relation to the communications to Robinson for the purposes of the case and the notes of solicitors' communications. It was accepted that Robinson would be called to give evidence and that his reports would be tendered as evidence. It was accepted by the solicitors for the claimants that when called to give evidence, the various assumptions and source information on which he based his opinion would then be able to be questioned because it was not possible to rely on the conclusions without exploring the material that gave rise to them. However, the claimants wished to maintain the privilege and protect the documents until that point in time. The judge said that there was no waiver at that stage because there had been no disclosure of the documents yet and the report had not yet been tendered into evidence.

There was an obvious tactical advantage in the timing of when the information must be provided. If it is not provided till the expert gives evidence, then the main cross-examination of the various applicant witnesses would usually be completed before then. Nicholson J indicated that it was still a possibility for the state and respondents to recall witnesses to cross-examine them if necessary even though that might result in some delay. The practical reality is that there would usually need to be good reason to recall witnesses and there is less of an inclination to do so if there are only a few small or ancillary points to be put to a witness. There was also an argument about public interest immunity.

A similar issue then came up before Madgwick J in the case of *Clarrie Smith v Western Australia*, decided on 20 April 2000.[12] That was a case where the state issued subpoenas to the consultant anthropologist, Dr Mana Waite, and the two assistant anthropologists working with him, Sally Babidge and Stuart Fisher, all of whom had been engaged for the native title claim. The subpoena sought production of all documentation recording primary source material such as handwritten or electronically recorded notes, sound recordings, video recordings and any records made of observations by researchers and of interviews of any persons, including the claimants, who provided information which was for the purpose of or incidental to the anthropological report; and ethnographic site surveys around the claim area, which included restricted reports provided to the claimants' solicitors and which were said to be have been prepared in anticipation of litigation under the Aboriginal Heritage Act. This was presumably for litigation challenging any consent that might be given by the Minister under the Western Australian Aboriginal Heritage Act to the damage or destruction of sites.

There were claims for privilege over the two types of heritage survey reports: those reports that were given to developers; and those restricted reports that had just been provided to the solicitors for the claimants. The court held that heritage survey reports were done for the predominant purpose of Aboriginal heritage assessments and not for the purposes of legal advice and for this reason they were not privileged.

In relation to the claims that some of the restricted reports were produced in anticipation of litigation under the Aboriginal Heritage Act, the court ruled that they did not appear to have been produced for the dominant purpose of use in proceedings and therefore were not privileged. It is not clear from Madgwick's reasoning what he meant by this. He could have been making a finding of fact that they were not produced for the dominant purpose of use in any legal proceedings or for any legal advice. If so, they would not be privileged. However, if he was asserting that the documents had to be created for the dominant purpose of use in the native title proceedings rather than other proceedings, then this is questionable. The general principle is that communications that are privileged because they were made in anticipation of litigation remain privileged even for the purposes of other litigation. As set out in the *Daniel* case, if the communications and notes were for the purposes of legal advice to be given on future acts, then they would be privileged. It would certainly be arguable that if the purpose of the restricted reports were for legal advice about rights under the Aboriginal Heritage Act or in relation to future act determinations, then these should have been privileged as well.

Madgwick J in this case differed from Nicholson J on the issue of waiver and the time when the source materials had to be provided to other parties. It was accepted that the source material documentation recorded matters that had been made for the dominant purpose of use in the native title proceedings and were, therefore, privileged at the start. However, Madgwick J decided that privilege was already waived at that point and it was not something that could be kept until the expert actually gave evidence. He said that because the report was going to be tendered it was clearly different from the claim book situation in the Warrumungu case, where a claim book was used to set out the nature of the case but was not part of the evidence. Madgwick J decided that it would be unfair to allow the expert report to stand as filed without disclosing the documents on which it was based. He was concerned that if one waited until Waite gave evidence, the state and other respondents could then seek an adjournment during the cross-examination of Waite to read the materials. This would be of inconvenience to the parties and the court and would cause greater delay and, therefore, they should have access to that documentation before the evidence was given. The source material was ordered to be produced but there were limitations placed as part of the balancing process required on the basis of public interest immunity.

Public interest immunity

The public interest immunity principle is one that has evolved over the last thirty years from the notion of Crown privilege where evidence could be excluded if it was against the interests of the state, for example to protect cabinet documents, defence secrets, police informers and so on. This has now been expanded to allow the objection to disclose documents or information if it is against the public interest to do so. The process then is one of balancing public interests by on the one hand ensuring all relevant evidence can be considered by a court at trial and, on the other hand, protecting confidentiality for certain matters. The categories of what can be objected to on the grounds of public interest are not closed and the courts are required to weigh these up and decide where the balance lies in each case.

In the case of *Aboriginal Sacred Sites Protection Authority v Maurice,*[13] which went to the Full Court of the Federal Court as part of the Warrumungu land claim, the court had to decide whether the Aboriginal Sacred Sites Protection Authority could be ordered to produce documents to the Aboriginal Land Commissioner for the hearing of the land claim. It was argued that information about sacred sites was gathered under a promise of confidentiality and that disclosing the information would cause dismay and resentment, preventing the future flow of information from Aboriginal informants. The Commissioner however had decided to require the information to be provided. The court reiterated the usual rule where one has to weigh up the public interest in maintaining confidentiality against the public interest in the information being available in the administration of justice, that is to ensure that all relevant information is before a court or tribunal to ensure a fair hearing. The majority of the court held that it could be argued that there was a public interest immunity that could arise in relation to such information. The proper protection of minority rights is very much in the public interest as is respect for deeply held spiritual beliefs. Justice Woodward said that there should be a special degree of protection and respect for the rights and beliefs of Aboriginal people, which would extend to cover both the Aboriginal guardians of the secrets and other persons to whom they extended their confidence.[14] However, the court held that the Commissioner was not wrong in the way he carried out the weighing up process to decide that the balance went in favour of disclosure of the material, which was subject to restrictions such as limiting the number of people who could be in attendance at the hearing at the time of that evidence and restricting the use of any information for purposes other than the land claim.

The issue has been argued in native title cases in Western Australia. As discussed earlier, in *Daniel v Western Australia* the State of Western Australia had issued subpoenas to anthropologist Michael Robinson during the course of the hearing into the Ngarluma/Yinjibarndi claim. Robinson had prepared an anthropological report for the native title claimants and the state was seeking access to all notes and recordings that he had of any interviews or conversations or observations of members of the claimant groups. The issue of public immunity privilege was raised on behalf of Robinson and the Anthropological Society of Western Australia along similar lines to those used in the *Aboriginal Sacred Sites Protection Authority* case. The court discussed the balancing of interests and decided that, because Robinson's expert report was going to be tendered in evidence and it was likely that the source materials would have to be revealed then, there was no great public interest consideration in not disclosing them earlier in the proceedings. Nicholson J held therefore that there would be no public interest immunity attaching to the documentation.

A similar view was taken by Madgwick J in the case of *Clarrie Smith v Western Australia*.[15] He accepted that protection in respect for Aboriginal rights and beliefs were matters in the public interest but the public interest immunity did not exist just to enable tactical advantages or disadvantages in litigation. He thought that the need for respect for rights and beliefs could be protected by restricted access so that the information could only be provided to the lawyers and the state's expert anthropologist and they could only have one copy of the document, which could not be reproduced and would have to be destroyed after the end of the trial.

Protection from disclosure

As there will generally have to be evidence given on oath claiming privilege, it is not possible to create a sham structure in order to avoid the need for production of documents. However, as can be seen from the cases discussed, much turns on the purposes for which the information and communications were made or commissioned in the first place and how information is recorded.

It appears that public interest immunity cannot be relied on as a means to protect the communications from disclosure in the long run when it amounts to source material for reports to be tendered or expert evidence. The Aboriginal Sacred Sites Authority case shows that confidential information could be ordered to be released to the other parties even when it is not otherwise the subject of any report by the person with the information. This is consistent with the law relating to public interest immunity in other contexts, which is that privilege is a narrow one and the trend is to order disclosure.

There has not been a clear case on the question of public interest immunity with respect to unpublished research carried out by people who would not be giving evidence in the case. If this was obtained confidentially in circumstances when it is not to be revealed to anyone, it remains to be seen to what extent parties will find out about these and seek to subpoena or whether on balance the public interest immunity claim would be upheld. It is clear that none of this would come within the category of client legal privilege. The communications that are most likely to be protected then are those that have been made for the purpose of legal advice or litigation.

Source material and legal advice

Client legal privilege applies where native title claim group members and other witnesses (for example, members of different groups) are interviewed in order to gather anthropological, historical or other evidence for the purposes of the native title hearing. It could also apply to information gathered for legal advice on the strength of a native title claim and on what is appropriate by way of mediation, whether on an intra-Indigenous level or with the state and other respondents.

To ensure that evidence can clearly be proven to have been gathered that way, it may be helpful if there could be a brief from the lawyers for the claimant group to the expert commissioning the work so that there is no dispute. It is also important that confidentiality be maintained over the research and the advice, otherwise the privilege could be considered as waived. The information collected should not be discussed with any third party other than other experts engaged by or on behalf of the claimant group for the purposes of litigation or legal advice. The fact that lawyers may then advise on or commission another report for the purposes of 'without prejudice' mediations after they have given the advice to their client should not result in the privilege over the initial advice being lost.

Heritage surveys and work program clearances

It is necessary to draw a distinction between the survey report or work program clearance report given to a third party developer on the one hand, and the process and purpose of conducting the surveys and of providing a report to the claimant group's lawyers on the other. Once an open report is given to a third party developer or the Aboriginal Cultural Materials Committee, it is likely that the report and its contents will no longer be privileged. This, however, does not necessarily mean that privilege for the source material for that is waived, particularly if the open report is a very basic one that simply says whether or not the work program is cleared.

As indicated in the *Daniel* case, where the purpose of the survey and the communications to the anthropologist or archaeologist in the course of the survey are collected by the consultant for the dominant purpose of being provided to the lawyer to give legal advice on such things as the rights and strengths of a future act determination hearing, or on an appropriate settlement agreement, or on the chances of a valid consent being given or opposed under section 18 of the Aboriginal Heritage Act, then this should be privileged. In the *Clarrie Smith* case, the survey reports for the solicitors were not held to be privileged as they were not for litigation or legal advice. It therefore could assist if the surveys are carried out for this purpose and not primarily for the purposes of providing a company with a clearance report. The motives that a company might have in funding the cost of the survey are arguably irrelevant. It is, for instance, quite common for companies to fund privileged and confidential legal advice to claimants about negotiations for future act developments.

There could then be an agreement for the lawyers and the claimants to advise the developer, in the form of a work program clearance report, whether or not the work is cleared. The contents of the work program clearance report cannot be privileged but this could be limited specifically just to the clearance of the work program without giving any confidential ethnographic information.

In this regard it is essential that the consultants be engaged by the Aboriginal group and not by the developers. It should be stated in the agreements with the developer and the consultants that the purpose of the survey and the provision of a report to the lawyers is for confidential legal advice to the Aboriginal group and not for the purposes of providing an open report to the company. A work program clearance report is something that can be agreed to be provided separately. This issue has not been fully tested but it could be a prudent course for Aboriginal groups to take.

Recording and filing information

Each person's personal methods will influence how information is recorded and filed. Consideration will need to be given to whether everything is to be recorded in the same book or document or tape or whether there should be different physical records of different types of communications. It is easier to separate items that have to be produced and those that do not if they are contained in discrete documents. Discovery and production can be organised by way of blanking out or covering up certain parts of documents that are privileged but this is a complicated process and invites queries. If notes relating to different items are categorised separately, it is easier to say which relate to privileged occasions and which do not, and everything said is recorded and how things are noted. Each consultant obviously needs to decide how to balance convenience with caution to ensure that disclosure is limited.

References in reports to other material

In the *Towney* case, the other parties were alerted to correspondence and draft reports by references made in the final report to these. There were also references to concepts that required an analysis of what Peter Sutton had said in his reports and correspondence. If these references had not been made, the other parties might never have known of these sources. This would not have mattered if Sutton's reports were going to be put into evidence as well, for example as a peer review report or a further expert report. If the material is not relevant as source material or otherwise for a final report, then consideration has to be given as to whether the other parties should be alerted to it by references in the reports lodged. This could be particularly relevant if there are reports or communications that contradict or criticise the expert report filed or earlier drafts of it.

It will be up to the consultants, the lawyers and the claimants to negotiate to what extent this could be done without causing problems of professional integrity. It is essential that there be free communication and exchange about these issues as the lawyers must recognise too that there may simply have to be limits to the extent to which their clients' interests can be protected.

Conclusions

The law relating to privilege over confidential communications with consultant experts is still developing and no one can be certain about what can be privileged and what cannot. However, it is necessary to bear these issues in mind when structuring contracts of engagement and to clarify the purpose for which one is carrying out the work. Mere confidentiality and codes of ethics do not appear to be sufficient to prevent disclosure of information. Clients and informants need to be warned about the real possibility that the information will not be kept confidential and may be able to be used against them.

The fact that client legal privilege has a greater chance of success than general public interest immunity means that greater protection is likely to be given to information obtained for legal advice or litigation. This may have the effect of having to interpose lawyers or legal briefs or agreements between the consultant anthropologists and the native title group members. By doing so, lawyers are not necessarily trying to be difficult or to take control but simply to use their best endeavours to protect the interests of their clients.

In some ways, rather than restricting the consultants, the greater the chance of documents not being disclosed, the more one can feel open to raising adverse points and having a full and frank discussion between the consultants and lawyers and clients. While it is essential that the exchange between all the consultants should continue to work out the best balance of the different interests and techniques, it must not be forgotten that the ultimate decision and privilege belongs to the Aboriginal people whose knowledge and information it is in the first place.

11

The Nharnuwangga, Wajarri and Ngarlawangga Consent Determination

Philip Vincent

THE NHARNUWANGGA, WAJARRI AND NGARLAWANGGA people's native title claim lies in the north-west of Western Australia. The claim, which was organised through the Aboriginal Legal Service, encompasses the upper reaches of three major river systems, the Ashburton, the Gascoyne and Murchison, and comprises a vast area of country—some 47 607 square kilometres in all, including nineteen pastoral stations (32 521 square kilometres), 2296 square kilometres of national park, 11 791 kilometres of vacant Crown land, reserve land and other areas.

The claim was heard in the Federal Court, the hearings having commenced in September, 1999. On 29 August 2000 the proceedings were settled by consent, and the Federal Court, presided over by Madgwick J, issued final orders, with the agreement of the parties. The orders, which come into effect upon certain events, include: a determination of native title over the whole of the area of the claim (excluding some peripheral station areas); an Indigenous Land Use Agreement between the native title holders and the State of Western Australia, in relation to exploration and development; and access agreements between the native title holders and the relevant pastoralists in relation to the exercise by the native title holders of their native title rights and interests over the pastoral leases.[1]

As pointed out by Madgwick J in his reasons for decision, this agreement was: the first consent determination of native title in Western Australia; the first consent determination arising out of a native title claim where the hearing has already commenced in the Federal Court; and a consent determination of native title in respect of a larger land area than has previously been achieved.[2]

Negotiations in this case towards a consent determination were not undertaken until after the trial had commenced and a considerable amount of evidence had been taken. According to Madgwick J, during the course of evidence it became apparent to him that there was a considerable amount of goodwill between claimants and some pastoralists having long family connection with the area. He therefore took the initiative of urging the parties to try to build on this goodwill through mediation.[3] Graeme Neate, President of the National Native Title Tribunal, was appointed mediator, and the parties entered into rounds of mediation on the claim area and later in Perth.

During the course of mediation, the applicants, with their legal representatives, met with representatives of the Western Australian Government's Department of Premier and Cabinet and the Pastoralists and Graziers' Association (who represented the majority of pastoralists).

Unfortunately, this initial round of negotiations broke down, and the parties recommenced the trial. Following further evidence, the trial judge again exhorted the parties to try to settle the action. The parties recommenced negotiations, this time without a mediator.

The framework for the settlement was finally agreed between the major parties, and drafting of the documents, which were necessarily complex, commenced. Eventually the parties were able to advise the court that the matter could be settled. The trial judge ordered that all parties to the proceedings (whether they had taken part in the hearings or not) be advised of the date when the orders to finalise the proceedings might be made. On the return date only one party that had not previously participated in the hearings, a mining company, appeared and specifically had input into the final form of orders.

The claimant group

The community of the Nharnuwangga, Wajarri and Ngarlawangga people is a relatively small one. Most of its members live at the community of Yulga Jinna, which is located on the claim area. The community is led by 'an indomitable man' (to use the judge's description), Clarrie Smith. The bulk of the older generation have lived and worked on the various pastoral station properties within the claim area. It is for this reason that they know, and are known by, many of the current pastoralist families. The Indigenous Land Corporation recently purchased Mulgul pastoral station, which is also on the claim area, for the group, and they are taking steps to re-establish themselves on this property. The trial judge, in his reasons for decision, by way of background, had this to say of the claimant group:

> The Yulga Jinna people and others who, according to what survives of traditional Aboriginal laws and practices, may speak for their communities authoritatively in respect of the land concerned, came together to present a unified claim on behalf of the Nharnuwangga, Wajarri and Ngarlawangga people over the much larger area now claimed. Evidence was heard by the Court at various places on the land concerned. There was evidence of the survival, despite the decimation of Aboriginal populations and their dispossession of their lands since the coming of white people, of a community observing so far as is possible, in modern circumstances, traditionally based laws and customs. Other evidence included rigorously criticised anthropological evidence and studies by two professional historians. The evidence also showed, again so far as is possible in modern circumstances and in the actual circumstances of the surviving members of the claimant groups, a continuing connection with the land in question. There were, however, live issues about all these matters.[4]

The pastoralists

Of the nineteen pastoralists who participated in the settlement of the action, eighteen were represented by the Pastoralists and Graziers Association. Two stations were owned by a mining company, and no doubt were acquired for the primary purpose of gaining access for mining and exploration.

To effect a settlement in which native title was to be granted over pastoral lease areas, it was necessary for the native title holders and the pastoralists to work out and agree a regime whereby both commercial pastoral activities and native title activities could coexist. This was eventually done. As Madgwick J remarked, in considering the finished product:

> the principal rules have been worked out as to the practical interaction between the native title holders and those such as the pastoralists who have other rights to be on and use the land. It is an important consideration in my mind, that it would probably not be possible for this Court to settle such a working out of on-the-ground practicalities without the agreement of the parties.[5]

The state government

For the purpose of the settlement, the applicants accepted that from the Western Australian Government's point of view, as representative of the wider community, it would be important to ensure that: the terms of the consent determination that was to be made were consistent with a fair view of the evidence and with current law; and that multi-use of the land, particularly including mining and exploration, could occur on an expedited basis for the benefit of the economy, while preserving legitimate Aboriginal rights and interests. A 'fair view of the evidence' is, of course in the eye of the beholder (eventually the judge), so inevitably the negotiation of the terms of the consent determination involved both sides making accommodations, while ensuring that basic requirements to protect their respective interests were met.

The terms of the consent determination

It was necessary for the consent determination order to address the matters referred to in section 225 of the *Native Title Act 1993* (Cwlth), as required by section 94A. The order provides that native title exists, on the part of the Nharnuwangga, Wajarri and Ngarlawangga people, over the whole of the claim area (amended by agreement to delete some peripheral pastoral lease areas), other than where it has been extinguished by law. The nature and extent of native title was set out as being:

(a) the right as against any other Aboriginal group or individual to be acknowledged as the traditional Aboriginal owners of the land;
(b) the right to hunt, fish and gather (including to gather ochre) for the purpose of satisfying their personal, domestic or non-commercial communal needs, including observing traditional laws and customs;
(c) the right to have access to and camp on the balance of the determination area in order to:
  (i) exercise the rights set out in (b);
  (ii) travel through and make visits to and take care of places that are of cultural or spiritual importance.

Consistent with the state of the law at that time, including principles decided in the Full Federal Court 2000 decision in *Ward*,[6] the determination contained the following constrictions. No native title rights were accorded in respect of minerals and petroleum. Native title rights and interests would yield to other granted rights and interests. Laws of general application would regulate and control the native title rights and interests (the extinguishment of the right to take fauna on nature reserves and wildlife sanctuaries that had been created prior to the introduction of the *Racial Discrimination Act 1975* (Cwlth) was specifically referred to).

Native title rights and interests were stated to have been extinguished in respect of enclosed and/or improved pastoral lease land and areas the subject of mining and like leases (other than on specifically 'Aboriginal-held lands', which benefited from the application of section 47A of the Native Title Act).

The determination also stated that the native title is not to be regarded as 'exclusive' of the rights and interests of others, and, to the extent of any inconsistency with other legally created rights, must yield to such other rights. This recognised the existence of other interests within the determination area, which is reflected in the comments of the trial judge, who said in his reasons, 'the evidence could support a conclusion that native title was, at least over considerable areas, non-exclusive'.[7]

For the purposes of the settlement of the action, determination of native title and the associated agreements were regarded by the parties as a 'package'. The orders of the court provided that the determination of native title would not come into full force and effect until the Indigenous Land Use Agreement, to be entered into between the native title holders and the state, was registered in the National Native Title Tribunal.

The pastoral access agreements provided access to the native title holders to all parts of the pastoral leases within the determination area. This was notwithstanding that such areas may be fenced or improved with resultant extinguishment of native title in line with the decision of the Full Federal Court in *Ward*.

The agreements therefore provided access rights over and above those available through native title under *Ward*, which, although subject to appeal to the High Court,[8] reflected the current state of the law and would, no doubt, have been regarded as binding by the trial judge. The rights are also greater than the access rights provided to Aboriginal people by section 104 of the *Land Administration Act 1997* (WA) to gain sustenance in their accustomed manner on unenclosed and unimproved portions of pastoral leases.

The agreements (called 'access protocols') will be memorialised on the Crown land title of the relevant pastoral leases under section 17(2) of the Land Administration Act so that the agreements 'run with the land' and are binding on subsequent pastoral lessees and title holders.

The basic scheme of the access arrangements reflected in the agreements is as follows. On occasions when the native title holders wish to have access to a pastoral lease, they notify the lessee of their intention, with a general indication of numbers, a contact person, the place people intend to go, proposed length of stay, which members will be using firearms, and camping places that will be utilised. The pastoralist can by notice object to a particular visit, issue directions and denote excluded areas from time to time on reasonable grounds related to the efficient operation of the pastoral lease. In case of unresolved dispute about such matters, then there is provision for arbitration. It is agreed that certain activities will not be undertaken by the native title holders without prior approval of the pastoral lessee.

These include interfering with plant, equipment and stock, using other than low-powered, low-calibre firearms, and camping at watering points. Mutual public liability insurance cover is provided for to address accident or damage arising from access.

Heritage protection is provided for, including a statement of recognition on the part of the pastoralists of the need to protect Aboriginal cultural heritage, particularly the protection of grave sites, and the undertaking on the part of the native title holders to advise the pastoral lessees of site notifications made under section 38 of the *Aboriginal Heritage Act 1972* (WA). Consultation is to occur between parties in relation to any employment or contracting opportunities on the stations.

The Indigenous Land Use Agreement

The Indigenous Land Use Agreement (ILUA) is to be entered into by the native title applicants and the Premier on behalf of the State of Western Australia. The intention is that it be registered in the National Native Title Tribunal as an area agreement under section 24CG(1) of the Native Title Act.

The agreement applies to all of the determination area other than areas where native title has been extinguished. The ILUA replaces the objection, negotiation and arbitration processes under the Native Title Act with the following alternative procedures. Mining tenements for other than productive mining (for example prospecting and exploration) will have, as a condition of grant, the requirement that the tenement holder enters into a standard form heritage protection agreement. Productive mining, general purpose mining leases, petroleum titles and proposed compulsory acquisition of native title will be subject to the procedures and compensation rights set out in Part 2 of the *Native Title (State Provisions) Act 1999* (WA) and the Land Administration Act 1997. This state legislation has been enacted pursuant to section 43A of the *Native Title Act 1993* (Cwlth), which provides that state laws can provide for alternative provisions to Native Title Act processes if they meet certain requirements, including that they 'provide for consultation'.

In relation to the arrangements for the prospecting and exploration phase of development, the current practice in the National Native Title Tribunal under 'right to negotiate provisions' means that the best that can be hoped for is an order that a heritage survey be conducted. No compensation, for example, has ever been ordered by the Tribunal. The undertaking by the State Government in the ILUA to make entering into a heritage protection agreement a condition of tenements is therefore an advance.

The standard form of the heritage protection agreement forms an annexure to the ILUA. It provides for notification of the company's proposed program of activity to the native title holders, and response by the native title holders (or their representatives) as to whether and what type of heritage survey may be required and who should be involved. Various levels of survey are provided for depending on the type of proposed activity. In the event of dispute, there is provision for arbitration.

In order to provide a cumulative record of information about areas to be avoided in exploration programs, the ILUA provides that basic details of surveys that have been undertaken be kept on a public heritage register, called the Nharnuwangga, Wajarri and Ngarlawangga Heritage Register, in the Aboriginal Affairs Department. The register will detail where, when and by whom surveys have been conducted, and give a summary of findings including the location of Aboriginal sites (which is defined to include any area surrounding the site that is reasonably required for the protection of the site). No sensitive material is to be included in the register. The desire on the part of the Government to establish this register obviously required careful consideration by the native title holders. After much thought they decided to accept the proposal, subject to acceptable drafting.

With regard to the applicable procedures covering productive mining, petroleum titles and compulsory acquisition of native title rights and interests, the state provisions to a large extent mirror the Native Title Act provisions. Instead of providing for 'negotiations' between parties concerning how or whether such development should proceed, the Native Title State Provisions Act refers to 'consultation'. Whether there is a material difference between these concepts at law has yet to be decided. Importantly, the state provisions, like the Native Title Act, include mediation and finally arbitration in the event of lack of agreement, albeit by a state body. Likewise, rights to compensation under the Native Title Act have never been tested, as no awards have ever been made in the National Native Title Tribunal or Federal Court. No distinction can therefore, in legal terms, be made in terms of qualification, quantum or otherwise between the two processes.

Conclusions

Settling litigation always requires courage on the part of the litigants. It inevitably involves accommodations in circumstances where the result of the court action cannot always be foreseen. In the highly charged political atmosphere of native title it undoubtedly required great courage from all parties. The results have shown that, with a degree of trust between claimants, pastoralists, miners and government, outcomes were achieved that have produced benefits for all parties. While the appropriateness of the terms of any settlement must be restricted to the particular case at hand, for a variety of reasons it would seem that this settlement can be regarded as a useful resource for the future.

12

Lawyers and Rats: Critical Legal Theory and Native Title

David Ritter and Frances Flanagan

THE DEEP UNPOPULARITY of lawyers in Australian society in general has a unique resonance in the context of native title. Lawyers are frequently seen to be the gatekeepers of a labyrinthine process that appears at times to benefit no one but the lawyers themselves, much like the law case in the opening pages *of Bleak House* by Charles Dickens: 'This scarecrow of a suit has, in course of time, become so complicated, that no man alive knows what it means'.[1]

The assumptions that lawyers profit from the troubles of others, communicate in incomprehensible jargon and hide behind veils of secrecy and hierarchy, are all too evident in the native title process. The role of lawyers is further complicated by the tensions that exist between them and members of other professions. Drawing on critical legal theory, we explore whether lawyers can be more effective for their clients if they adopt a position that is critical of the native title process.

Historically, a liberal rational view of human relations has been the prevailing discourse governing lawyer–client relations. Clients are seen as independent actors who freely undertake to consult with lawyers when necessary. The lawyers, independent of extrinsic factors, objectively act in their client's best interests, which are defined strictly in terms of the legal problem at hand. This conservative view 'requires that law practice be confined to the realm of manifest conflict and segregated from the realm of intact social relations'.[2] The lawyer is required to pursue 'with the utmost skill, aggression and diligence the client's objectives, as long as they do not violate the law' until such time as the lawyer is dismissed by the client, or the dispute has been resolved.[3] Conceived in such terms, a lawyer's professional roles and obligations are distinctly apolitical.[4]

This view of the lawyer–client relationship has found expression in the milieu of native title. An entirely ethically appropriate position for a lawyer may be to take instructions purely from the applicants on a native title claim.[5] Having taken such instructions, the lawyers must then endeavour to win the case. This adversarial program will involve a rigorous guarding against disclosure of information to third parties or respondents, an unwillingness to co-operate with other applicant groups (whose success may diminish the size of the prize at the end of the litigation) and a refusal to countenance settlement negotiations where the evidence is strongly in the applicants' favour. Indeed, the most oft-levelled attack on lawyers in a native title context is that they are overly preoccupied with an adversarial and litigation oriented approach.[6] Even in the context of future act negotiations, traditional approaches may be found wanting: 'hard edged negotiation often requires an adversarial approach, whereas native title interests may prefer to be longer term stake holders in a development'.[7]

The relationship between native title lawyers (here meaning only those lawyers who are acting for native title claimants) and their Aboriginal clients challenges many received notions of lawyer's roles. The ethical requirement that lawyers be 'objective' and keep their clients at arm's length[8] is difficult to maintain in a context in which Aboriginal people may be acutely dependent on lawyers in a broad range of matters that extend beyond the paradigm of the exchange of instructions for legal advice.[9] There is also, perhaps, a recognition that most lawyers who work for native title claimant groups do so out of personal conviction.[10] It is also an area in which the clients, because of their position of social and economic disempowerment, are most unlikely and unable to complain if they are not happy with the service they are getting.[11] Simply put, if you are a native title lawyer and you do something negligent or unethical, you are likely to get away with it. This is an odious and uncomfortable thought, but one that should not be ignored. There is no code of ethics particular to lawyers practising in native title, no requirement that such lawyers undergo cross-cultural education, no national association and no system of accreditation.

The ambiguity in the relationship of native title lawyers and their clients extends to the issue of the lawyer's obligation to avoid a conflict of interest. If a native title lawyer were to withdraw every time deep divisions occurred within a native title claimant group, every native title claimant lawyer in the country would be conflicted out of operation within a matter of weeks. The very concept of Native Title Representative Bodies is problematic in terms of conflicts. Lawyers employed by land councils, although employees, are required to appear qua themselves (or at least under the name of their principal legal officer) on behalf of particular native title claimant groups. This becomes difficult if the duty of the lawyer to the client (the native title claimant group) is contradicted by the lawyer's duty to the employer, or even conflicts with the employer's obligations under the Native Title Act.[12]

The politics of mediation and negotiation

The early ethos embedded in the Native Title Act was to encourage settlement of native title questions by negotiation and mediation.[13] However, the use of mediation is not a panacea. An uncritical substitution of mediation for litigation will not remedy many of the inherent structural limitations in the native title process.[14] While mediation has the potential to embrace more imaginative outcomes than litigation, the process has its own problems, not least of which is that it might be seen as an example of what Miller has called the 'pacification of Indigenous outrage'.[15]

In mediation, particularly the interest-based mediation that is favoured by the National Native Title Tribunal, parties are encouraged to focus on their interests, rather than their rights, and to compare those interests against measurably fair criteria.[16] In practice, what these lofty ideals entail is the categorisation of Indigenous expression as either legitimate or illegitimate. It is all very well to encourage parties to focus on interests, rather than rights, but it is not clear how this is achieved where there is a manifest power imbalance and where the legal rights of one party simply overwhelm the legal rights of the other. Similarly, the concept of objective standards of fairness, although a noble aspiration, can flounder in a cross-cultural context. Fairness is, at a fundamental level, situationally and culturally contingent. Rather than fairness, pragmatism may be a much more effective cross-cultural touchstone.[17]

Critical legal theory

Critical legal studies, or critical legal theory, has an eclectic and diverse set of origins.[18] It draws its content and its inspiration from jurisprudential realism, post-structuralism, Marxism and feminism. It is 'a form of critical jurisprudence that utilises the tools of deconstruction to attempt to demystify a legal liberalism, exposing the law as inherently indeterminate'.[19] As Geoffrey Leane has pointed out, there is no one theme or theory that links the diverse writings of the critical legal theorists, except perhaps the 'critical' descriptor: 'It is more in the nature of the movement than a theory'. Fundamentally, most critical legal theorists would see legal doctrine as 'mere legitimating ideology'.[20]

The purpose of critical legal theory criticism is not to introduce a new orthodoxy or a new hegemony.[21] We see the critical legal theory project as an attempt to unmask prevailing legal doctrines and institutions, and to come up with a more substantively just institutional arrangement for law, with the understanding that any new institutional arrangement must itself be further interrogated.[22] It is a project founded on a commitment to continuing critique and inquiry. The aim is 'to unfreeze the world as it appears to common sense as a bunch of more or less objectively determined social relations and to make it appear as . . . it really is: people acting, imagining, rationalising, justifying'.[23] Critical legal theory requires, above all, a realisation that law is made by those on the riverbank and not those who are drowning.[24]

The two chief (and related) features of the critical legal theory movement might be seen as, on the one hand, a commitment to the relentless interrogation of legal institutions and doctrines and, on the other, a scepticism towards the notion that real social justice is founded on rights. In terms of the first tenet it is counter-hegemonic.[25] It is an exercise in deconstructing legal institutions and doctrines, known generally as 'trashing'. The critical legal theory project is aimed at exposing hierarchies, false binaries and power relations latent within liberal legal discourse. It also involves a rejection of the ideology of legal liberalism as conferring on legal doctrine a false air of naturalness, resulting in unjust social structures acquiring the appearance of inevitability.[26]

The imperative to expose and challenge assumptions about the inevitability of social arrangements arises from the notion that:

> the most effective kind of domination takes place when both the dominant and dominated classes believe that the existing order, with perhaps some marginal changes, is satisfactory, or at least represent the most that anyone could expect, because things pretty much have to be the way they are.[27]

If an 'order of things' is just accepted, then important features of society can come to seem fixed or unalterable, and alternatives will be difficult to even conceive.[28] Criticism—trashing—is thus seen as a means toward social emancipation.

The second and related fundamental tenet of the critical legal theory movement is a distrust of rights discourse. Classically, social reform movements have concentrated on achieving greater rights, but critical legal theory treats the quest for rights with scepticism:

> Rights are granted to, or bestowed upon, the powerless by the powerful. They are ultimately within the control of those with authority to interpret or rewrite the sacred text from which they derive. To enjoy them, one must respect the forms and norms laid down by those in power. One must especially avoid excesses in behaviour or demands. Rights are never 'owned', merely loaned, and all too easily manipulated away or neutralised by the dismissal of their potentially transformative promise as fantasy.[29]

While scholars share a wariness of rights, there is no accepted alternative critical legal theory position. Some commentators take the view that rights discourse[30] is positively harmful for disempowered groups because even to engage in rights discourse is 'incompatible with a broader strategy of social change'. Such theorists 'view the extension of rights, although perhaps energizing political struggle or producing apparent victories in the short run, as ultimately legitimating the very racial inequality and oppression that such extension purports to remedy'.[31] Rights, then, are seen as hazardous because they offer an illusion of social change that can be confused with the real thing. The danger of rights discourse is that sight of real objectives is lost. According to this view, if 'experiences of solidarity and individuality' were not passed through 'the filter of the language of rights, we would be in a better position to address the political issues on the appropriate level'.[32]

It may be difficult to accept the critical legal theory critique of rights in the abstract because of the extent to which the pursuit of rights has historically dominated the progressive sociopolitical agenda. In this vein, one of the more common attacks made on critical legal theory is that it is largely theoretical and lacks practical focus. Notwithstanding such criticism, a number of critical legal theorists have concentrated specifically on the practical implications of critical legal theory.[33] Following this tradition, the problem of rights discourse is considered at length in the material context of native title and it is argued that critical legal theory has very specific implications for a native title lawyers' area of practice. Indeed, it is argued that this approach provides the most appropriate and useful theoretical framework for a native title lawyer because it both explains what it is that native title lawyers find themselves doing, and facilitates that work.

Critical legal theory and race theory

Although critical legal theory is itself clearly radical, it has been heavily attacked from within the left by critical race theorists who are suspicious of the white and academic origins of critical legal theory.[34] If critical legal theorists condemn prevailing jurisprudence as law made from the riverbank, then critical race theorists distrust critical legal theorists as academics writing theory from the riverbank. Critical race theory is defensive of rights, evincing a discomfort with the part of critical legal theory that rejects rights-based theory. Obviously, it is much easier to 'trash' the concept of rights when you and your kind are replete with those self-same rights. In this context, a differentiation might be made between (usually white) lawyers seeking rights and Indigenous people seeking rights. There is clearly a politics of 'who' here. The seeking of rights and the recognition of rights will have different connotations for different people depending on their situation: for those who have been denied rights both historically and in their own lives, an academic abandonment of rights may seem a terrible and dismal proposition.[35]

In this respect, critical race theory clearly emerges as an appropriate corrective to elements of mainstream critical legal studies.[36] Yet such correctives do not merit the abandonment of the critical legal project. Rather, the emergence of critical race theory might be seen as the vindication of the critical legal movement. Critical legal thinking should, of course, be subject to the same trashing, and the same unmasking, decoding and analysis as all other jurisprudence. Even sceptics must be regarded sceptically or their scepticism simply becomes a new form of faith.

While the positive project of the critical legal theory movement should be to interrogate and reform the institutional arrangements of law, this does not necessarily entail an abandonment of rights. Rather, it simply calls for a critical analysis of the meaning of rights in their social context. The pursuit of rights may validly form part of an agenda of social equity without a complete adherence to rights discourse. Thus, critical race theory and critical legal theory are here seen as different strands of a broader critical legal movement, engaged in the hot pursuit of social justice.

Native title is, by definition, 'a right' and the native title process is generally seen as one of establishing and determining rights. As Brennan J said in *Mabo*, the 'term "native title" conveniently describes the interests and rights of Indigenous inhabitants in land, whether communal, group or individual, possessed under the traditional laws acknowledged by and the traditional customs observed by the Indigenous inhabitants'.[37] Thus, native title is a portmanteau idea under which the 'native', the Indigenous, is conditioned by a non-Indigenous conception of 'title'.

The Native Title Act is a largely self-contained system for the determination of native title rights and as between native title and other competing rights. Aboriginal people (characterised as applicants for the recognition of rights) are permitted to make applications for a determination of native title (rights).[38] Such applications are made to the Federal Court, which must (after either mediation[39] or litigation has resolved the matter) make a determination of native title (rights). Such a determination must state the determined rights with some considerable specificity.[40] In the period after an application for a determination of native title has been lodged, the application may be eligible for registration[41] in order to access interim rights, such as the right to negotiate[42] with respect to future use of the claimed land. Thus, within the native title process, when 'Aboriginal peoples strive for recognition, they are constrained to present their demands in the normative vocabulary available to them . . . even though these terms may distort or misdescribe the claim they would wish to make if it were expressed in their own languages'.[43]

Mabo was promising enough: the Aboriginal group in question achieved a determination, as against the whole world, of a right to use, occupy and enjoy their traditional lands. However, since then, the courts and the legislature have incrementally limited native title. Transformative and chaotic common-law actions like *Mabo* have made way for a streamlined and workable system for the determination of native title.[44] The burden of proof has seemed to get harder,[45] a *sui generis* title 'as against the whole world' has become a mere 'bundle of rights.'[46] The propensity to extinguishment has also increased.[47] This gradual reduction is, perhaps, in the nature of rights as 'the person [or nation] who wants to "recognise" a right can choose the necessary measure of value, the necessary consequences, and the necessary level of generality'.[48]

In order for contemporary Aboriginal associations with land to be accorded status as administrators of native title rights, they must be determined by various non-Aboriginal sources of authority (courts and governments) to meet certain ostensibly objective criteria. The purpose of the native title process is not to determine what is fair.[49] There must be an identifiable community or group[50] that can demonstrate a continuing[51] traditional connection[52] with the land or waters in question from the time of sovereignty[53] through to the present day. Further, this connection must not have been extinguished[54] by government action or washed away by the tide of history.[55] Native title rights will only be respected, so long as they are capable of recognition within the law of Australia and do not fracture any of its skeleton of principle.[56]

The effect of these various doctrinal and institutional arrangements is to entrench and perpetuate existing power relations between Aboriginal and non-Aboriginal interests. The depoliticisation of the native title process and the invocation of principles of objectivity and neutrality foreclose any possible enquiry into substantive justice within those power relations.[57] Confining Indigenous aspirations and the search for substantive justice to an application for a determination of native title may be to abandon the material pursuit of social equity.

The emptiness of native title rights as a vehicle for achieving social equity is amply illustrated by two striking examples. The first is the *Yorta Yorta* case, in which mediation 'failed': the matter went to trial and the claimant group lost.[58] The result was a determination of no native title over the area in question. The second example is the *Clarrie Smith* case for the Nharnuwangga, Wajarri and Ngarlawangga people's claim in which, although the matter went to trial, negotiations were reconvened and 'succeeded', with the native title claimant group achieving a positive determination of native title.[59] Ostensibly, these two cases are opposites. Yet what both reveal is that whatever way the coin lands, Indigenous political aspirations and lived realities are obscured and frustrated by the application of the native title rights process.

Many of the inherent limitations of rights discourse are displayed by the Yorta Yorta case.[60] In that case, Olney J found that the native title of the Yorta Yorta peoples had been washed away by the tide of history as long ago as the late nineteenth century. Olney emphasised that the native title determination process was not a political one, but rather a purely legal exercise in applying the facts to the law:

> [A native title claim] is not about righting the wrongs of the past, rather it has a very narrow focus directed to determining whether native title rights and interests in relation to land enjoyed by the original inhabitants of the area in question have survived to be recognised and enforced under the contemporary law of Australia.[61]

His Honour seemed, with respect, irritated at the applicants' attempt to politicise the case, remarking that he was being asked to engage in 'social engineering', 'political correctness', and 'righting the wrongs of past centuries'. The applicants subjected the court to 'frequent, and in some instances, prolonged outbursts of what can only be regarded as righteous indignation . . . at the treatment they, and their forebears, have suffered at the hand of the . . . authorities'.[62]

After shifting the terms of the debate (ostensibly to strict legalism), Olney J articulated a historical and political narrative, in which the Yorta Yorta did not maintain the legally required connection with the land or with their traditional laws and customs. In Olney's judgment, colonisation is constructed as an inevitable and natural force. His Honour temporally and morally distanced the native title claim from the history of colonisation that gave rise to it. In his view 'the law of native title . . . is in a present . . . absolved from any responsibility for that which has been washed away'.[63] In *Yorta Yorta*, the law of native title acted to de-legitimise the political struggle and aspirations of the Yorta Yorta people and ruled out any appeal to fainess or equity under the cloak of (purportedly) value-neutral legal principles.

Before focusing on the *Clarrie Smith* case, we want to emphasise that in no way do we seek to be critical of the native title claimant group in question. What that group decides about their own country and society is their business, not ours. Rather, our comments are structural observations about the legal limitations of the determinations and the way in which the determination has been perceived. We have also carefully restricted our comments to matters of public record.

On 30 August 2000, the *West Australian* announced on its front page that the consent determination in the *Clarrie Smith* case was a 'title win'. On page 8, the newspaper carried an array of effusive comments from various stakeholders about the success of the 'landmark deal'. However, on the same page, in figurative and literal small print was a short analysis entitled 'What Aboriginal claimants get'. The section merits repeating in full:

- Recognition of the applicants as traditional owners of the claimed area.
- The right to hunt, fish and gather for personal, non-commercial use in order to carry out traditional laws and customs.
- Access to camp on the land and to visit and care for places of spiritual importance. This includes areas of the pastoral leases where native title may have been extinguished legally.
- Expedited procedure for mining, prospecting and exploration, which includes compulsory heritage protection.
- The right to future compensation for productive mining or compulsory acquisition of land.

What the small print reveals is that, although the Nharnuwangga, Wajarri and Ngarlawangga people now had a formal determination of native title, in obtaining that determination they had actually lost major rights. Most significantly, they lost the right to negotiate. This means that, although the group has the only current determination of native title that is not subject to appeal in Western Australia, as a direct result of this 'achievement' they are the only registered native title claimant group that does not have a right to negotiate with mining companies over their traditional land.

Lost also to the group is the extraordinary value of uncertainty. While a native title claim is extant and undetermined (even within the constraints of the Native Title Act), its unknown dimension (that is, its Indigenous content[64]) is discursively destabilising. Indeed, uncertainty may actually deliver greater bargaining power and a greater opportunity to achieve substantive justice than any determination of rights. As Altman and others have described it, the more the right to negotiate is confined by a limiting set of legal precedents, the more non-Indigenous interests are able to call the bluff of native title claimants.[65] In contrast, as long as there is uncertainty about the process and about the consequences, Indigenous people are able to use that uncertainty to persuade mining companies that it is in their interests to settle matters by negotiation.

In a sense, this decision is exactly the kind of result that the colonising power intended the native title process to achieve. Indigenous political aspirations have been subverted and then converted into a determination of 'rights'. These rights are neatly quantified and are entirely subject to a 'workable' and 'timely' process that enables them to be extinguished in the future, should it become desirable to do so. Under section 13 of the Act, the determination is final and can be the only one for its area. Further, the Aboriginal people in question appear happy with the result, which has also achieved wider community acclaim. Arguably, the *Clarrie Smith* case marks an instance of what Miller has described as 'the allure of rights', deceiving an oppressed group of Indigenous peoples into 'accepting a minimal grant or a pyrrhic victory'.[66] Undeniably, there are benefits in a successful native title claim, but such success also marks deep colonisation: 'a subsumption of Aboriginal and Torres Strait Islander being under the commodity form of Anglo-Australian property law'.[67]

Confronting ambiguity

Although the rhetoric of native title is one of advancing the 'self-determination' of Indigenous people, the practice suggests the contrary. The *Mabo* case made it clear that Australian sovereignty was non-justiciable by Aboriginal people and the native title process denies Aboriginal people the necessary internal sovereignty to govern their own affairs. In order to obtain native title rights Aboriginal people must all agree with one another, not overlap, agree on boundaries,[68] develop an internally consistent theory of their case and comply with innumerable laws, guidelines and regulations: such conditions are deeply antithetical to Aboriginal groups enjoying any inner sovereignty.[69]

The fabric of pre-colonial Indigenous society was predicated on the relationship between Indigenous people and their land or 'country'. Successive Royal Commissions have seen the displacement of Indigenous people from these lands as a fundamental cause of Aboriginal dislocation, alienation and disempowerment. However, a determination of native title is only a statement of rights: it cannot reconnect Aboriginal people with their land in some form of magical reconstitution. It cannot of itself have any impact in terms of Aboriginal social and economic well-being. Native title rights must be seen as what they are: limited, contingent and vulnerable. As Woodward J said when heading the inquiry that foreshadowed the introduction of land rights legislation in the Northern Territory, 'in truth, the granting of land rights can only be a first step on a long road towards self-sufficiency and eventual social and economic equality for Aborigines'.[70]

Recasting the role of native title lawyer

The pursuit of native title rights and the native title process should not be abandoned. Rights are useful to the extent that they support rather than impede political actions and we do not advocate their abandonment as a goal. However, a slavish adherence to the pursuit of rights should give way to an agenda of social equity that embraces rights as just one of a series of options to achieve substantive equity. As Miller asserts, 'In terms of the Indigenous struggle for land rights, reliance on legal gains is but one element of an overall strategy for securing social justice'.[71] There are a number of features of the native title process that are not themselves the pursuit of rights. Under a traditional view of legal processes they would be seen as mere incidents of native title practice. However, when viewed through the prism of critical legal theory they assume central significance.

There is a transformative power in the native title process. Peter Gabel and Paul Harris have encouraged lawyers to think of themselves as building power and breaking images, an aspiration that is highly applicable to the native title process. The first principle of such a practice must be:

> to subordinate the goal of getting people their rights to the goal of building an authentic or unalienated consciousness. This obviously does not mean that one should not try to win one's cases; nor does it necessarily mean that we should not continue to organise groups by appealing to rights. But the great weakness of a rights oriented legal practice is that is does not address itself to a central precondition for building a sustained political movement—that of overcoming the psychological conditions upon which both the power of the legal system and the power of social hierarchy in general rest.[72]

Native title lawyers can consciously direct their efforts to removing the psychological conditions upon which the disempowerment of Aboriginal people are built. Working in such a way, lawyers can—in partnership with their clients—develop strategies that go beyond rights consciousness to expanding Aboriginal people's sense of personal and political power.

Gabel and Harris advise lawyers to seek to develop a relationship of genuine equality and mutual respect with their clients. It is arguable that such genuine equality will ever be achieved between an (educated, privileged and usually non-Indigenous) lawyer and a group of (structurally disadvantaged) Aboriginal people (the possibility of achieving absolute parity in the relationship between lawyer and client is also limited by legal doctrines, such as fiduciary obligation and conflict of interest, but it can remain a guiding ideal). However, the 'critical vision sees the lawyer as an actual or potential member of the same community of interest as the client'.[73] This is not an attempt to own the perceptions of Indigenous people, rather it is an acknowledgment that a lawyer's own moral and political commitments at least give the lawyer a vicarious share in the client's political position. In a sense, it merely acknowledges 'a basic fact of contemporary law practice—that lawyers commonly make, and have to make, judgments in terms of their own moral and political commitments about what the client's interests are'.[74]

The value in transforming lawyer–client power relations does not lie in making lawyers feel better about themselves. Rather, as suggested above, the importance of this approach is that native title lawyers, by removing the hierarchies and barriers between themselves and their clients, make all lawyers and all law more accessible and intelligible to Aboriginal people. In this context, ways of talking between native title lawyers and their clients are crucial in achieving 'an acceptable intercultural language' to facilitate a relationship of equity. Back and forth exchanges in the form of 'let me see if I understand what you said', 'let me rephrase what you said and see if you agree', 'is what you said analogous to this example in my culture?', or 'can you acknowledge this analogy?'[75] can help achieve genuine understanding. Such ways of communication are perhaps very different to 'normal' lawyer–client exchanges and reflect a realisation that native title lawyers should be 'animated by the ideal of practice as a process of constituting or reconstituting non-hierarchical communities of interest'.[76]

The native title process offers a forum for unmasking laws as unjust and discriminatory. In order for it to be used in this way, native title lawyers must bring to their practice a critical analysis of the meaning of native title rights in their social context. Native title lawyers should conduct themselves in a way that demystifies the symbolic authority of the state.[77] It is a matter of reshaping the way legal conflicts are represented in the law by bringing out the true socioeconomic foundations of legal disputes. This may be achieved by talking frankly to claimants about the balance of power in mediation and negotiation. This also requires lawyers to critically consider their own role in negotiation. Lawyers should discourage claimants from surrendering to a passive role in which they depend on the lawyer to fight their battles for them. In the words of Noel Pearson, lawyers should ensure that their clients have 'the right to take responsibility'.[78]

There are a number of ways that these ideas may be applied in native title practice. An obvious means is to simply acknowledge, openly, what Aboriginal people already know: the native title process is 'whitefella' law—and a lot of it just does not make any logical or moral sense. This means simply admitting to one's clients that the native title law is a racist and pragmatic compromise;[79] that no amount of 'just terms compensation'[80] can justly compensate for the disaster of colonisation; and that governments would act against the interests of those seeking to establish native title.[81] It is to acknowledge, as did French J in his then capacity as President of the National Native Title Tribunal, that:

> The process of determining whether or not native title exists, where its existence is contested, is likely in a significant number of cases to involve consideration of complex historical property dealings and defunct property statutes. States, Territories and significant mining interests are vigorous in their pursuit of extinguishing events against native title claims. Challenges to acceptance of native title claims rely in large part upon such arguments. The process must seem perverse to those who maintain their association with their country and upon whom Indigenous tradition confers responsibility for that country. The operation of past grants of interests to irrevocably extinguish native title, regardless of the current use of the land, reflects a significant moral shortcoming in the principles by which native title is recognised.[82]

Statements of this kind militate against the 'chilling effect' of litigation and negotiation on political struggle.[83] Native title lawyers must, however, guard against using such admissions as rallying cries for the righteousness of the native title cause, because to motivate Indigenous groups toward uncritical oppositionalism is simply to further their disempowerment. Instead, the aim must be to follow such disclosures with a presentation of pragmatic choices, such as the suggestion that while no compensation will ever be enough, something is better than nothing.

Native title rights may be weak, but they can be used as leverage to achieve benefits that go beyond mere rights. As Altman has observed:

> historical precedent shows that land rights and native title have been used as economic leverage in negotiations to ensure the provision of: financial payments, employment and training opportunities, concessions for Indigenous contract businesses, and other benefits, such as the provision of government-like services.[84]

He cites, as an example, that the main lever used in the Queensland Century Mine Agreement, purported to be worth $100 million over twenty years to various native title groups in the Gulf Region, was the threat of delay.[85] In terms of the way in which native title lawyers act for their clients, an identification of this potential means that the lawyer will always be looking for strategies that go beyond mere determinations of rights.

Critical legal theorists identify counter-narratives as a 'powerful means by which oppressed groups can undermine presuppositions that make social structures seem fair and natural'.[86] Counter-narratives enable individuals to challenge legal institutions and doctrine by using the logic of non-Indigenous law against itself. Critical legal theorists speak of the precipitant result as a 'crisis in legitimacy'. Such crises occur when disempowered individuals 'force open and politicise a contradiction between the dominant ideology and their reality'.[87] Ritter has argued that the *Mabo* decision itself was caused by such a crisis.[88]

Conclusions

Within the native title process, the assertion of rights should be seen as just one element of a considered political campaign to remedy the fundamental power imbalance between Indigenous and non-Indigenous people within Australian society. This proposition suggests a recasting of the role of the native title lawyer: rather than just seeking determinations of legal rights, it is the project of the native title lawyer to redress power disparity. As former Social Justice Commissioner and lawyer Mick Dodson put it, as 'soon as you move beyond a general statement of rights to the ways in which rights are exercised, the map loses its clear definition and the boundaries have to be negotiated'.[89]

Engagement with the legal work of native title in the manner that we have suggested presupposes a level of social inquiry and understanding into Indigenous realities by native title lawyers. A commitment to substantive justice necessarily involves a reliance on social enquiry, without which the impact of legal institutional arrangements on society cannot be understood. Lawyers, however, are not trained with the skills to engage in social inquiry and cross-cultural understanding. Such skills are the province of social researchers and operatives of various sorts, including anthropologists. Thus, a critical legal approach to the practice of native title inexorably lends itself to a greater respect—by lawyers—for the methodologies and advice of anthropologists and the like. Accordingly, critical legal theory offers great promise as a theoretical framework for interdisciplinary understanding between lawyers and anthropologists.

If native title is to deliver on its promise then, paradoxically, native title lawyers must look beyond the legal process of native title to see what lies behind it. We must relentlessly interrogate what we are doing and why, attempting to unmask and decode the process—even as we serve it. Our own actions should be the subject of inquiry and scrutiny, based on the criteria of whether we are empowering our clients and challenging social injustice. The alternative is a bleak one: to act merely as functionaries in a faceless production line for the determination of mass-produced rights; to deliver no greater social justice than would be expected of an assembly line; and to let pass this opportunity to grasp, humbly, at the holy grail of individualised justice.

13

Reflecting on Past Practice: The Alice Springs Arrernte Claim

Mandy Paul

THE CURRENT CONTESTATION over Australia's Aboriginal history in parliaments, the media and the courts reminds us that history has the ability to shape understandings of the past and the present, and, through that, possibilities for the future. Questions about what happened in the past, and how, as a nation, Australia should respond, resonate in the debate over the Stolen Generations. Not so many years ago, it was the debate following the High Court's 1992 *Mabo* judgment that exercised the public imagination in a similar way. Australia's black history is one of the themes that dominated public discourse in Australia in the final decade of the twentieth century, and will continue to do so for some years to come.

What underlies this debate is a shift in Australian historiography. The practice of history has come a long way since Stanner's accurate description of the 'great Australian silence'.[1] It was in part the new historiography of the 1970s and 1980s, led by people such as Henry Reynolds, that changed the way in which many, including law-makers, understood the history of the dispossession of Australia's Indigenous peoples.[2] This new history also provided some of the arguments that enabled the *Mabo* decision to transcend the decision in *Milirrpum v Nabalco* (the Gove case) of two decades earlier.[3] This is what Australia's current Prime Minister, John Howard, lambasts, this new 'black armband history', and why, inspired by the national pride shown by people present at his speech at Gallipoli on Anzac Day 2000, he called for a return to the teaching of history as facts rather than 'issues'.[4]

But the history of dispossession is not something that can be simply discounted as issues. It has had a great impact on native title cases, including the Alice Springs Arrernte native title case, *Hayes v Northern Territory*. The importance of having historians involved in the native title process, and the potential of contemporary historiography, forms the basis of this chapter. I draw on my own work as native title historian at the Central Land Council from March 1995 to April of 1999 to explore how a small slice of the history of dispossession played a major part in the Arrernte claim.

The Alice Springs Arrernte native title application was lodged with the National Native Title Tribunal in August 1994 and accepted in April 1995. The application was for determination of native title in relation to the land and waters of 166 parcels of Crown land within the municipal boundaries of the town of Alice Springs. At the time of application, the parcels of land were vacant Crown land, Crown land subject to reserves and various leases, and Crown land 'set aside' for various purposes. Historically, much of the land had been subject to pastoral leases. The applicants comprised Arrernte people from Mparntwe, Antulye and Irlpme estate groups. After a period of unfruitful mediation, the case was referred to the Federal Court. Hearings in the case, *Hayes v Northern Territory*, commenced in July 1997, and ran for thirty-five days over the next year, concluding in February of 1999.[5]

Olney J delivered a draft determination and his reasons in September 1999. He found native title to exist in all or part of 113 of the lots claimed. However, he found that the applicants' native title rights and interests did not give them the right to possession, occupation, use and enjoyment to the exclusion of all others. He also found that those rights and interests must yield to rights conferred by other interests to the extent of any inconsistency. In September 2000, the applicants, through the Central Land Council, and the Northern Territory Government embarked on negotiations towards an Indigenous Land Use Agreement, both parties having appealed certain aspects of Olney's findings.

Extinguishment and history

Questions of the legal extinguishment of native title generally fall within the domain of lawyers. In the Alice Springs Arrernte case, the Northern Territory Government argued that a vast number and variety of tenures, both historical and contemporary, constituted extinguishing acts. These included everything from occupation licences and miscellaneous leases to pastoral leases. The Northern Territory Government sought to distinguish the pastoral leases in this case from those referred to in the 1996 *Wik* case in general.[6] Further, they argued that the issue of pastoral leases without a reservation in favour of Aboriginal people, in the period of 1912 to 1924 (following the transfer of the Territory from South Australia to the Commonwealth) had extinguished native title rights.

The research behind the arguments made on these points by the Central Land Council was an example of how fruitful detailed historical research using archival material can be; of the way in which historical research and legal argument can inform each other; and how such collaboration can yield positive results. As a general rule, the conventions of legislative interpretation mean that the legislation itself, any explanatory memorandums, and possibly the second reading speech, can be consulted for guidance when seeking the intention of legislation. In this case, the provision for the inclusion of a reservation clause in favour of Aboriginal people in pastoral leases, present in earlier South Australian legislation, was omitted from the 1912 Crown Lands Ordinance, and subsequently reinserted in the 1924 Crown Lands Ordinance. The legislation itself, and the parliamentary debates, did not assist in determining the intention of the 1912 Ordinance on this point. There was, however, material held in National Archives relating to the drafting of the Ordinances, as well as other archival and published material that shed light on the political and administrative context. The historical interpretation turned on the context, sequence and meaning of a particular set of drafting memos in which the clause making provision for the reservation, present in the earlier drafts, was omitted. The legal argument turned on whether the drafting disclosed a clear and plain intention to extinguish native title rights.

Through examination of the context—the Commonwealth's first attempt at making land law, and the appointment of Baldwin Spencer as Special Commissioner and Chief Protector of Aborigines in the Northern Territory—we were able to argue that when the Minister's wishes were expressed to omit the clause for a reservation on the basis that provision would be made in Aboriginal law, there was not a clear and plain intention to extinguish rights.

In his reasons, Olney J declined to distinguish South Australian Pastoral Leases from those in *Wik*. In relation to the 1912 Crown Lands Ordinance, he adopted the reasoning in the applicants' submissions. He stated that, rather than manifesting a clear and plain intention to extinguish native title rights, 'those responsible for the drafting and promulgation of the Ordinances were desirous of ensuring that proper provision should be made for the protection of Aboriginal rights'.[7]

While the detail of this argument has been amply discussed in an article by Jamie Dalziel,[8] a lawyer employed by the Central Land Council who worked on the case, attention needs to be given to the method, especially the gains that can be made when people from different disciplines—in this case historians and lawyers—work together. This was not the only example during the preparation and conduct of the case; there were others, including the development of arguments relating to the drafting and effect of the Aboriginal Ordinance in relation to areas that were proclaimed prohibited to Aboriginal people, and arguments in relation to the validity of particular pastoral leases.

Historians can also bring to bear their knowledge of the way information (particularly that in government files) is collected, organised and stored during some of the processes involved in litigation. This knowledge yielded positive results when historical and legal expertise was pooled during the process of discovery and the filing of documents in the Alice Springs Arrernte case.

However, there are occasions when sitting in an office with a lawyer and talking history can feel like time travel. The person across the desk is asking for a chronology of facts or just the documents—is reaching for the positivist, empiricist historian. We are back in 1967, before second-wave feminism, before the publication of E. P. Thompson's *The Making of the English Working Class*, before the new Left, and before the 1967 referendum and Stanner's 1968 Boyer lecture—in short, before the flowering of social history and all that has changed in the practice of history since. This approach is not hard to understand. As Heather Goodall has reminded us, history and law have a shared tradition of positivist, empirical notions of evidence.[9] Many lawyers feel comfortable with this kind of history, some so comfortable that they do not see a need for historians at all. It is this kind of thinking that was enunciated in the 1998 *Bellevue Crescent* case, where Justice Young of the Supreme Court of New South Wales distinguished between what he called 'the facts of history' (which he admitted as evidence) and what he called social history, 'analyses as to why certain things happened' (which he did not admit, although he did read it and decide he could take judicial note of it if necessary).[10]

History has moved on since 1967. The practices of history and historiography have been shaped by the new histories that arose out of the social movements of the late 1960s and 1970s. New fields of historical enquiry, such as women's history and social history, have led to the development of new approaches, including oral history. There has been fruitful cross-fertilisation with ethnography. In the late 1990s, history has engaged with postmodernism, post-colonial theory and cultural studies. In Australia, Aboriginal history has emerged as a field, and has undergone development, challenges and transformations of its own.[11] It has been particularly affected by the interventions of Aboriginal people and engagement with Aboriginal understandings of time, the past and authority.[12]

The silence has been replaced by many voices, including Aboriginal voices. There is no single 'Aboriginal history', just as there is no single 'history'. Good history has not abandoned its empiricist roots, and continues to use traditional methods of interrogation and contextualisation of sources. However, the sources, the subject of enquiry, and the questions posed may be new, as may be the level of reflexiveness on historical practice. To not employ such history in the native title context is to miss out on half of the contribution history can make.

Historical interpretation

The historical research on pastoral leases in the Alice Springs Arrernte case went to the court as part of a legal submission. This meant that interpretation of the documents was minimised by being couched in legal language as assertion and legal argument. One common fallacy of what might be termed a 'common sense' view of history is that documents and other sources do not need interpretation; that they 'speak for themselves' and that therefore any interpretation is at best suspect and at worst unnecessary. However, it is not only historians' knowledge of the way historical sources are collected and organised but also our understandings of the ways in which such material is created that can be used to good effect in native title contexts. That is, attention needs to be paid to the conditions of production of historical sources as well as their content, both apparent and latent—we need to practice historical analysis.

Documents, for example, embody different layers of information. The first is literal. We can, in Australia, usually pick up a historical document and read it. Ration records from Northern Territory pastoral stations in archival files might contain lists of people rationed, the content of rations and the frequency of distribution. On a literal level these could be very useful. They may list names and familial relationships, ages and occupations of people receiving rations on a particular station.

However, a researcher who has a detailed knowledge of the conditions of production of such documents can read them in a way that reveals much more than their literal meaning. The file can be situated in the larger system of which it is a part, and the governmental and administrative regimes that produced it can be explained, such as the relationships between rationing and wages. Knowledge of comparative material may illuminate the particular case: were rations on this station particularly meagre? Did that contribute to population movements? The researcher may consider what social relations produced the documents. Was the person assigning non-Aboriginal names to those receiving rations? Did the administrative practice that produced the document mean that only certain categories of people would be listed? Are women listed? Was the pastoralist overstating the rations distributed in order to subsidise a marginal operation? Then there are wider questions, such as why this document has survived. What related documents have not? What other material might shed light on aspects of station life on which this document is silent? A similar argument can be made for the benefits of a thorough and clearly interpretive approach to the use of other types of historical sources, including oral history.

The need for historical interpretation is also exemplified by the way Olney J used historical sources in the *Yorta Yorta* case, which was effectively to read selected nineteenth-century works as literal truth, requiring no contextualisation, interrogation or interpretation. This can be contrasted with the sophisticated reading of some of the same sources provided by Deborah Bird Rose.[13]

Yet another example is the possible interpretations of Peter Gunner's mother's thumbprint, on which so much hung in the 2000 Northern Territory Stolen Generations test case.[14] Did she speak English? Can we establish whether the contents of the form giving consent to have her son removed to St Mary's in Alice Springs was explained to her? Did she share the official's understanding of the meaning of making her mark? Was the form in common use? Did she know the official involved?

Continuing connection with country

The other side of the coin from extinguishment, the other major element of proof of native title, can be glossed as 'connection'. Crucial to the establishment of native title is demonstration of continuing connection by the applicants with the country that is subject to the application or litigation. There will be many cases in which connection will be fiercely disputed by those opposing the applicants. The historical record is a rich source of evidence of connection, and the exercise of rights, over time. Two of the basic methodological tools in any good historian's kit can contribute to the documenting of historical connection. The first is archival and library research, and informed interpretation of such material. The second is oral history. Since the 1970s oral history has developed a sophisticated methodology and theoretical basis, one that addresses preliminary research, collection, transcription and the interpretation of oral history material. Recently, much attention has been paid to the place of memory and narrative in history, and those working in Aboriginal history have engaged with Aboriginal oral traditions.[15]

Good oral history practice requires more than simply sitting down with someone in a creek bed and turning on a tape recorder. This idea—of historians doing some form of fieldwork—is a source of disciplinary boundary skirmishes between those trained as historians and those trained as anthropologists. While there is potential for collaboration, it is unlikely that researchers from those different disciplines will be coming to fieldwork with the same background information, or asking the same questions.

Expert reports

The most obvious way to present detailed historical research and analysis relating to historical connection to the court is in an expert report. Of course such a report will only ever be secondary to the most important evidence of historical connection, which will come from applicants in the witness box. In the Alice Springs Arrernte case, the Crown filed an expert report by Peter Donovan, a consultant historian who had previously written a history of the Northern Territory and a history of Alice Springs, this latter commissioned by the town council. The Central Land Council on behalf of the applicants filed an expert report by Dick Kimber, a respected local historian who has been researching the area and its people for some twenty-five years. The report filed by the Crown had a more detailed focus on non-Aboriginal land use; that filed by the Central Land Council had a broader historical sweep and more emphasis on the presence and connection over time of the applicants and their ancestors. During the lead-up to the hearing, the report by Peter Donovan was withdrawn. This left the report by Dick Kimber in evidence for the court, and its author was not called for examination.

Kimber's expert report served a number of functions. First, it provided a detailed context for the oral evidence of the applicants. Second, it served as general background information for the court, which came to the case with no particular knowledge or understanding of the history of the area. The report discussed the specific history of the colonisation of the country of the Arrernte people, including non-Aboriginal land use, and the impact of restrictive legislative regimes. It also documented examples from the historical record of the exercise of native title rights over time. Further, because of the time-depth of records in the region, the report located the named ancestors of applicants in that story.

Perhaps there are ways in which the report could have been improved—by the incorporation of oral history, for example. Notwithstanding this, an expert report by a historian who will be recognised as such by the court is a vital part of presenting the best possible case in native title proceedings. Crucially, a sophisticated history will provide critical analysis of its sources. Any early texts that discuss the applicant group can be located in their own historical context—explaining the particular interests of the author who may also be a local leaseholder, for example, or locating the texts in the genre, of which texts such as 'pioneer tales' or even 'ethnographic studies', may be a part. Such explication should assist the court to avoid literal readings of such sources, while providing guidance as to their 'reliability' in terms of historical evidence.

A good historical report, then, will be one that seeks to draw on contemporary historiography while simultaneously keeping a weather eye on the requirements of the legal system, including the 1995 Commonwealth Evidence Act, relevant practice directions and orders of the Federal Court, and developments in case law.[16] Julie Finlayson argues that: 'written records in native title claims are likely to gain greater status and credibility as evidence under the general provisions of the Native Title Amendment Act 1998 and directly as a consequence of changes to the rules of evidence'.[17] I hope she is wrong if this development is related to a diminution in the status of the oral evidence of applicants and a privileging of non-Indigenous accounts. It is vital, however, that those working to maximise the benefits of the native title process for applicants make full use of the widest range of sources possible. At the same time, we need to push at the boundaries of the courts' understanding by presenting rigorous, scholarly history that a court will recognise as such. This may sound like a difficult task. However, it barely rates, compared to what is being required of Aboriginal communities in order to engage successfully in the native title process.

On the second day of hearing in the Alice Springs Arrernte case it became apparent that the Northern Territory Government was going to put its considerable resources into fighting the case on questions of extinguishment, and also on questions of the composition of the native title holding group (a 'wide' or 'narrow' model of taking country) and the nature and content of native title rights. Historical connection was not at issue. As Olney J said in his reasons for judgment:

> it is appropriate to observe that there is no dispute that the whole of the claimed land is part of the country recognised as the traditional land of the ancestors of the members of the claimant groups at and prior to the settlement of that land by non-Aboriginal people.[18]

The considerable historical research undertaken into connection was put to good use in the conduct of the case. Apart from the expert report, such research was used in the compilation of background documents and witness statements to assist in the questioning of applicants in court, and also contributed to the development of legal arguments on the extinguishment side of the case.

Law and history as systems of knowledge or discourses or disciplines are integrally related, and there is an interaction between systems of knowledge embodied in Aboriginal cultures and the Western discipline of history. Knowledges historians are working with in the context of native title include other Western disciplines, such as anthropology, archaeology and linguistics. What we are dealing with are the ways these different systems see and understand each other. This is not just a theoretical discussion. These perceptions are worked out in the native title process, and this has tangible and real results, most significantly for native title applicants.

Those of us from different disciplines need to remind ourselves that there are two primary systems of knowledge within which we are operating: Aboriginal law and knowledge, and the Australian legal system. As Rosemary Hunter has pointed out, such different discourses are historically specific, and can and do affect and transform one another.[19] Working with a range of disciplines provides an opportunity to engage in new, positive relationships across boundaries. Complementary and co-operative strategies can be facilitated in a number of ways.

First, there is a need for a real and mutual recognition of the skills and expertise of those trained in other fields. This has wider application than in the relationships between the disciplines of history, law and anthropology, and extends to other disciplines such as linguistics, geography and archaeology. This needs to include a willingness to relinquish a measure of disciplinary power in order to improve overall results. Second, adopting a process of joint field research would enrich both the information collected and communication between all involved. My brief experience of such fieldwork suggests that it has significant potential.

Third, a strategy of regular exchange of information during the research phase is necessary, so that, for example, information from documentary sources can inform linguistic and anthropological research, and new understandings gained in other fields can spark ideas and new research angles for the historian. Also important is the inclusion of the historian in an information loop relating to the development of legal argument, so that she or he can contribute ideas or suggest research avenues. Advice of legal staff may be necessary to ensure that such collaborative work methods do not attract charges of 'contamination' in court.

Fourth, there is a need for regular exchanges of information with the applicants during research. Feedback from field research may not be very controversial, but informing applicants of the contents of, for example, files found in the archives, appears to be. Arguments about legitimate transmission of knowledge and tradition need to be had, and heard.

Finally, consideration needs to be given to the writing of joint expert reports. This may be particularly productive in contexts where ethnographic or other texts produced in the nineteenth century are significant sources.

Conclusions

The new history in Australia has produced rich resources for historians and all Australians. There are now raised voices where there used to be silence. For those working in native title not to embrace and benefit from this shift is to fail to grasp a powerful tool in the struggle for the rights of Australia's Indigenous peoples.

14

Three-legged Elephants: Native Title Histories

Neville Green

It was said that the Buddha visited a city where monks quarrelled about what was the correct doctrine. Buddha told them that in ancient times a wise king brought together all the people of his town who had been blind since birth. They were given the task of describing an elephant. Some were taken to feel the head, others the ear, the tusk, the belly, a leg or the tail. Each was told by their guide that what they held was an elephant. When the king asked each in turn to describe the elephant, the responses varied and each person claimed that their version of the elephant was the only true one.

Just as we cannot grasp the truth of the elephant by a description of one part, neither can we come to an understanding of native title history without a knowledge and appreciation of its many parts. In the case of the blind people and the elephant, the responses at least had a pragmatic base. This is not always so with native title history where each interested party has an expectation arising from a personal concept of history and history methodology. These interested parties include a judge, Aboriginal applicants, lawyers, the other parties represented by the lawyers, and of course the historians.

In September 1998 the Federal Court of Australia issued *Guidelines for Expert Witnesses*. These guidelines were developed co-operatively by the Federal Court, the legal profession and the Law Council of Australia. The need for such guidelines arose from a shared concern that an expert witness may be uncertain of his or her role. The legal profession is now obliged to provide any expert witness, including historians, with a copy of the guidelines. There are three defining aspects to the guidelines:

1. An expert witness has an over-riding duty to assist the Court on matters relevant to the expert's area of expertise.
2. An expert witness is not an advocate for a party.
3. An expert witness's paramount duty is to the Court and not to the person retaining the expert.[1]

The guidelines also set out, in eleven points, the form of the expert's written report.[2] The structure of a history report will vary, not only from one historian to the next, but also between cases. Usually the essential elements of a report will consider the issues that relate to Aboriginal people on and off the land under claim. These may include: the first encounters with explorers and what they reveal about identity, population and land usage; dispossession through settlement, both overt by freehold and covert by pastoralism; the names of the first and subsequent pastoralists and the names of Aboriginal people associated with that land throughout the period under review, always alert to reference to Aboriginal occupation, identity and continuing beliefs and customs; displacement by police, pastoralism and mining; containment (control) by legislation, employment, missions, reserves and ration camps; depopulation by conflict, disease, removal and migration; and liberation via income, mobility, education, recognition and access to land.

Several major resources need to be searched for the different information they may hold. There are journals of explorers, though these are few and far between. The Colonial Secretary's Records provide the correspondence to and from the Governor, especially prior to responsible government in 1890. Police files, while rarely providing observation of Aboriginal culture and their identification by language or 'tribe', are a mine of names that may be identified as applicant ancestors in relation to a particular locality. Aboriginal files categorise people by fractions of Aboriginal blood, though rarely by language groups, but nevertheless are useful as a background to significant events, such as the removal of applicant ancestors. Prison records contain thousands of names and can reveal some of the causes of removal. There are pastoral station records, especially the census records maintained by the Native Welfare Department from 1950 to 1971. As well there are the diaries of pastoralists and visitors, station and mission journals, books, articles, newspapers and other sources. Historians only have access to the personal files of Aboriginal people when the applicants make such records available for research.

The volume of primary records to consider for a history report is considerable, the volume of archived records massive. In the Ngarluma/Yinjibarndi case, for example, it was estimated that there were 12 000

Department of Land Administration land tenure files, not to mention the files created by other government departments.[3]

A history is only as good as the evidence that can be brought to the topic. Historians would agree that evidence of European and Aboriginal relationships is incomplete and that only a little Aboriginal history has found its way into archived documents. In the 1960s archaeologist John Mulvaney and anthropologist W. E. H. Stanner, among others, brought to wider attention the neglect of Aborigines in Australian historical writing. In the two decades that followed, historians such as Henry Reynolds, Bain Attwood, Anne McGrath and Richard Hall took up the revisionist challenge, which has come to be known, in some quarters, as 'black armband history'. Matching this output was a growing number of personal histories written by Aboriginal people themselves.

How does native title history differ from general history?

History reports for native title purposes represent an emerging form of history that demands far more fine detail than a manuscript for general publication. Cambridge historian, G. R. Elton, described this attention to detail as a 'crawl upon the frontiers of knowledge with a magnifying glass' adding that:

> Research work of this journeyman kind deserves to be judged by the only tests it seeks to satisfy: is it honest and exhaustive, has it asked questions that are right and adequate in the context of the problem, has it found reasonable answers, does it prove the author to have learned his trade?[4]

In Western Australia as many as twenty professional historians and researchers from the various land councils, government agencies and the private sector are poring over archived files that have previously attracted little academic interest. Ultimately the amount of native title history research that is taking place in Australia today will revolutionise the history of Aboriginal and European relationships and uncover many hidden aspects of Aboriginal lives and circumstances.

Perhaps I am being overly optimistic, for this can only happen if the research and reports get into the public domain and are not embargoed for thirty years. The need to make native title history research available for general history is even more imperative with the emergence of a group of 'white armband' historians determined to show that Henry Reynolds and others have exaggerated the impact of European settlement upon Australian Aborigines.

In Australian Aboriginal history it is the research rather than the actual writing that is time-consuming. Around 60 per cent of a project is research, 30 per cent writing and 10 per cent is referencing, editing, proofing and presenting. In an ideal situation, historians can do their own research and writing, but native title history, with deadlines linked to Federal Court schedules, does not present the 'ideal situation'. The pressure to produce reports that can be defended in court has encouraged a trend towards a hierarchy of lead historian, assistant historians and researchers. Ideally the lead historian will have a broad knowledge of Australian history and qualifications in Australian anthropology and Aboriginal studies. A good assistant historian will identify sources, suggest themes to explore, supervise the research and serve as a proofreader and critic of the draft report. When the report is filed it is the lead historian who will stand in the witness box and accept responsibility for all its facts and all its flaws.

The assistant historian may also be given the task of critiquing an opposing historian's report. In some respects the assistant historian is serving an apprenticeship and in doing so will develop a professional regard for other historians. There should be no 'black hats' and 'white hats' in native title history. Professional integrity is especially important when we are called upon to review the history reports filed on behalf of other parties. Michael Barker QC refers in this volume to a cynical American legalistic view of experts as 'saxophones' playing to the lawyer's tune. This is similar, in some respects to Henry Reynolds' warning, at a history conference in 1994, that historians may become courtesans in the native title process. We should therefore resist any pressure to do a 'hit job' on our colleagues or skew the report merely to please our client or employers.

The quality of the results of the research depends very much upon how the research task is defined. The researcher, the third and vital link in the history process, must understand the task and be able to work quickly and efficiently through the sources and not be led astray by interesting but irrelevant data.

While a large proportion of the time required to produce a native title report is consumed by research, probably as much as 60 per cent of the Aboriginal history data collected is not incorporated into the final report. What should happen to this additional information? It can remain on the computer as a growing database, be printed in synopsis volumes for in-house reference or be filed with the historian's report.

In the Miriuwung Gajerrong land claim, or *Ward* case,[5] Cathie Clement's history report was accompanied by a volume of extracts from sources. This allowed the judge, lawyers and other historians to see beyond the report itself and to gain some insight into how she had interpreted the source documents. Christine Choo used a similar presentation in her history report for the same case and for the *Clarrie Smith* case, the Nharnuwangga, Wajarri and Ngarlawangga people's claim.[6] She took this approach to a new level by cross-referencing the report to accompanying volumes of extracts of sources, each subdivided into appendices, tables and numbered items.

However, while filing resource volumes gives access to the sources used for the report, it also allows the introduction into the case of any irrelevant and even misleading information that an enthusiastic researcher might have gathered. While the extra information may look impressive it can leave the lead historian quite vulnerable in the witness box.

The authors of native title history reports have been generally accused of bias, the suggestion being that key documents are ignored if they do not support a particular point of view. While this may sometimes be the case, it is quite risky in native title reports. With the Federal Court guidelines in mind, the lawyers on both sides are alert for partisan sentiments being expressed in the reports. Whatever we have written in our major theses, or had published, can be brought to bear on our testimony. As to the suggestion that documents are 'overlooked', a historian preparing a report for other parties would certainly pick up whatever had been omitted. An astute historian who knows the territory can easily detect what has been 'missed'—not only a three-legged elephant but also one with five legs. How would these omissions be explained to the court? It would soon be exposed as the work of a devious or incompetent witness, and the credibility of the whole report would be thrown into doubt.

If our duty is to the court, then it is obvious that our reports must be as complete and unbiased as possible. If the facts are there then they must be presented. One issue that is still unresolved for professional historians is the distinction between fact and opinion. Is the historian as an expert witness expected to assemble facts, offer opinion or do both? In one case (not for native title) a report I had written was criticised as having too many facts and too few opinions. I was sent off to write a page of opinion and this was criticised because I had based my opinions on the facts in my report.

Contextual relevance

There is a view held by some lawyers that historians must contain themselves to those events that occurred within the boundaries of a particular native title claim. 'Is it relevant?' they may ask of an incident that occurred 50 kilometres outside the claim. Occurrences can have a ripple effect like tossing a pebble into a pool. A single act of possession by James Cook on a remote island off the northern tip of Cape York on 22 August 1770 had awesome relevance for every Aboriginal person east of 135° longitude. A proclamation by Charles Fremantle near the mouth of the Swan River on 2 May 1829 still has relevance for all Aboriginal people in Western Australia. If historians yield to pressure and shed the context of historical events we have a three-legged elephant; lopsided and incomplete.

J. H. Hexter used the term 'tunnel history' to refer to history specialisation. G. R. Elton, whose *The Practice of History* was once required reading for history students, responded, 'there is really nothing wrong with thinking in tunnels, provided one remembers that there is earth above and around the tunnel, and that the shape and direction of the tunnel are governed by the constitution of the substance about it'.[7]

I use the word 'context' instead of 'substance'. Context can be the experiences that shaped political attitudes; and the legislation that imposed harsh and discriminatory laws upon a minority group. It is the social attitude of the dominant population that accepted as right and just the existence of such laws. It is the social dynamics of employment, arrest, imprisonment, dispossession, powerlessness, disorientation and substance abuse, social welfare and Aboriginal responses to all of these.

A contextual view of history method can puzzle lawyers and a judge who may not understand the relevance of context. It can anger Aboriginal applicants who may not see the relationships between past and present events or between the practices that occurred in other parts of Australia. There are silences in history. There are missing pieces. Voices have been muted, documents lost, events unrecorded. Sometimes the silences of history can only be interpreted in the context of other regions, other voices, other documents and other experiences.

Events in the Kimberley, Western Australia, such as the massacres at La Grange in 1864 and at Forrest River in 1926, are impossible to prove in court using only the few documents and fragments of oral narrative that survive, but the probability that they occurred can be enhanced in the context of violent reprisal that characterised the Australian frontiers.

Elton says that not all the past is recoverable:

> Historical study is not the study of the past but the study of present traces of the past; if men have said, thought, done or suffered anything of which nothing any longer exists, those things are as though they had never been. The crucial element is the present evidence, not the fact of the past existence.[8]

Oral evidence

Is the historian obliged to accept what Aboriginal people say is their history? Is that history any more than an inherited memory? To what extent can Aboriginal voices unlock the silences of Australian history? If the Aboriginal version of history is ignored do we have a three-legged elephant? These are questions we do engage with, but rarely to the satisfaction of Aboriginal claimants. A number of Aboriginal people are regarded as the custodians of the culture and history of their groups and their voices will be heard in the court, but rarely appear in the historian's report.

There are two main reasons for such omissions. First, an expert should not include in a report information that Aboriginal informants can present to the court themselves. Second, for legal reasons a historian may not have access to the Aboriginal custodian of an oral history.

Some historians are reluctant to include in a written report information that cannot be referenced to a document that can be presented to the court. Oral history is not something that is unwrapped, displayed and rewrapped with its integrity intact. It may be nebulous and ephemeral. It may have intangible fragments of fact. It may be a personal or an inherited experience. Unfortunately, we, like the blind citizens with the elephant, cannot reconstruct the past from the piece of memory we clutch to our hearts. We may restructure the collective fragments into a narrative of people, places and events of the past, but we can never recall the total history of a society or a community or even relate our own life histories and be accurate in every detail.

Conclusions

In an ideal situation, with a fair-minded government and a well-chosen team, intending Aboriginal applicants can become aware of the potential resources before they engage professionals. In a native title case in which I appeared, I was dismayed when an applicant approached me for a copy of my report. His lawyer had not given him access to it. Perhaps before he gave evidence, it was understandable to shield him from 'contamination'. Nevertheless, how many applicants ever get to see the reports we experts have written about their families and about their history and culture? In the not too distant future our reports should be directly accessible to Aboriginal people, and to the general public as well.

15

Working as a Barrister on the Miriuwung Gajerrong Native Title Claim

Michael Barker QC

In the United States expert witnesses are sometimes referred to by the slang term 'saxophones', an expression plainly intended to infer a lack of impartiality: the lawyer hums the tune and the expert plays it like a musical instrument. No doubt, people trained in the disciplines of anthropology, linguistics, history and the like who belong to professional institutes and who subscribe to professional codes of ethics would be somewhat taken aback if it were suggested that, to the extent they act as expert witnesses in native title proceedings, they lack impartiality.

For many such people, accommodating the law and legal processes is a requirement that has only confronted them relatively recently and pejorative statements about expert witnesses are something new. Yet, common-law courts have accommodated expert witnesses in court proceedings for centuries. More than one public inquiry into the role of expert witnesses in Australia has observed that opposing experts are as much a part of the litigation process as opposing parties, solicitors and barristers.[1]

The major problem has been (and is) that, in many areas of litigation, the expert witness has become something of a professional witness, earning a living from such an activity and, in many instances, appearing more as an 'advocate' than an impartial 'expert' seeking to advantage the court with a scholarly or informed opinion. For this reason, many recipes have been advanced to remove the ingredient of partiality, including proposals that there be court-appointed experts (where an expert is truly required) or the removal or dilution of the right of a party to claim client legal privilege in respect of the lawyers' legal communications with their expert witness.

In 1998 the Federal Court of Australia issued *Guidelines for Expert Witnesses*. The guidelines endeavour to make the function of the expert witness more an 'officer of the court' than advocate of a party. Expert witnesses must be furnished with the guidelines before filing reports and giving evidence in proceedings, and reports filed by an expert witness must be endorsed with a declaration stating that the witness has made all 'desirable and appropriate' inquiries, and that nothing of relevance has been withheld.

Whether or not people from the disciplines of anthropology, linguistics and history would be righteously indignant at the suggestion they might be considered 'saxophones' when called to give expert witness in proceedings, there is no doubt that, rightly or wrongly, the opposing parties, their lawyers, and other expert witnesses will assume a certain degree of partiality on behalf of such expert witnesses. They will seek to illustrate such partiality to the court so that the opinions of that witness will be accorded little or less weight than they might otherwise have been.

As a result, it is incumbent on every expert witness called in native title proceedings to be aware of this long experience of the law with expert witnesses and to gain an appreciation of the function and role of expert witnesses in native title proceedings. Courts will in effect treat native title proceedings and expert witnesses involved in them no differently from other proceedings. However, that is not to say that such experts in native title proceedings are unimportant or are unable to make significant contributions on behalf of the parties and in assisting the court in making the factual findings required in native title proceedings. The proceedings in the Federal Court in the Miriuwung Gajerrong native title claim bear out the accuracy of this statement.[2]

The *Miriuwung Gajerrong* determination

In the Miriuwung Gajerrong native title claim, proceedings in the Federal Court under the *Native Title Act 1993* (Cwlth), the trial judge, Lee J, determined that native title existed in land and waters in the east Kimberley region of Western Australia and an adjacent portion of the Northern Territory known today as the Keep River National Park; that the native title was held by 'the Miriuwung and Gajerrong People' in respect of all of the claim area, save for Boorroonoong (Lacrosse Island) where it was held by both the Miriuwung and Gajerrong people and 'the Balangarra People'; and that the rights and interests of the common-law holders of native title derived from, and were exercisable by reason of, the existence of native title and, in particular, included the right to 'possess, occupy, use and enjoy' the relevant claimed area.

Significantly, Lee J found that native title is 'a right to the land itself' not a mere collection or 'bundle of rights'. Lee J also determined that, save for the total extinguishment of native title in some portions of the claim area comprising roads and other 'improvements', native title had not been extinguished. He held that, given that native title inheres in the land itself, the common law does not recognise its 'partial extinguishment'. Consequently, there could not be a finding of extinguishment of native title unless a 'clear and plain' case of total extinguishment was established.

The Full Federal Court decision on appeal

Western Australia, the Northern Territory and other parties appealed the determination of Lee J to the Full Court of the Federal Court. In *Western Australia v Ward*, the Full Court (three judges) unanimously upheld the trial judge's determination that native title existed and was held by the Miriuwung and Gajerrong people (and, in respect of Boorroonoong, Lacrosse Island), by both the Miriuwung and Gajerrong people and the Balangarra people).[3]

However, the Full Court, by a majority (2:1), held that the trial judge was wrong in finding that native title was a 'right to the land itself' and that there could not be 'partial extinguishment' of native title; and that there had not been total extinguishment of native title, in any event, over large portions of the claim area. The majority found native title comprised a 'bundle of rights' and so could be separately and cumulatively extinguished over time.

The majority specifically found that native title had been totally extinguished on land that was the subject of historic pastoral leases and had been enclosed by way of fencing; and that an area of land set aside and used (albeit physically used only in part) for the purposes of the Ord Irrigation Project (including Lake Argyle), totally extinguished native title.

On 4 August 2000 the High Court of Australia granted the Miriuwung Gajerrong people special leave to appeal against the decision of the majority of the Full Court in respect of the 'bundle of rights' issue and many of the extinguishment issues. The appeal was heard in 2002.[4]

The experts and the issues

Important aspects of the *Miriuwung Gajerrong* determination at trial and on appeal in the Federal Court concern the findings and reasoning of the trial judge as to the proof of native title and the identity of the people who hold native title area. The decision on these aspects is highly instructive and likely to provide something of a guide or precedent, although not a 'template' or 'model', for other claimant groups throughout Australia.

The manner in which native title was proved in the *Miriuwung Gajerrong* case also helps to elucidate the role and function of expert witnesses, such as anthropologists, linguists, historians and archaeologists, in native title proceedings. The decision confirms the view that the evidence of such experts may assist in the proof of native title by adding to, explaining or complementing the direct testimony to the court of the claimants, but cannot substitute for the testimony to the court of the claimants. Nor can the opinions of expert witnesses substitute for those of the trial judge, in the sense that the opinions of experts do not usually bind a trial judge and are unlikely to do so in native title proceedings. Ultimately, the judge must find: whether native title exists; and, if so, who holds the native title; and whether there has been any extinguishment of native title.

Depending on the evidence before the court, there may be various options as to what the trial judge may find and the opinions of expert witnesses bearing on such issues may be persuasive or at least helpful.

The trial judge in the *Miriuwung Gajerrong* case was plainly assisted by the testimony of expert witnesses in dealing with the issue of what he called 'Aboriginal connection with the claim area after sovereignty' and the particular questions of whether the applicants represented a community identifiable with the Aboriginal people in occupation of the claim area at sovereignty; and whether that community had maintained connection with the land by observing, as far as practicable, the traditional customs, laws and practices of its predecessors.

The trial judge had particular regard to four areas of evidence. The first of these was the historical evidence, which included parts of a report from archaeologist Dr Robin Gregory (filed by the Northern Territory), historical aspects contained in the 1939 ethnography by Dr P. M. Kaberry, *Aboriginal Woman Sacred and Profane*, a history report by Dr Neville Green (filed by the State of Western Australia), various publications including oral histories by Dr Bruce Shaw (called by the first applicants), Dr Cathie Clement's history report (filed by the Northern Territory), Dr Christine Choo's history report (called for the first applicants) and historical passages to be found in the works of the anthropologists Professor Ronald Berndt and Professor Kenneth Maddock.[5]

Second, there was the linguistic evidence, including the reports and evidence of Ms Frances Kofod (a linguist called by the first applicants), together with aspects of a report by Dr Bruce Sommer (called by the state) and the published linguistic material of Dr A. Rumsey.[6]

Third, was the anthropological evidence, including the published works of Professor Elkin, Dr Kaberry, Professor Radcliffe-Brown, and R. M. and C. H. Berndt; as well as the reports filed and evidence given in the proceedings by Mr Kim Akerman (called by the first applicants), Associate Professor Will Christensen (called by the first applicants), Dr Kingsley Palmer (called by the second applicants), Mr Kim Barber (called by the second applicants), Ms Kim Doohan (called by the Balangarra people and the Kimberley Land Council), and Professor Kenneth Maddock (called by the state).[7]

Last, there was genealogical evidence, including the testimony of the claimants, and charts prepared by anthropologists called on behalf of the applicants and the Kimberley Land Council. There were also genealogical charts and field notes made by Dr Kaberry in the 1930s as part of her PhD fieldwork in respect of people then living within a part of the claim area.[8]

The trial judge made primary findings in the case in reliance on both expert evidence and extensive evidence of the claimants themselves. These findings related in particular to the 'primary' evidence of the applicants concerning their social organisation and connection with their traditional country and the rights and interests enjoyed by them in relation to their traditional country;[9] the genealogical testimony of the claimants to the court; and the evidence of the claimants concerning their observance of traditional laws, customs and practices to maintain connection with the prior community and with the land.[10] The trial judge also considered the issue of the 'boundaries' of the Miriuwung and Gajerrong land and again regarded the primary evidence of the claimants, as well as historic and ethnographic records and related expert evidence touching on the issues, in the course of making findings.[11]

Proving the present, not the past

Adducing primary evidence from claimants on these various matters is critical to the task of proving that native title has survived sovereignty and exists today. The task of proving native title is not dependent on proving what the details of the system of social organisation and rights and interests in land of a group of Aboriginal people were at the date of sovereignty. Rather, the common law of Australia, as explained in *Mabo v Queensland (No 2)*,[12] assumes change from sovereignty to the present, including change in social organisation and the nature of rights and interests enjoyed in relation to land by members of a community or group.

In a critical passage, sometimes overlooked by those concerned with proof of native title, Brennan J (as he then was, and with whom Mason CJ and McHugh J agreed) observed:

> The incidents of a particular native title relating to inheritance, the transmission or acquisition of rights and interests on death or marriage, the transfer of rights and interests in land and the grouping of persons to possess rights and interests in land are matters to be determined by the laws and customs of the Indigenous inhabitants, provided those laws and customs are not so repugnant to nature, justice, equity and good conscience that judicial sanctions under the new regime must be withheld [footnote omitted]. Of course in time the laws and customs of any people will change and the rights and interests of the members of the people among themselves will change too. But so long as the people remain an identifiable community, the members of whom are identified by one another as members of that community living under its laws and customs, the communal native title survives to be enjoyed by the members according to the rights and interests to which they are respectively entitled under the traditionally based laws and customs as currently acknowledged and observed.[13]

This passage highlights the task claimants for native title, and the court ultimately, have in proceedings under the Native Title Act. The claimants need to give evidence of their current rights and interest in relation to land. It matters not that, since sovereignty, the rights and interests of members of a people among themselves may have changed. As Brennan J has stated, they 'will change'. If those rights and interests proved are 'enjoyed ... under traditionally based laws and customs', then they will survive to be enjoyed 'as currently acknowledged and observed'.

In other words, it is for the claimants to show what their rights and interests are in relation to land under their traditionally based laws and customs, as currently acknowledged and observed. Their task is not to prove that the rights and interests they enjoy today are the same, or substantially the same, as those that governed their ancestral community at sovereignty.

Once it is appreciated that the focus of the common law rule as to whether native title has survived is whether the current laws and customs under which rights and interests are derived are traditionally based, the role and function of a witness, including an expert witness, who might be called to help prove the survival of native title begins to fall into place.

History

A historian is called by claimants principally to provide an account of the written historical record pertaining to a claim area. Depending on the issues in a particular case a historian's evidence may venture beyond the conventional and provide a contemporary view of past reality. The history reports in the *Miriuwung Gajerrong* case identified references to Aboriginal people historically in the claim area and confirmed the primary evidence concerning the presence of an organised Aboriginal society in the claim area at sovereignty. However, they also emphasised that the historical record is often 'silent' as to the presence and activities of Aboriginal people beyond legal and other official processes. Nonetheless, the historical evidence highlighted the use of the claim area by Aboriginal people that confirmed the maintenance of connection over a number of generations.

Interesting issues arise concerning the role of oral history in native title proceedings. Ordinarily there will be no role for the historian to speak on behalf of the current applicants through the preparation of an oral history, as the claimants must do that for themselves by giving evidence to the court. However, it is possible to imagine circumstances where an oral history of a particular issue, drawn from current claimants, might prove relevant, helpful and admissible. There is no impediment to members of the applicants giving direct evidence of their own histories and the history of their community, including evidence of the laws, customs, practices and traditions handed down to them and to their community by their ancestors. In this sense the oral history of the claimant group may be presented to the court.

There is no role for historians to express opinions about the anthropology of the claimant community or its ancestor community: to do so would usually go beyond the disciplinary expertise of the historian. However, it is to be expected that, to the extent that the historical record is incomplete, has gaps in it or needs to be interpreted having regard to other historical facts or knowledge historians have gleaned as part of their disciplinary studies, the historian should set the historical record straight or put it in a proper context and help to complete it or explain the gaps. In doing so, all accepted and contemporary means of providing a relevant history may be employed.

In the *Miriuwung Gajerrong* case three history reports went into evidence, on behalf of the first applicants, the state and the territory. Dr Clement's report (for the territory) was admitted by consent of the parties and did not attract any controversy among them. It contained a very useful chronology of historic and ethnographic events. Those of Dr Choo and Dr Green were the subject of extensive cross-examination of the witnesses. Dr Green's report for the state was questioned, among other reasons, because it purported to provide an 'ethno-history' of the claim area when the first applicants believed it failed to do so in any comprehensive manner. Dr Choo's report was questioned because the state perceived she had expressed opinions going beyond the function of a historian.

Choo's report also attracted some objections from Counsel for Western Australia because, in dealing with a question relating to which Aboriginal families had resided on which pastoral stations over a number of generations, she had purported to have regard to some personal communications with some of the claimants. The state complained that her evidence in this regard was based on hearsay in circumstances where the informants were not clearly identified and the state had lost the prior opportunity to cross-examine her informants (who may have earlier given evidence in the proceedings). Counsel for the first applicants accepted that, in all the circumstances, such evidence should not be admitted. Evidence had already been led from the primary claimants concerning such matters and so the deletion of such references in the history report did not disadvantage the claimants' case.

The objection illustrates the propensity of lawyers to object to hearsay evidence and other evidence that appears not to have a basis in an expert report. That is not to say, however, that hearsay evidence is always immaterial to the giving of expert evidence. If so-called hearsay is gathered as part of the recognised methodology of a discipline for the purpose of expressing an expert opinion, then the hearsay will be admitted on that basis, at least, and may also be admitted as to the truth of the matters asserted in appropriate circumstances.

In the *Miriuwung Gajerrong* case, the history expert called by the first applicants was not called primarily to provide an account of what the claimants themselves had said or would say in evidence. The taking of an oral history was not part of the historian's brief. However, an oral historian, Dr Bruce Shaw, was called. Shaw had, during the 1970s and later (but long before *Mabo*), published a number of significant oral histories following extensive interviewing of members of the claimant community who had since passed away. The quality of his work was such that the court accepted his oral histories and the recorded statements of persons since deceased as reliable and authoritative. The trial judge found that the stories of the deceased persons 'provide substantial links between Aboriginal society before and after European contact'.[14]

There has been and probably will continue to be some debate about the appropriate methodology for the taking of oral histories and the form of their publication. The ultimate point of the debate is whether or not a reliable account of what people say or have said appears in the published work. The work of Dr Shaw was of a high standard and the published work was verified by the original hand-typed manuscripts he had orally confirmed with his informants.

Depending on the circumstances in any given case, there may or may not be oral histories of the type that Shaw had taken in the Miriuwung and Gajerrong claim area. Where they exist, however, they do provide, as the trial judge found, considerable evidence of the laws and customs of the ancestors of a current community and of their possession, occupation, use or enjoyment of the claim area in the period linking the present with the past.

To the extent that witnesses, such as the claimants themselves or expert witnesses who have dealt with the claimant community over a number of years are able to do so, statements made by deceased members of the claimant community, while hearsay, may go into evidence. Whether or not they will be considered authoritative statements on any relevant issue will depend on a number of factors, including the status of the deceased person, the circumstances in which the statement is made, the clarity of the making and receipt of the statement, and the degree of support that a contentious statement may have had in the community in the past and in the present.

Archaeology

Archaeological evidence can also be useful in a native title case in establishing the fact of prehistoric and historic Aboriginal settlement of a claim area. It is not necessary to prove the antiquity of such settlement, only that at the time of sovereignty Aboriginal people possessed, occupied, used and enjoyed the claim area. In some instances, however, patterns of use observable by an archaeologist after sovereignty may permit the archaeologist to express the opinion that certain sites have been used not only in the present but for thousands of years before the present. The 'present', in this context, may well, on evidence available to the archaeologist, be after the date of sovereignty and at about the date of, or even after, contact with European settlers in the claim area. However, as with historians, ethnographic opinions expressed by an archaeologist will usually be found wanting in a native title proceeding. Those opinions are best expressed by the duly qualified anthropologist.

Anthropology

An anthropologist called for claimants in native title proceedings is not called to put into evidence a 'claim book' or report that accounts for the pre-history and archaeology, history, oral history, ethno-history, or a narrative about what the claimants currently say about their system of social organisation and the rights and interests they claim under their traditionally based laws and customs, as currently acknowledged and observed. Rather, in most cases such an anthropologist will be expected principally to provide a critical, disciplinary analysis of the claimants' current system of social organisation, and their rights and interests in relation to land, usually informed by 'participant observation' and regard to relevant literature.

In some instances, the anthropologist called by the claimants may have enjoyed a long association with the claimant community and may exhibit deep knowledge of the community's present culture, laws and practices and their evolution.

The statements of deceased people relevant to the matters in issue made to another person, while technically hearsay, may be adduced in evidence. An anthropologist who has had a long association with a claimant community is likely to have gained much information from informants who were knowledgeable and senior in the community, but who have since passed away. The anthropologist may therefore be in the position of reporting to the court on the basis of views not only of current members of the community but also those of significant deceased people, and these views may form the basis of the critical, disciplinary analysis contained in the report.

In the *Miriuwung Gajerrong* case Associate Professor Will Christensen was called by the first applicants to give anthropological evidence. He had not had the benefit of a long association with the claimant community and was engaged by the first applicants not long before the hearings commenced. However, he was familiar with the general region by reason of fieldwork conducted earlier in his career. By contrast, the second applicant group (some members of three 'local groups' or 'estate groups' in the Keep River National Park area) called Dr Kingsley Palmer who, like Christensen, had only limited fieldwork experience in the area, and Mr Kim Barber who had a longer association with the community, especially through the conduct of 'heritage surveys' for members of the community over a number of years. A report cowritten by Kingsley Palmer and Barber was filed on behalf of the second applicants. Christensen would explain later the approach he took to the writing of an initial report in the circumstances in which he found himself, and, following the giving of primary evidence, the preparation and filing of a supplementary report.

Respondent parties who wish to call anthropological evidence will usually be in the position of calling a person with relevant qualifications and experience in the discipline but without any relevant fieldwork experience in the claim area or knowledge of the claimant community. When put in such a position, the role of the anthropologist for a respondent is different in a number of important ways from that of the anthropologist called for a claimant community. The claimant's anthropologist may be expected to have developed a relationship of trust and confidence with the community, and through a degree of participant observation, will have come to understand the subtleties of social organisation, and rights and interest in and in relation to land or waters. These subtleties may not be immediately apparent to the more remote anthropological observer (or 'celestial' observer, as one anthropologist has put it!) of the court proceedings in which members of the claimant group address such issues.

Nonetheless, anthropologists who give evidence based on participant observation and anthropologists who give evidence on the basis of a general expertise and keen examination of the direct evidence in any given case are both capable of making meaningful contributions to the proceedings, although one would ordinarily expect that a court will be most aided in an understanding of the claimant community's system of organisation, laws, customs and practices, by the anthropologist who has had the closest association with the community. Yet, in relation to broader concepts of anthropology, not necessarily to be drawn from a study of the claimant community, the general competence of the anthropologist called to give evidence by a party may be important. In all cases, however, as observed earlier, the key issues in native title involve the trial judge having to make primary determinations of fact as to whether native title exists and, if it does, who holds it. The anthropologist can provide helpful opinion and understanding on these issues, but the opinions of an anthropologist, like those of other expert witnesses, do not bind the judge.

It is clear enough that the role anthropologists have played traditionally in relation to the making of land claims under the *Aboriginal Land Rights (Northern Territory) Act 1976* (Cwlth) is not immediately referable to the conduct of native title claims and the function of anthropologists and other experts in relation to them. The land claim procedure was and remains an administrative one, strictly speaking, whereas native title proceedings are conducted according to the common-law rules articulated in the Native Title Act and the usual court processes of the Federal Court (albeit modified to suit native title circumstances). The primary evidence of claimants themselves is, as noted earlier, critical to the proper conduct of native title proceedings. In a proper sense, expert witnesses are ancillary in the evidentiary process, and do not lead it.

In the future, there is reason to think that the role and function of anthropologists will develop as the jurisprudence relating to native title itself develops. Land claims in the Northern Territory historically and the native title applications made and heard in court to date have involved more traditionally oriented Aboriginal claim groups. Many of those groups have been, to various degrees (in some cases a considerable degree), the subject historically of anthropological 'study'. In many forthcoming claims under the Native Title Act, the claimant group may not have been previously 'studied' ethnographically to any great extent and may not appear as traditionally oriented as claim groups who have gone before them. The function of the anthropologist in analysing and helping to explain why the rights and interests asserted in relation to land or waters by such claimant groups are derived from a 'traditionally based' set of laws, customs and practices will be of increasing importance, as will the requirement for acute anthropological analysis of the nature of 'rights and interests' held traditionally in relation to country. To put the point more directly, as claimant groups cease to resemble the 'estate group' model of social organisation represented in classical anthropology, the task of anthropologists in helping to explain to the court the 'traditionally based' system will become of increased importance.

Similarly, it may well be that the role of anthropologists in the making of native title claims will be bifurcated, so that anthropologists will in the future not only be engaged by native title claimant groups for the purpose of giving expert evidence following participant observation, but also be engaged, often as members of a team, in the important task of providing expert advice, with other expert advisers, to the lawyers involved in the preparation and presentation of the evidence of claimant groups. A distinction has traditionally been drawn by the law between expert witnesses and expert advisers. Anthropologists in particular may expect to become more involved with both claimant groups and respondents as expert advisers in native title proceedings. Indeed, the conduct of the Miriuwung Gajerrong claim and the particular role of Associate Professor Will Christensen in the circumstances of the case tend to confirm that likelihood.

Genealogies

The question of genealogies was also important in the Miriuwung Gajerrong claim. The question was raised whether genealogies could properly be adduced and received into evidence without primary witnesses being called to verify much of the information therein. The alternative was that the genealogical work conducted by anthropologists itself required skill in the application of a disciplinary methodology that qualified the genealogies as expert reports admissible in evidence in their own right as to the truth of their contents.

In the event, genealogical evidence was adduced by the direct evidence of the claimants as well as by the charts prepared by anthropologists. The expert written genealogies also relied upon earlier ethnographic work conducted in the field by Phyllis Kaberry.

The trial judge noted that the first and second applicants adduced substantial oral evidence from witnesses on kin relationships and connections with their forebears and that the evidence was largely consistent with genealogies prepared by the anthropologists. However, the trial judge further found that the preparation of the genealogies:

> involved distilling information from a broad context of ethnographic material and it involved the application of skill and expertise of anthropologists. I was satisfied as to the reliability of the methods employed by the anthropologists in preparing the charts having regard to the general consistency of the content of the charts with the tenor of the 'primary' evidence of the applicants. The charts as received in evidence were not restricted to the expression of opinion by anthropologists but were also evidence as to the truth of the statements contained therein. Genealogies duly prepared by anthropologists employing their specialised skill and understanding of the structure and culture of a society represent not only an appropriate field of expert evidence but also a record of statements made to the anthropologists, the record of which is likely to be reliable, statements made being appropriate to be admitted in a case of this nature.[15]

On appeal, the state challenged the reception into evidence of genealogies prepared by an anthropologist called on behalf of the Balangarra people. Unlike the first and second applicants, the Balangarra people did not adduce substantial oral evidence to support the genealogies. However, there was some direct evidence in that regard. On appeal, the Full Federal Court held that the trial judge was entitled to rely on the evidence, including genealogical evidence, of an anthropologist called by the Balangarra people on the basis that the evidence was supported by 'limited primary evidence' of witnesses.[16] These findings suggest that it will prove difficult simply to have an anthropologist tender written genealogies without there being appropriate direct evidence from the claimants to verify the substance of the written genealogies.

Linguistics

Linguists can also be of immense importance in helping to prove native title. As with other expert witnesses, the evidence of a linguist can bear directly on the questions of whether the applicants represent a community identifiable with the Aboriginal people in occupation of the claim area at sovereignty; and whether that community has maintained a connection under its laws, customs and practices.

The evidence provided by linguist Frances Kofod, called by the first applicants, that the Miriuwung and Gajerrong languages were related, from the same family of languages, and had 'taken centuries to evolve', plainly had a bearing, with other evidence, on the likelihood that it was the Miriuwung and Gajerrong people respectively who had, since sovereignty, belonged to the country claimed by them to be their traditional country.

It was never asserted by the applicants that language alone established the 'connection' of the claimants with the traditional country claimed. Dr Sommer, called by the state, submitted in his evidence that certain words, which were not of the Miriuwung or Gajerrong languages, were used to describe locations and features in the claim area, and that this suggested the possibility that the Miriuwung and Gajerrong community had taken over habitation of the area from another group or groups. To that suggestion, the trial judge found:

> It may be thought that in the absence of any evidence that such an event had occurred subsequent to the formation of the colony, there would be little room for such speculation. It was made clear by Ms Kofod (the linguist called by the First applicants) that the extent of the use of the Miriuwung language in respect of features in the claim area, coupled with ethnographic material relating to widespread Dreaming and spiritual connections with the land for Miriuwung and Gajerrong people, speak quite forcefully of lengthy occupation of the relevant area and make it most improbable that the Miriuwung and Gajerrong were first connected with the land some time after 1825 or 1829 (the sovereignty dates in the NT and WA).[17]

In other words, the *Miriuwung Gajerrong* decision emphasises how linguistic evidence when combined with other ethnographic evidence can permit an inference to be drawn confidently that the people who today speak languages associated with the claim area are members of a community that was associated with the claim area at the time of sovereignty.

Frances Kofod was in a position to give reliable ethnographic evidence to the court that underlay her expertise as a linguist. The trial judge noted that her report and evidence was 'instructive', and that 'she had observed and studied speakers of Miriuwung and Gajerrong languages for periods of 3–4 months in each year between 1971 and 1974 and again in 1986 and on numerous periods in 1987 and 1988'.[18] Kofod worked with fluent speakers of the languages, had been involved in the establishment of the Aboriginal language centre at Kununurra and had become familiar with the community. The trial judge found her to be 'an impressive witness whose evidence could be relied upon'.[19]

In short, in the course of becoming effectively fluent in the Miriuwung language herself (a facility she did not claim for herself) and studying the Gajerrong and the nearby Gija languages, Kofod had relied upon key informants, some of whom had since passed away. She was able to advise the court of statements made by deceased people on matters of relevance in the proceedings.

The trial judge's findings

The trial judge, having heard the primary evidence and the evidence of the expert witnesses, ruled that native title existed in the claim area (save in some portions where it had been extinguished), and was held by the Miriuwung and Gajerrong people (and jointly by the Miriuwung and Gajerrong people and the Balangarra people in respect of Boorroonoong, Lacrosse Island).

The finding that the 'people' held the native title has been of particular interest to anthropologists and lawyers. The finding that the larger 'community' or 'tribal group' held the 'communal native title' was made against a background of the first applicants asking for such a determination and the second applicants asking that the finding be that (in the Keep River area of the claim in which most of them were particularly interested) native title was held by 'local groups' (or estate groups).

The trial judge considered that the evidence in the case demonstrated 'substantial consistency' with the concept of a 'tribal group' advanced by Elkin in 1938 in *The Australian Aborigines*:

> As described by Professor Elkin, such a group is comprised of people related by actual and implied genealogy who occupy and are in a definite area of territory and hunt and gather food over it according to rules which control the behaviour of smaller groups and families within the tribe. The identity of the tribal group is reinforced by shared use and possession of language. The sub-groups make the community work by acting as the economic units which take sustenance from, and are responsible for the upkeep of, the land and for the protection of sites of religious or ritual significance for the community according to traditional laws and customs that have been handed down from Dreamtime figures. Sub-group reliance upon kinship systems and lines of descent provided order in the community.

The trial judge also commented:

> The exogamous nature of the sub-groups, (which according to the anthropological evidence was historically the case with Miriuwung and Gajerrong sub-groups), meant that there were contacts, ties and understandings between the sub-groups. The older men and women of the community, with authority based on knowledge of laws and customs and of secret matters, were drawn from the sub-groups to organise ceremonial activities and rituals, such as initiation, for the 'tribal' group.[20]

He therefore considered from anthropological opinion that 'local groups' constituted the relevant native title holders, but explicitly found on the evidence that the 'laws and customs', of which there was much primary evidence, were 'the laws and customs of the community, not laws and customs of the sub-group'.[21] The 'community' was the 'Miriuwung and Gajerrong community', which the judge found had 'an ancestral connection with the Aboriginal community, or communities, which occupied the claim area at the time of the assertion of sovereignty in the State and Territory'. The trial judge therefore found that 'it follows that the communal title in respect of the claim area is the title of the Miriuwung and Gajerrong people'. (He found similarly in respect of the 'Balangarra people' regarding the shared interest over Boorroonoong, Lacrosse Island.)

In the *Miriuwung Gajerrong* case, the evidence disclosed that the Miriuwung and the Gajerrong were perceived as separate 'tribal' communities at the time the earliest ethnographic work was done in the claim area. The evidence plainly disclosed that the Miriuwung and the Gajerrong had long had their own laws and customs and that today they largely share in ceremonial activity, without affecting the right of each group to speak for their traditional country. In essence, the trial judge, having determined that native title existed and was held by the people, left it to 'the people' to administer their own system of native title. There was no need for the court to attempt to codify the traditionally based system as currently acknowledged and observed.

In the northern portion of the claim area, the ethnographic and historic evidence suggested that the original inhabitants either operated under a different 'tribal' name from the Gajerrong affiliation ascribed and used today, or had distinct local group names. In the event, the trial judge found that the Gajerrong people historically had shared the occupation of that portion of the claim area with other groups, but were today the sole occupants.

In a portion of the claim area in the south, Aboriginal people who claimed to be Gija or Malngin by tribal affiliation gave evidence that they shared interests in that portion with the Miriuwung claimants. However, because they had not made a formal application the trial judge did not make a finding of shared native title in their favour. On appeal, the Full Court found that, in an appropriate case, the court may indeed make a finding of native title or shared native title in respect of an area, notwithstanding that a group of Aboriginal people represented in the court has not made a formal application under the Native Title Act, although for other reasons they found it unnecessary to do so in this case.[22]

Conclusions

The Miriuwung Gajerrong claim indicates that experts in anthropology, linguistics, history and related disciplines do not so much have to engage in a boundary crossing exercise when they become involved in the law and native title proceedings, but work within agreed boundaries on the understanding that together their evidence will complement that of the others and help establish, with direct evidence from claimants and to the satisfaction of the court, that the claimant group is an identifiable community whose ancestors occupied the claim area at sovereignty, and which community today, albeit in a changed way, enjoys rights and interests in relation to land under traditionally based laws and customs. The brief given to each expert so engaged should be designed to achieve this understanding.

While expert witnesses are important in introducing evidence that might not otherwise find its way onto the court's record and in aiding the court's understanding of some complex ethnographic, linguistic, historical and prehistorical matters, it is plain enough as a result of the Miriuwung Gajerrong experience that the direct evidence of the claimants themselves provides the foundation to the proof of native title. The proof of native title is not dependent on what rights and interests in relation to land the ancestral community had at sovereignty, but on whether the rights and interests in relation to land the community currently acknowledges and observes are enjoyed under traditionally based laws and customs.

16

Working as an Anthropologist on the Miriuwung Gajerrong Native Title Claim

Will Christensen

THE MIRIUWUNG AND GAJERRONG are two closely related language groupings with contiguous traditional countries in the north-east Kimberley region of Western Australia and adjacent areas of the Northern Territory. Their combined territories stretch across some 200 kilometres from their northernmost extremities, including seas and offshore islands, to their southernmost extremities south of the artificially created Lake Argyle, a product of the Ord Irrigation Scheme that took shape from the late 1950s. The Cambridge Gulf in Western Australia constitutes, in broad terms, the westernmost point of their combined territories, while 200 kilometres or so away the Victoria River in the Northern Territory marks their easternmost extremity.

Today there are perhaps five hundred to six hundred people of Miriuwung or Gajerrong descent. Many identify themselves as solely one or the other, while some characterise themselves as 'half-half' or 'mixed' Miriuwung and Gajerrong. Others again describe themselves as 'half-half' or 'mixed' with other language groupings found in the region, particularly with the Gija to the south, the Malngin to the south-east, the Ngarinyman to the west and south-west, and the Jaminjoong to the east and north-east. Adding a further dimension of complexity, it seems likely that some of the people who now identify as Miriuwung and Gajerrong are descended from people identified in the past, at least in some circumstances, as Gooloowarrang, Doolboong, and Wardenybeng. The latter identities, submerged if not altogether forgotten until given new life by the native title process itself, have gnawed at the edges of the joint Miriuwung Gajerrong claim.[1]

Most people identifying as Miriuwung or Gajerrong live within their ancestral territories broadly defined or in the adjacent areas. They are now a minority in the lands taken as a whole that were once exclusively theirs, though they continue to constitute a large percentage of the population away from the main township of Kununurra. The changing population balance has its roots in the steady growth of non-Aboriginal numbers initiated by the Ord Irrigation Scheme, the major components of which were completed in the 1960s and early 1970s.

The Miriuwung and Gajerrong live today in a variety of circumstances. Some continue to live and work in the region's pastoral stations, until the 1960s the main source of employment for the then preponderant Aboriginal population. A number of those stations are now Aboriginal owned and run. Other Miriuwung and Gajerrong people live in the small communities built over the last quarter of the twentieth century in various parts of Miriuwung and Gajerrong territory. These communities are generally situated on small government reserves or excisions from pastoral stations and national parks, and a few exist tenuously on land for which no formal tenure has been granted. Other Miriuwung and Gajerrong people live in the large Aboriginal communities found in surrounding areas. Many live in or near Kununurra, a township established in 1963 as part of the Ord Irrigation Scheme, and now the region's administrative and commercial hub. A smaller number live in or near Wyndham, a port on the Cambridge Gulf established in the 1890s to service the developing pastoral industry. Wyndham lies a short distance from Gajerrong country. Until Kununurra came into existence, it was the only significant centre of non-Aboriginal population in the region.

Kununurra lies squarely within Miriuwung country, as do the associated irrigated farming properties and major infrastructural developments such as irrigation channels, Lake Argyle, the main reservoir for the irrigation scheme, and Lake Kununurra, the direct feed into the irrigation channels. Kununurra is one, if not the, major fulcrum of contemporary Miriuwung and Gajerrong activities. There is much movement backwards and forwards between Kununurra and the other places where Miriuwung and Gajerrong people live. It has a powerful draw in the region, because of its shops, schools, medical facilities, courts, sporting facilities and activities, community services, and the other things that large towns provide. But on the other side of the equation is a strong and, if anything, deepening concern at the individual and family level to sustain close connections with 'country'. That concern is manifested in a variety of ways, not least by the continuing efforts to build and sustain communities on or close to places or areas of special significance to particular groups and individuals. The emphasis on maintaining links to country is also demonstrated in patterns of visitation to and movement between communities, in recreational activities, and in the socialisation and education of the young.

Significantly in the present context, Kununurra is home to what is now generally known as the Miriuwung and Gajerrong Land Council or, to give it its full title, Miriuwung Gajerrong Families Heritage Aboriginal Land Corporation. The Land Council was established in 1979 and formally incorporated six years later as an agency to serve the needs of Miriuwung and Gajerrong people and their communities. That remit has, virtually from the start, placed it at odds with the Kimberley Land Council, based in Derby and now with an office in Kununurra, and the Northern Land Council, based in Darwin. These are the two large regional land councils that serve the broader regions embracing Miriuwung and Gajerrong country. A battle for influence—for the right to represent and speak directly for the Miriuwung and Gajerrong people—has been a recurrent theme in the Miriuwung and Gajerrong Land Council's relationships with these two bodies. The Miriuwung Gajerrong native title claim has brought new force and focus to that battle.

The Miriuwung Gajerrong claim was one of the first to be filed under the provisions of Australia's native title legislation. The Native Title Act was promulgated in 1993, with the associated administrative structures and protocols coming into existence the following year. Almost immediately, the Miriuwung and Gajerrong Land Council started preparing a claim. Early discussions, largely fruitless it seems, were held with the Kimberley and Northern land councils in relation to the intended claim. The land councils had both, by this time, been designated as representative bodies under the provisions of the Act, as had the Aboriginal Legal Service of Western Australia. The latter's mandate as a representative body was not regionally specific, opening the way for it to act within regions for which there were also regionally based representative bodies.

Early in the piece, the Miriuwung Gajerrong claimants, the 'first applicants' as they were later officially described, made a number of far-reaching decisions.

The choice of the Aboriginal Legal Service of Western Australia as the representative body for the claim was perhaps the most important of these decisions, a choice that alienated some potential claimants. Their disenchantment actually had little or nothing to do with the Aboriginal Legal Service itself, and much more to do with how the Miriuwung and Gajerrong Land Council was seen as manoeuvring the Kimberley and Northern land councils out of the claim leadership.

The overall boundaries for the claim were also set at an early stage. The area to be claimed included much but by no means all of what was generally understood to be Miriuwung and Gajerrong country. Areas not included were of three types. First were areas thought to be beyond claim by virtue of past or present usage or administrative decision. Second were areas where there was thought to be conflict with possible claims to adjacent country. Third were most of the seas and offshore islands to which claim could have been made. In this regard, Lacrosse, Kanggarryu and Pelican islands were included in the claim area, but surrounding seas and smaller islands were not. With this third category of exclusions from the claim area, it might be more appropriate to use the words non-inclusion or deferral given that the door had been left ajar for a supplementary claim at some future point.

The various exclusions from the Miriuwung Gajerrong claim area were motivated largely by the desire to minimise the likelihood of conflict with other potential claimants, partly by the desire to reduce the research burden. The exclusions reduced but did not remove the scope for conflict with other potential claimants, though that did not become apparent for quite some time, and then only bit by bit. As events eventually unfolded during the trial process, the Miriuwung Gajerrong claimants made a number of significant concessions to other parties, though none that seriously compromised their initial position. Thus, for example, the claim boundaries were reined in a little near Goosehill, on the north-west margin of the claim. Overlapping Balanggarra interests in Lacrosse Island at the head of the Cambridge Gulf were also acknowledged, albeit reluctantly, as were overlapping Gija interests in the Lissadell area to the south. Suggestions made during the trial process that these areas were not really Miriuwung or Gajerrong at all were vehemently resisted.

The inclusion in the claim area of land that might once have been referred to as Gooloowarrang, Doolboong, and Wardenybeng also carried the potential for conflict. At the outset, the main concern in this regard was not with the conflicting or alternatively constructed claims of the sort that eventually took shape, but rather with the play that opponents of all and any native title rights in the areas concerned would make of the apparent Miriuwung Gajerrong succession to land that once belonged to others. The claimants were not about to back away from conflict on this score. They had three strong arguments on their side. First, the areas in question are now thought of as being Miriuwung or Gajerrong. Second, the current customary law owners of these areas are now thought of as Miriuwung or Gajerrong. Third, the variation of labels notwithstanding, an unbroken line can be drawn between the current and pre-colonial owners of these areas as defined in customary law.

Another major decision that was made early in the piece was that the claim would proceed in three stages. Stage One, some 7900 square kilometres in all, would comprise Crown lands in Western Australia and the

Northern Territory thought to be open to claim. Areas with varied tenure types and histories came under this heading, including the Keep River National Park in the Northern Territory, Lake Argyle and its surrounds, and a pastoral station vested in the Aboriginal Lands Trust of Western Australia on behalf of the Aboriginal community who lived on and managed it. Stage Two was to consist of pastoral leases in Western Australia and Stage Three of pastoral leases in the Northern Territory.

It was also determined that a composite Miriuwung Gajerrong claim would be made. In the terminology then used, the claim was to be made by the 'Miriuwung and Gajerrong Peoples'. When I eventually came on to the scene, I equated the 'Miriuwung and Gajerrong Peoples' with the Miriuwung and Gajerrong people as a whole. Others saw things differently, equating the 'Miriuwung and Gajerrong Peoples' with that section of the two communities aligned with the Miriuwung and Gajerrong Land Council.

Other things also swung, or were seen as swinging, on the decision to mount a composite Miriuwung Gajerrong claim. The novelty of a composite claim of this sort caused consternation, for some perhaps simply because it was novel and would make novel demands. For others, the novelty of the composite claim was seen as involving some sort of anthropological heresy. Two things particularly aroused concern: the suggestion that language groupings were being advanced as Indigenous landowning entities in their own right; and the suggestion that undifferentiated community ownership of land was being proposed.

The major decisions having been taken, the battle to win acceptance for the claim was then enjoined. Stage One of the Miriuwung Gajerrong claim was filed with the National Native Title Tribunal in 1994. The hope at the time was that the claim would be settled through negotiation and mediation. That soon proved impossible, not least because of trenchant opposition to the claim by the Western Australian State Government. Coming to the conclusion that mediation between the various parties was not likely to lead to an agreed position, the President of the National native title Tribunal referred the matter to the Federal Court in January 1995. After a number of preliminary legal skirmishes, the case proper got under way later that year, with Justice Michael Lee presiding. Various expert witness reports were filed soon thereafter.

In March 1996 I was on study leave from Western Australia's Curtin University of Technology. My course was set on a project (on education systems in selected countries of the Indian Ocean region) unrelated to my prior teaching and research on Indigenous Australia. The Aboriginal Legal Service of Western Australia approached me in the midst of this new venture, requesting that I serve as anthropological consultant for their clients.

Approaches to other anthropologists had failed for one reason or another. I was also told that the claim would be seriously disadvantaged if a knowledgeable anthropologist could not be found more or less immediately.

Three weeks after the initial approach I commenced work on the claim. I had managed in the meantime to speak with a number of the claimants and to get their and my university's approval for my involvement in the Miriuwung Gajerrong claim. I believed at the time that my own role was a stopgap measure and would end or be reduced once an alternative appointment was made. An anthropologist who could go the full distance with the claim was required, however long that might prove to be. Preferably that person would be someone with lengthy prior research experience in the area.

In taking on the job, I had little idea of what lay ahead, but I suspected that more would be entailed than I had initially bargained on. As it happened, I worked on the Miriuwung Gajerrong claim on and off for twenty-two months. The culmination and formal conclusion of my involvement came in January and February 1998, when I spent five days in the Federal Court being examined as an expert witness. The day after my final court appearance I made a long-delayed return to academic duties at Curtin, my prior study-leave plans having been indefinitely postponed.

In the weeks after my return to Curtin, the case continued in the Federal Court. Further expert witnesses were examined. Final submissions by counsel were made in March and April. Justice Lee handed down his decision on the *Miriuwung Gajerrong* case in November of that year. Lee found emphatically in favour of the claimants on most points of contention. Michael Barker QC, the barrister representing the Miriuwung Gajerrong claimants, has outlined the main elements of Lee J's decision and its wider significance in chapter 15 of this volume.

Predictably, considerable controversy was aroused by the *Miriuwung Gajerrong* decision. Many welcomed Lee's determination. Others, notably the Western Australian Government and powerful industry groups, opposed it vehemently. Some of the negative reaction was driven by local factors, including developmental plans for the areas affected by the decision, but its perceived ramifications for claims elsewhere in the state and nation inspired much of it.

An appeal against Lee's finding followed. Various parties, led principally by the Western Australian Government, joined the appeals. The Kimberley Land Council and the Northern Land Council, acting on behalf of clients they saw as disadvantaged or excluded by the Lee decision, sought alternative declarations. A Full Court of the Federal Court heard submissions and appeals on the contested matters in Perth in July and August 1999.

Courtroom evidence in relation to these matters occupied fifteen days, making it one of the longer appeals in the Federal Court's history. The Court's decision on the appeal was handed down in early March 2000.

All three members of the Full Court found in favour of Lee's findings of fact, but two (Beaumont and von Doussa JJ) found against his determination on various matters of law. The two found that Lee had misconstrued the legal essence of native title and what was required for it to be extinguished permanently. They also found that, at a more specific level, he had miscalculated the effects of particular legislative and administrative decisions and actions on the persistence of native title in the *Miriuwung Gajerrong* context. Justice North dissented from the majority view, coming down strongly in support of all aspects of the original determination. From the Miriuwung Gajerrong viewpoint, the appeal judgment had a twofold effect. It cut substantially the area over which native title was to be granted; and it drastically curtailed the scope of the native title rights and interests deemed to have survived over the remaining areas.

The *Miriuwung Gajerrong* case went before the High Court in 2002. The facts of the claim, as found by Lee and upheld by the Full Court of the Federal Court, were not at issue in the High Court appeal. Solely at issue were the matters of law on which the majority of the Full Court of the Federal Court overrode Lee's original determination. The High Court's resolution of these matters would have major implications for native title claims elsewhere in Australia, and perhaps internationally.[2]

The work context

The work situation that awaited me when I became engaged in the claim was defined by four main factors. The first of these had to do with the timing of my engagement. The claim process was already well advanced, and a broadly based research plan had been formulated by the Aboriginal Legal Service. Much work—anthropological, archaeological, ethnohistorical, historical and linguistic—had been completed. More was in progress, including ongoing historical research by Christine Choo, and the compilation of genealogies by anthropologist Kim Barber. Other research work had been initiated or planned by the Kimberley Land Council and Northern Land Council, each representing interests either not represented or uncomfortable with aspects of the first applicants' claim.

The Miriuwung Gajerrong claim had been in the Federal Court for over a year by the time I came on board. The legal preliminaries had been largely dispensed with, and a broad timetable had been devised for the submission and hearing of evidence. Of immediate relevance to me, the

Federal Court had stipulated that a further anthropological submission, for which I would come to be responsible, had to be filed, with the deadline just six weeks away. That timetable provided only the barest opportunity for reviewing existing evidence and for seeking first-hand claimant confirmation on the cardinal points of the claim. It allowed no room for delay and little or no scope for returning to first principles.

The second factor influencing my work was the conflict and contention surrounding the Miriuwung Gajerrong claim. At the time of taking on the job, I had fair warning of the divisions, but I had little understanding of their origins, extent or ramifications. I had no real grasp of how persistent and debilitating to all concerned those divisions would prove to be.

Refusing to acknowledge any substance to the Miriuwung Gajerrong claim, the Western Australian Government had used its considerable resources to oppose the claim by every means and argument available to it, including procedural ploy. That hostility, incidentally, persisted right through to the hearing of the High Court challenge. A recent change of government seems to have produced a different stance. Much more could and, indeed, should be said about the State Government's stance in relation to the Miriuwung Gajerrong claim than is possible here. I was disappointed though, in truth, not surprised by the Government's position.

There was also strong local opposition to the claim. The received wisdom was that such opposition was to be expected. My experience in this respect ran pretty much true to form. Non-Aboriginal opinion in the region, to the extent I could gauge it, ran solidly against native title generally, and perhaps even more strongly against claims close to home. I consoled myself with the thought that, when the claim was successful, the negative attitudes and fears would yield to more positive and constructive feelings.

While I was, in a sense, girded for direct opposition to the claim, I was not ready for the bitter divisions between those who were ostensibly united in supporting it. I was introduced to the conflict unexpectedly. While still pondering what I had understood to be the Aboriginal Legal Service's confidential approach to me, I received two disturbing telephone calls, both clearly aimed at persuading me to reject the offer. The calls, each unofficial, came from persons associated with the other representative bodies. I was told that this was 'the land claim from hell'. One of the callers asserted that it would be better if the present claim were to fall over and be replaced by one with a chance of success. Various allegations followed, principally to do with the breakdown of negotiations between the various representative bodies and the Miriuwung and Gajerrong Land Council.

I was troubled by the accusations I had heard, and disturbed by the description of the Miriuwung Gajerrong claim as the 'land claim from hell' for which no help could be held beyond 'falling over' and being replaced by something better. There was no time for delay. I hesitated briefly before signing on as a consultant for the first applicants. Two things persuaded me. One was the view, reinforced in lengthy conversation with Michael Barker QC, the first applicants' barrister, that a failed application would make another application less, rather than more, likely of success. The second consideration was that the evidence available to me showed that the Miriuwung Gajerrong claim was anchored appropriately on the correct people and was proceeding with their support. It also seemed to me that even those expressing concern abut how the claim was being advanced were not opposed to its fundamental substance, but were looking toward various forms of refinement and extension. I believed that whatever forms of refinement and extension were required could be achieved as the claim progressed.

The hoped for resolution of differences did not come. Right up to the time I finally stepped down from the witness box, I was uncertain of and worried about where the representative body wrangling was leading and how it would reflect on the evidence presented. With more than a hint of dread, I wondered how that wrangling would affect my own examination in court. I wondered too what arguments would be put when it came time for final submissions.

The third factor was the most important, to my mind. This factor was the fundamental agreement between the Aboriginal claimants and their representatives that the right people were going forward for the right country. Sadly, this fundamental agreement was in constant danger of being obscured, denied and even subverted in a climate of ill-will.

I began my involvement in the Miriuwung Gajerrong claim with a strong sense, based upon my prior experience in the region and my examination of the correspondence relating to the claim, that the fundamentals of the claim were sound, if rather idiosyncratically expressed. I ended my formal involvement knowing a great deal more about the nuances and complexities of the claim, and still firmly convinced that, in its essentials, the claim was reasonable and soundly based. Lee's judgment vindicated that position. My hopes that the claim would eventually come to be accepted by all representative bodies, however, were misplaced. I should have known better. To be told in advance of taking on the consultancy that this was the 'land claim from hell' should have told me more than it did. I was naive about the politics, and I was naive in thinking that the issues of anthropological contention would eventually yield to the evidence.

I am still struggling for perspective on the conflicts pitting claimant group and representative bodies against each other. There is a history to these tangled conflicts that long precedes native title, and there is every reason to believe that they will find new focuses when the immediate native title issues are settled. But that is not to make light of the differences between the various parties to the Miriuwung Gajerrong claim, nor to treat the divisions as simply the product of idle politics. The size and complexity of the claim made some differences almost inevitable. There were, for example, genuine issues to do with overlapping interests, demarcation, and the apparent exclusion of eligible claimants. There were also questions to do with desired outcomes with respect to prescribed body or bodies corporate. These were all substantive issues calling out for some sort of resolution.

Then there were issues to do with the methodology of the claim process—to do with strategies and methods for achieving the desired outcomes. Among these issues were questions of carriage: who would represent the claimants; how the case would be presented; how the research agenda would tie in with the broader approach to advancing the claim, and so on.

Both methodological and substantive issues, as defined here, were highly charged. They were and still are real and important issues worthy of careful examination and discussion. In the circumstances then prevailing, these issues were swallowed up and became subordinate to the main political cleavages. That fact, together with the adversarialism encouraged by the formal legal process, meant that once positions were taken, they were no longer open to negotiation, notwithstanding the occasional gestures in that direction. The one light that shone brightly for me throughout was the conviction, strengthening by the day, that the claim mounted by and on behalf of the first applicants was legitimate and important to their future. Complexities and distracting arguments aside, Miriuwung Gajerrong claimants represented by the Aboriginal Legal Service are acknowledged by all Aboriginal parties in the region as the rightful claimants for the areas in question. That was borne out in the courtroom, with minor dispute and qualification, and has since been acknowledged by each of the representative bodies, notwithstanding their differing views as to how the claim should have been structured.

Lee J succeeded admirably in sorting the wheat from the chaff in regard to the various issues of contention. The fact that he was able to find so strongly in support of such a complex and far-flung claim testifies, without doubt, to the overall strength of the Miriuwung Gajerrong claim. The claim was built upon a solid foundation of agreement, and this point ought not be lost sight of or underestimated.

The fourth factor was uncertainty about just what was required to prove native title, and about the role of expert testimony in the process. The latter translated for me into various issues of anthropological interpretation and evidence. Was so-called 'estate group analysis' necessary to sustain the claim? If so, was that approach compatible with the composite Miriuwung Gajerrong claim as it had previously been formulated? If it were not essential, would it be helpful? To what extent would the proving of native title require the demonstration of certain types of continuing cultural orientation (language, religious observances, knowledge of country)? How would the evidence of variation and change within the Miriuwung and Gajerrong communities sit with the presumed requirement to demonstrate continuity of association with the areas over which native title was being sought? What is the contemporary nature of Miriuwung Gajerrong communities and what does that mean from the viewpoint of how relationships to the land are now sustained and articulated?

I started on the Miriuwung Gajerrong claim with my own hunches as to the anthropological evidence likely to be required to demonstrate the continued existence of native title. Had I been free to do so, and had time allowed, I would probably have proceeded with what has become standard anthropological practice in gathering and marshalling what I took to be the required evidence. That is to say, I would have attempted to delineate and map the many landowning units (for which the expression 'estate groups' is as good as any other on offer) within the overall Miriuwung and Gajerrong groupings. I would also have wanted to understand and describe the interconnections between those estate groups and others. It soon became evident that what I had in mind in this regard was simply not possible given the time and other constraints imposed by the Federal Court process, nor was it consistent with the overall evidentiary strategy being pursued by the Aboriginal Legal Service on its clients' instructions.

The main tasks and challenges

The Aboriginal Legal Service was determined that the Miriuwung and Gajerrong claimants themselves would carry the greater part of the burden of presenting evidence to the court, and it was equally determined that 'estate group analysis' would not provide the framework within which evidence would be led or presented. The call in this regard was not mine. If I was to play a constructive role in relation to the Miriuwung Gajerrong claim, it would have to be within the constraints of the Legal Service's evidentiary strategy.

In taking on the work on behalf of the first applicants, I took on a job that was multifaceted and open-ended. There were three highlights to that involvement. The first was the preparation and submission to the court of an initial anthropological report (June 1996). The second was the preparation and submission to the court of a final anthropological report (November 1997). The third was my courtroom examination as an expert witness (January–February 1998).

Other tasks, not possible to describe here in any detail, were also important elements of my overall anthropological contribution to the Miriuwung Gajerrong native title claim. Those other activities included preparing an affidavit relating to the hearing and examination of certain types of evidence; revising genealogies; reviewing reports filed in the court or circulated by other parties; preparing reports for circulation to selected other parties; reviewing courtroom evidence of other expert witnesses; participating in discussions between legal counsel and claimants; and providing general advice to counsel on anthropological matters bearing on the claim.

As stated earlier, the Miriuwung Gajerrong claim was well advanced by the time I became involved. Two annotated bibliographies had been produced for internal purposes. Historian Christine Choo had already presented three lengthy and detailed historical reports. Bruce Shaw, an anthropologist and oral historian, had submitted an oral historian's report. Frances Kofod had filed a linguist's report. Richard Fullager had filed an archaeologist's report. Kim Akerman had filed an anthropological report. Sadly, ill health prevented Akerman going the full distance with the claim. Kim Barber was preparing genealogies on behalf of the Aboriginal Legal Service.

It was early April. I was told that the court had allowed that a Supplementary Report could be filed by 17 May, some six weeks ahead. In the event, it was filed in early June. I was given a wide-ranging brief as to the issues to be tackled. It was understood that only so much could be achieved in the time available, and that I would have little scope for original research. There was little time to reflect on the exercise, but two thoughts were strong in my mind. I had to address issues where the claim was potentially vulnerable, and I had, in effect, to establish my credentials for further participation in the process as an expert witness. By doing so, I would be able to contribute later in the piece, principally, I expected, in the context of courtroom examination.

I was almost immobilised at the start by the magnitude of the task before me. Where did that task begin and end, and how could the final product be presented to best advantage? I eventually filed a 116-page report that brought together all of the available evidence to which I had access.

In compiling my report, I chose a format unlike any other I have seen used for a similar purpose. I decided that no point would be served by beating around the bush or by going down ethnographic sidetracks. Nor, I concluded, would I gain added credibility by pretending disinterested scholarship. I had to nail my colours to the mast as to the propositions I was supporting. I had to be bold, but I also had to be capable of defending whatever position I took.

The framework for my initial report was provided by the issues that were central to the Miriuwung Gajerrong claim: pre-sovereignty occupancy and ownership; pre-sovereignty systems of rules, customs and laws; claimant links to forebears and predecessors; an identifiable claimant group; and continuities between past and present patterns. The available evidence was interrogated in relation to these issues. The same format was used a year and a half later when I was given the opportunity to file another report.

My final report was presented six weeks after the Miriuwung Gajerrong witnesses had finished giving evidence, and just eight weeks after I was informed that an additional submission would be allowed. The lack of notice and compressed time frame made the task formidable. Nevertheless, I welcomed the opportunity, seeing in it a chance of responding to evidence heard by the court since my initial submission. I also hoped that the exercise would help prepare me for my forthcoming courtroom examination, as it did.

The additional submission did not mean I could file new evidence or open up new lines of argument. Instead, I could comment upon or add information on specific issues that had been raised. That new evidence included 5000 pages of court transcript, together with the information in reports filed since my own initial report, particularly those filed by Maddock and Barber and Palmer.[3] Working within those constraints, I was able to work in some of the results of the detailed work I had undertaken since the filing of my initial report, including work on the historical anthropological literature. In this context, I drew heavily on Phyllis Kaberry's published work, field notes and genealogies. I also drew on records left by Joseph Birdsell and Norman Tindale in connection with their 1950s work in the north-east Kimberley.[4] I was also able to work in some material gathered at first hand. With this last, I had to be careful not to overstep the mark, at which I could only really guess, by introducing material that could be seen as putting respondents to the claim at legal disadvantage.

The third highlight of my involvement in the Miriuwung Gajerrong claim was the courtroom examination as an expert witness. That examination, in Perth in late January and early February 1998, lasted some five days in sum, stretched over eighteen days. The experience of being in the witness box was gruelling and stressful, but not nearly as stressful as the days of waiting and of watching other expert witnesses being examined, all the time wondering whether I would hold up as well when my time came. During my time in the witness box, I was questioned in relation to a wide range of issues bearing on the Miriuwung Gajerrong claim, including matters touched upon in the field notes I had been required to produce for the court's benefit. My evidence gave rise to over 500 pages of transcript.

Some of the questions I faced were designed to test my credibility as an expert witness, both on a general professional level and specifically in relation to the Miriuwung Gajerrong claim. Other questions were directed toward confirming or challenging the ethnographic facts and interpretations upon which the Miriuwung Gajerrong claim rested. Two things served me particularly well in the latter regard. One was the intensive work I had undertaken on the region's early anthropological records. Kaberry's field notes and genealogies from the 1930s, together with Birdsell's and Tindale's journals and correspondence from the 1950s, were especially useful here. I was also served well by being able to 'read' in contemporary anthropological perspective the evidence tendered to the court by other witnesses, both expert and 'primary'.

Reflections on the experience

For the reasons given, my experience working on the Miriuwung Gajerrong claim was not what one would normally hope for or expect in such situations. The unusual nature of that experience may mean that it has little to offer anthropologists or other expert witnesses working elsewhere. On the other hand, the very atypicality of my experience may make it of some interest, particularly to the extent that it forced me to grapple with issues that might not otherwise have been brought into focus.

One of these issues, which loomed large for me throughout my involvement in the claim, was the question of professional specialisation and division of labour. The formal brief I was given by the Aboriginal Legal Service was couched in terms that could well have applied to a native title claim anywhere in Australia. That brief, incidentally, had been drawn up months before I was initially contacted, and at a time when a more conventionally defined research role for the anthropologist was still contemplated. The matter of dovetailing with the work of other expert witnesses was not mentioned, the assumption apparently being that the various specialists would be working in parallel and not in contact with one another or one another's work. Legal counsel would grapple with how the various expert contributions were to be pieced together.

Seen thus, the issue of professional boundaries and co-operation was not one that ought to have bothered me. Increasingly it did. The absence of any substantial opportunity to build an argument from the ground up, from my own original field research, was a major factor in that respect. Particularly early on, I had to rely disproportionately upon existing written records, some specifically anthropological, others not. Various other professional specialisations had already contributed to the Miriuwung Gajerrong claim. What was I to make of these other disciplinary contributions? Could they be drawn upon in a way that added substance and credibility to my own analysis and presentation of evidence?

In the event, I plumped to make as much use of those materials as I could. My motivation came partly from a sense of not otherwise having enough to draw upon for the purposes for which I had been engaged. I was also genuinely convinced that the materials produced by the other professional specialisations were properly open to anthropological scrutiny and use. I remain convinced of that.

Deepening knowledge of the available literature added to my conviction that more was to be gained than lost by drawing broadly on all existing documentary materials regardless of their disciplinary provenance. The main point about the existing documentary materials was how incomplete and fragmentary they were. A reasonably strong and convincing picture could be drawn, but only if all available sources were open to use. That picture could never have emerged if some sort of self-denying ordinance had been in operation where the anthropologist read only the anthropological, the historian only the historical, the archaeologist only the archaeological.

I had to read the total available literature, through anthropological eyes to be sure, but giving neither privileged nor prejudicial treatment to one source as opposed to another simply on the basis of its disciplinary origin. I resisted then, as I would now, the suggestion that the various disciplines join only at the seams. The disciplines intersect in terms of their themes, topics and methods of inquiry. With the intersections come opportunities for corroboration and contradiction, and these were potentially crucial in the adversarial trial process in which we were engaged.

The realisation that much was to be gained by trawling all available sources did not mean that I had to be anthropologist, linguist, historian and archaeologist all in one. I was quite at ease accepting that the examination of primary archival material was a task for the historian, just as primary ethnographic and genealogical research was a task for the anthropologist. Moreover, I had absolutely no interest in getting involved in another expert's examination of primary data. Why, without some particular cause for doubt, would one want to repeat or even poke one's nose into the work undertaken by someone specialised in a field other than your own? However, when that work, or the information on which it was based, reflected, as it did, on issues falling within my primary area of interest and expertise—issues such as continuity of association, cultural continuity, identity, and the like—I had no compunction in treating them as valid sources. They were there to be mined and interrogated, as it were, and brought within an anthropological perspective. What was the alternative? Ignore the intersections? Retreat to a stereotyped anthropology? Accept a modular, compartmentalised notion of scholarly and professional disciplines? Leave the gaps, the overlaps, the contradictions, the corroborations to others to make whatever sense (or play) they might make of them?

Were we asking these things of, say, physics and pharmacy, we might with conviction say that it is better to stay within the boxes. But in the *Miriuwung Gajerrong* case, we had expert witnesses in socio-cultural anthropology, social history, ethno-history, oral history, human geography, archaeology, descriptive and historical linguistics, and socio-linguistics. One could hardly think of a more tangled set of disciplinary overlaps and intersections. (Sociology, for which an argument could well have been made, would have confounded the picture still further.) In that context, it was impossible to think of the various specialisations representing discrete pieces in the jigsaw.

When it actually came to working with the substantive matters dealt with by the various disciplines, I was struck by the essential congruence of evidence. That congruence might have gone unobserved and unremarked had disciplinary pigeonholing been the order of the day. My ability to identify and demonstrate the significance of that essential congruence was, I think, one of the valuable things I was able to bring to the Miriuwung Gajerrong claim. Part of that demonstration of congruence had to do with highlighting factual overlaps and complementarities; part had to do with pointing out thematic consistencies and patterns. If I had to gloss the latter with a single word it would be perspective. It was perspective related to cultural process and change. My various contributions to the hearing of the Miriuwung Gajerrong claim helped to put Miriuwung and Gajerrong cultures in the active as opposed to passive voice and in the present as opposed to past tense. In this I aided, and in turn was aided by, the other expert witnesses working on behalf of the Miriuwung Gajerrong claimants. In that sense, each of us was stronger for standing alongside the others, even if we worked essentially in isolation one from the other.

If working in a multidisciplinary context on issues that cannot be really pigeonholed was an essential part of my experience in the Miriuwung Gajerrong claim, so also was working in a situation that precluded the lengthy original field research that would normally be expected in such circumstances.

Conclusions

The terms of my involvement in the Miriuwung Gajerrong claim were far from ideal. I was acutely aware throughout of the difficulties and dangers associated with the restricted opportunities for original field research. At the same time, it also seemed clear to me that any decision on my part to decline or continue involvement in the claim would have jeopardised the claim's chances of success without in any way adding to the chance of success of an alternatively constructed claim. What then could I contribute and how would that contribution be made?

The challenge confronting me in each of the major phases of involvement in the claim was how to advance what was known and certain while leaving the door open to matters requiring further investigation and sharper specification. Others will be better judges of whether I was equal to that challenge or, indeed, whether it was a challenge anyone could meet. Perhaps, some might conclude, the challenge was pulled off in this particular instance, but only by virtue of having the back-up of a skilled and supportive legal team, an exceptionally focused and informed trial judge, and a strangely ill-prepared opposition.

Striking the right balance was difficult. It involved speaking plainly and honestly to the available evidence, all the time emphasising the things that really counted. Appearances notwithstanding, the things held in common by the various representative bodies and their clients outweighed the things in dispute.

In presenting the argument I was advancing, I had to be careful not to be pre-emptive as to matters where more discussion and data were required. That sometimes required me to argue in the abstract rather than the concrete. Plainly, the Miriuwung Gajerrong claim area had been identified long in advance of my arrival on the scene. The evidence initially available to me, vindicated by the great bulk of evidence subsequently presented, said that the claim area could properly be described as Miriuwung and Gajerrong, notwithstanding the various complexities already mentioned (especially to do with the Doolboong, Gooloowarrang and Gija). I said so in my report, but made it clear that to support the Miriuwung Gajerrong claim was not necessarily to deny rights and interests asserted by other groups. Of course, any such assertions would need to be substantiated, but such rights and interests could be acknowledged without injury to the Miriuwung Gajerrong claim in its essentials. Similarly, genealogies had been prepared for the greater number of people identifying as Miriuwung and Gajerrong. The implied listing was not comprehensive and not presented as such. The intent of the Miriuwung Gajerrong claim, as I understood it, was that all persons identifying and identified as Miriuwung or Gajerrong were contemplated as part of the claim.

The point here is that the case was being argued broadly on behalf of the Miriuwung and Gajerrong people, not on behalf of some finite listing or some particular organisational expression or section of the Miriuwung and Gajerrong communities. There were matters of detail, I assumed, that would inevitably have to be dealt with after rather than before the claim was resolved. Experience now tells me that the less unresolved at the point of determination, the better.

As to the apparent anthropological novelty of the Miriuwung Gajerrong claim, the view I took and am prepared to defend is that the novelty was more apparent than real. A composite language grouping claim may well be novel. But framing a claim in these terms is not to say that the language groupings are themselves the landowning units, or that more narrowly defined relationships to land have ceased to exist. I made this clear in my initial report, and repeated it without hesitation in later testimony.

Did the claim imply that the two language groupings had merged and become indistinct, I asked. No, I answered. The two are 'closely related but separable' and 'situated within a broader regional Aboriginal society'. Does the use of the labels Miriuwung and Gajerrong in the claim imply the existence of uni-dimensional and unchanging identities and relationships to land? No, I could say with confidence. The labels are 'glosses on more complex realities'. Do the Miriuwung and Gajerrong constitute landowning units in themselves? Again, I could aver that 'rights and interests vary within. At the heart of Miriuwung and Gajerrong communities are social and territorial rights, interests and responsibilities differentiating individual from individual and estate group from estate group'. And, further, 'Miriuwung and Gajerrong people have rights and interests in country further afield, that is to say in land not usually glossed as Miriuwung and Gajerrong, and likewise people further afield have rights and interests in so-called Miriuwung and Gajerrong country even though they might not think of themselves or be thought of as Miriuwung or Gajerrong'.

Finally, in terms of reflecting on my experience in the Miriuwung Gajerrong claim, I want to comment on how native title claims are framed and by whom. The Miriuwung Gajerrong claim was framed idiosyncratically. Much of the discussion surrounding the Miriuwung Gajerrong claim, and presumably other claims as well, has been predicated on there being a right way and a wrong way for claims to be structured. For some anthropologists, a composite language grouping claim is alien to their sense of what is appropriate. Lurking there somewhere is the suggestion that the more closely claimant entities reflect pre-sovereignty realities, the more anthropologically sound and defensible they are. There also seems to be the suggestion that any overarching entity (in this case the composite Miriuwung Gajerrong grouping) is bound to fracture and fragment. That might well be a possibility but who is to decide whether the advantages of consolidation outweigh the disadvantages?

One thing that has to be recognised is that claimants will and do make choices as to their preferred means of advancing their claims. We have to respect the right to such choices, due regard being paid to the interests affected by those choices, and we have to expect that diversity will come with choice. Anthropologists and other expert witnesses must decide whether or not they can work within the constraints of the choices made. They too face choices.

In addition to lamenting the 2002 High Court decision in relation to this claim, and the impact this will have on the claimants, my final point has to do with choice, and more specifically with what might be called informed choice. As expert witnesses and advisers, anthropologists and others should be capable of conceiving and examining alternative native title scenarios. We should be able to contrast alternative scenarios and show their varied advantages and disadvantages. Presumably, we all want native title applications to be successful, and successful in both the short and long term. That being the case, the ideal should be to contribute to identifying and elucidating choices. I would have liked to have had more opportunity to contribute in that respect to the Miriuwung Gajerrong people.

17

Working as a Historian on the Miriuwung Gajerrong Native Title Claim

Christine Choo

THE DISCIPLINE OF HISTORY can offer significant insights and evidence in relation to the determination of native title. The particular contribution of history emerges from the requirement under the Native Title Act for the applicants of native title to show continued use and occupation of the claim area by the applicants and their ancestors. There are many different ways in which the expertise of historians can be applied in the native title process. In addition to identifying possible sources of historical evidence, historians can provide contextualisation and analysis of the relevant primary and secondary historical material, an account of contact history for the region in which the claim is located as well as advice and comment on the historical materials and reports lodged by other parties involved in the claim. Historical research can also uncover information and evidence that may be relevant for analysis by one of the other experts engaged in the process, such as anthropologists, linguists and lawyers.

What native title claims have highlighted for non-Indigenous Australians is the complexity and richness of the many Indigenous traditions across the country—there is not one but many Aboriginal cultures—and the depth of Aboriginal connections with the land: 'When people speak of owning country, they speak to this understanding—that country is known and cared for by the people whose rights and responsibilities are inalienably bound to it . . . An important part of ownership is learning and teaching'.[1]

The existence of native title claims means that Australians can no longer ignore the presence of Aborigines and the impact of colonisation on their lives. The excuse that Aboriginal people are invisible in the archival records, making their history too difficult to tell, is no longer tenable. Careful archival research undertaken for native title claims can show the continued presence of Aboriginal people in the claim areas. This information, used in conjunction with anthropological, linguistic, archaeological and other evidence, can corroborate the claims of the native title applicants to their country.

Historical research often shows clearly that Aboriginal people were present in archival records in spite of consistent attempts in the past to render them invisible. Where their presence is not identifiable, historians have a responsibility to attempt to contextualise and explain the silences in the records. Professional historians have contributed to 'breaking open' the archival sources to enable the emergence of new understandings and new meanings in the texts. This is one of history's strengths. Ann Curthoys captures some of the challenge of the historian's work when she reminds us that new questions lead to finding new records or the reading of old records in a new way.[2]

Historical research in the native title context raises complicated questions about the nature of historical evidence. The paucity of existing research on contact history (and Aboriginal–European relations) in Australia, and particularly in Western Australia, leaves serious gaps in the story of regional settlement and its impacts. There may be many versions or views of this contact history embedded in the documentary sources where they exist. Consequently, the historical research process often involves intensive search, analysis and interpretation of documentary sources and primary archival material that may never before have been interrogated for the purpose of writing a history of contact in a specific region.

The evidence assembled by historians and the opinions they formulate are part of an intensely political process in which a number of different perspectives are pitted against each other. Where the process reaches litigation, these opinions and perspectives end up being presented in court. Often the same historical material may be subjected to analysis by historians working to very different briefs. Hence the brief to the historian outlining what is required by the legal team is of utmost importance. Not only should the brief provide clear guidelines or questions to be addressed by the expert, it should also enable an expert to define the boundaries of her or his professional expertise more clearly. While it is vital for experts of different professional backgrounds to co-operate with each other, it is even more important for them to be aware of the limit of their professional expertise and not overstep their disciplinary boundaries, particularly in the context of litigation. The danger that their credibility will be eroded in the process of litigation is ever present.

The brief to the expert determines the questions to which the expert is required to respond, and it is in the discussion of the brief that an important dialogue between lawyer and historian can and does occur. However, in the context of the native title process we have a long way to go towards improving the dialogue between lawyers and historians, between historians and anthropologists, between the legal processes and historiography. The dialogue between and among these groups must continue and improve in order to clarify mutual understandings of our particular professional expertise and professional boundaries. Some lawyers, like many other people, think that 'anyone can do history'. Lawyers therefore need to be educated about the uses of history, the value of historical evidence and the particular professional expertise that historians can offer. Historians have a responsibility to prepare themselves for increasing public scrutiny of their profession and its methodologies. They must also develop the confidence to deal with these issues in forums such as the court and in highly litigious circumstances that demand a different approach to the poetics and construction of the historical narrative from those required of academic historians.

Another significant aspect is the problem of reconciling the historical research itself and the language of the historical reports with the imperatives of the judicial discourse, particularly with its notion that an objective truth can be discovered and its demand for 'facts'. The rhetoric of objectivity that is at the heart of judicial treatment of historical evidence often obscures the senses in which both the analytical process and the facts it interrogates reflect the power relations associated with race, gender, ethnicity, class, and so forth. The historian and historical narrative inserted in this process have both didactic and performative functions. Thus it is important for the historian to take the needs of the particular audience, in this case the judiciary and the court, and their context, into account in the production of relevant reports and in giving evidence.[3] As an 'expert witness' the historian is bound to provide all relevant information, including the parameters of the report, previous experience and opinion, to the court in accordance with the guidelines outlined by the Federal Court of Australia and the Law Society of Australia, so that they are recognised and taken into account to the extent necessary by the court.[4] Such a duty should dispel any suggestion that the evidence given by expert witnesses is biased and therefore unacceptable. However, one of the most frequently used methods of interrogation in court is to attack the credibility of the expert witness both directly and indirectly. As this is to be expected, the expert must be prepared not only to clarify opinions and conclusions under cross-examination in court, but also for that opinion to be challenged.

Representations of the past

One of the most significant aspects of historical evidence is the question of cultural difference and different knowledges. Representations of the past are culturally specific. Western historiography is embedded in the tradition of written discourse and the idea of linearity, while the conceptions of time, place and story that emerge from various Aboriginal epistemologies are vastly different and sometimes incomprehensible to those from the Western tradition. Furthermore, the tendency of Western judicial discourse to value written traces of the past over other traces, for example individual memory, story, dance and visual art, often suppresses and obscures minority voices, rendering them invisible and inaudible. Linear and progressive history moves to incorporate the Other, a process Prasenjet Duara has aptly described as a means that involves 'totalization and closure in order to destroy or domesticate the Other'.[5] James Scott writes of 'the imperialism of a high-modernist, planned social order' that excludes 'the necessary role of local knowledge and know-how'.[6] However, if historians are to account for the silences in archival material, particularly important for native title cases, and to illuminate issues of social and cultural oppression, then they must challenge the orthodox notions of evidence and methodology.

Historical narrative and the historian's credibility are critical. The question of 'reading against the grain' and the interpretation of silences in the texts and in the available information on the lives of Aboriginal people are of vital importance in historical analysis in the context of native title. The work of Inga Clendinnen is instructive. In her 1999 Boyer Lecture and her *Reading the Holocaust,* Clendinnen encourages the careful examination of the texts and the world views of the participants in the stories that are provided. She suggests that what the historian has to offer is a 'middle voice' in action 'whereby the reader is brought into a constructed, controlled, directed engagement with the texts, and is invited to join the writer's search for their meanings'.[7]

Historians can and do discover new material that throws fresh light on perceptions of the history of Australia. The gaps in understandings of the history of non-Aboriginal occupation of this country are gradually being filled through the historical research and analysis undertaken in relation to native title claims. In the process, Aboriginal people have the opportunity to tell their side of the story of the occupation of their lands by non-Indigenous people, and the histories of non-metropolitan regions are told. Another outcome is that Aboriginal Australians are gaining access to documentary material and archival sources including photographs, oral history recordings, administrative files, diaries and other records relating to their communities, families and their lands. Until recently most of these sources have been inaccessible to Aboriginal people and their communities because of geographical, social, financial and cultural barriers.

Finally, a revision of Australia's history raise questions about the place of the discipline of history in the education of future generations of Australians. What histories and what story of Australia do we tell? Not only is Australian history rich in texture but it is also many-hued, with stories of Indigenous and non-Indigenous citizens from a range of cultural backgrounds still waiting to be told and to be heard. These are the stories for which each one of us must make room. While parts of them may be extremely difficult for us to accept, reflecting as they do the darker side of our history as a nation, they must nevertheless be told in order to enable us to honestly recognise this dark underside and to move on towards healing the nation. Yet the problem of creating social practices and institutions through which diversity can flourish remains.[8] Herein lies the challenge of the movement towards reconciliation between Indigenous and non-Indigenous Australians of all cultural and ethnic backgrounds.

Lessons from the Miriuwung Gajerrong claim

Preparation for the *Miriuwung Gajerrong* case, the first to reach litigation in Western Australia, was a challenge. One comforting feature was the fact that all parties concerned were exploring this novel process together. It was a professional and personal challenge to be working at the 'cutting edge'. If I had known what I now do about the litigation process, I may never have entered the fray. What did I learn from the experience?

I learned about the primacy of the legal process in the preparation for native title claims. The process is circumscribed by relevant legislation; it is determined within the legal context and is driven by the professional expertise of the legal team who have a commitment to their clients. Professionals from backgrounds in history, anthropology and linguistics contribute to the process from their particular perspectives and areas of expertise by addressing briefs from the legal team and bringing forward evidence to support their responses to these briefs. It is the lawyers who ultimately have the primary responsibility to argue the case for the native title applicants or respondents. It would be advisable, however, for the experts to work as closely as possible with the lawyers in order to ensure that all aspects of their contribution and argument are understood by the legal team. This will also ensure that the lawyers can gain optimal advantage from the evidence of the experts. Unfortunately the legal profession still appears to have limited knowledge and understanding of the work of historians and thus historians themselves and the profession of history can appear to be on trial.

I became acutely aware of the utmost necessity for clear and ongoing communication between the lawyers and expert witnesses, starting with the brief and then throughout the process. It would also be useful to engage in ongoing conversations with other experts working on the case in order to share relevant information that would benefit from analysis by another discipline. Historians can contribute in a variety of ways. They can be engaged as consultants to provide the legal team with an overview of the historiography and methods of history, or they may be engaged to provide a peer review of the historian's report that is to be tabled as evidence. A historian with expertise in a particular local area or topic may be engaged to give an opinion on that relatively narrow specialisation while another may develop expertise in the history of the claim area in the process of undertaking original research for the purpose of the native title claim. Regional and local history, tenure history, the history of industries such as mining and pastoralism and of missions each have a place in providing valuable evidence in the native title process. Whatever the particular specialty or expertise of the historian, this must be communicated to the legal team and ultimately the court with clarity and in a manner that enables the court to understand the underlying assumptions and methodology of the historian. It is the historiography that will provide the key to the historian's perspectives and conclusions and to the level of their acceptance by the court.

The particular professional expertise and analysis of historians can provide valuable insights into the historical and ongoing connection of applicants to the claim area. Thorough analysis of archival and documentary sources is vital for a sound comprehension of contact history. Such analysis can draw out evidence on the presence of individuals, families and groups in the claim area. It can show that groups of Indigenous people not only occupied the land, but that they hunted and gathered bushfood; that they engaged in ceremonial and other activities on the land; that they used implements; engaged in the maintenance of marriage and other social relationships and activities; and raised children on the land. Historical evidence can also show how Indigenous groups and individuals responded to the occupation of their lands by foreign invaders by resisting, accommodating or maintaining their own space in relation to the presence of the foreigners. It is important for the historian to make available contextual and interpretive information to enable the court to understand the full relevance of the historical evidence.

It is advisable for the historian undertaking primary research and presenting the report in court to visit the claim area or country, particularly if they have not previously done so. Such a visit will enable the historian to gain a better understanding of the geography and a sense of place, which are vital to the history of the place and its people. Very often the necessity of these visits is not appreciated by the legal team, who would prefer to keep the historian in the archives. Another significant step in the process of finalising the history report is to discuss the elements of the report with the appropriate people, including the applicants, in order to identify significant gaps in the historian's understanding of the documentary history. This does not constitute an oral history, nor should it be construed as such.

Finally, all expert witnesses have a responsibility to the court. However, the litigation process can be extremely stressful: the credibility of the witnesses is challenged; the veracity of the witnesses' claims is tested; the analyses and methodologies of the witnesses may be interrogated. As witnesses may be intimidated by the court proceedings, they should be carefully prepared by the lawyers for the processes of litigation. This preparation should include information on court protocols, for example the need to address the judge at all times, and the importance of speaking with clarity and honesty. Even with this preparation, which of course ought never to amount to 'schooling', the court appearance will be full of surprises.

Conclusions

What I was most unprepared for in the experience of being an expert witness on the Miriuwung Gajerrong claim was the way in which the profession of history, its methods and very existence, came under enormous scrutiny. The values and assumptions of the profession as well as that of the witness were challenged. I felt I had to develop the hide of a hippopotamus to survive the court process. This leaves me with enormous admiration for native title applicants who, with great patience and determination, endure the indignity of having to prove their entitlement to land that has been theirs all along.

Afterword

The native title epoch has fostered a time when disciplines central to native title claims have been drawn to work more closely together. Historians, linguists and especially lawyers and anthropologists are now engaged on collaborative work to an extent that has not occurred before. From such circumstances, the potential strengths and limitations of each discipline, as well as the possibility of contesting, crossing and complementing disciplinary contexts, has become increasingly evident. Native title has introduced a need to be aware that just as there are cultural and political processes embedded in the Australian legal system, so too are certain processes apparent in the relevant disciplines. At the heart of each contribution is how conceptual, methodological, ethical and practice issues in native title might be better communicated and acted upon, not only intra-discipline but also across disciplinary boundaries.

While most of the contributors to this volume have highlighted ways in which the disciplines might work more effectively together, some have made the point that better attention should be paid to native title legislative requirements, and others have shown the different emphases and approaches that practitioners within the same discipline might adopt. Suggestions range from ensuring that epistemological concerns and research data are regularly shared among practitioners and claimant groups, to making more effort to find out what each discipline actually does, to collaborating on the writing of reports. 'Silences' in the written record should be fully investigated, linguistic change over time addressed in claims and prompted in the courts, and Indigenous customary laws accorded the same intellectual and administrative status as other legal systems. From the evidence presented here, the legal 'boundaries' of the Australian court clearly need to be modified or pushed to embrace the value of cultural and historical matters, as these reflect Indigenous knowledges and practices in the field of what has come to be known as native title law. Alongside aspirations that the forum in which claims are heard might become less adversarial is the cogent hope that the burden of proof on showing whether or not native title has been extinguished will be more equitably and knowingly shared.

However, just as conversations and actions on redefining work practices and cross-disciplinary engagement re-emerge, shifts in the legal framework of native title law have taken place. The first of these occurred on 8 August 2002 when the High Court handed down its judgment on the appeal against the Miriuwung Gajerrong claim.[1] By a 4:3 majority judgment, the High Court reversed some of Lee J's 1998 findings in favour of the Miriuwung Gajerrong (and also the determinations of the Full Federal Court in 2000) and directed certain matters back to the Federal Court for further consideration. There is little doubt that this latest decision will disaffect native title claimants and maintain the cultural privilege and authority of Australian courts of law. In the process, it will also create new sets of practice questions for anthropologists, linguists, historians and lawyers with respect to the recording, analysis and representation of cultural data on behalf of or in conjunction with Indigenous claimants.

A focus on the *Miriuwung Gajerrong* appeal encapsulates and explains the current situation, especially as it poses two distinguishable sets of questions that will affect future native title claims and associated work practices. The first concerns the nature of native title—what it is, how it is sustained, what is required to prove its existence, and what the relationship is between native title in customary law and native title as now legislated. The second concerns how and when Indigenous customary rights and interests in land might be extinguished or suspended.

Specifically in relation to the *Miriuwung Gajerrong* appeal and with an obvious flow on to other claims, the High Court has now determined that past actions have affected native title in the following ways with respect to extinguishment and pastoral and mining leases.[2] Pastoral leases in Western Australia and the Northern Territory, extinguish native title to the extent of their inconsistency with traditional usage. The right to hunt and gather traditional foods is held to be consistent with the rights conferred by pastoral leases, whereas the right to burn the land is inconsistent, for example. The native title right to control access to land is similarly held to be inconsistent with the rights conferred by pastoral leases. Mining leases partially extinguish native title, including the right to control access to the land. Of significance too is that the High Court determined that native title rights to fish in tidal waters have been partially extinguished. Determinations such as these will have far-reaching consequences for Miriuwung and Gajerrong communities, as well as for other Indigenous communities and economies in a range of settings across Australia.

The overall implications of the High Court's decision for the Miriuwung and Gajerrong groups are severe. The decision will influence broader patterns and applications of native title law, as well as the aspirations of current and future claimants throughout Australia. It will also raise a number of practice issues for anthropologists, lawyers and others, including how to respond to the new procedures and how best to advise applicant groups.

It is now clear that native title virtually anywhere within the Miriuwung Gajerrong claim area will not have the force given to it by Lee J in his 1998 decision. Reductions in the scope of native title include rights to control access to land, rights to minerals and petroleum, and rights in cultural knowledge about the land. Allowing that these are reductions of the rights previously enjoyed, the High Court's judgment implies that native title has been partially extinguished across the entire Miriuwung Gajerrong Stage One claim. The judgment sets what might be described as the theoretical limit or potential precedent of native title recognition. That limit is the starting not the end point for native title recognition. The further judgments made by the High Court with respect to full and partial extinguishment reduce the native title actually granted or capable of being granted to the Miriuwung and Gajerrong to a fraction of the theoretical upper limit of recognition, itself a long way from full beneficial ownership.

On 12 December 2002 another defining judgment occurred, this time regarding the Yorta Yorta claim in Victoria. In appealing Olney J's 1998 judgment that the 'tide of history had washed away any real acknowledgment by the Yorta Yorta of their traditional laws and customs',[3] five out of seven High Court judges upheld Olney's original determination. It was found that while the Yorta Yorta 'had once observed traditional laws and customs [they had] ceased to do so'. In accordance with native title legislative requirements, it was claimed that the 'forebears of the claimants had ceased to occupy their lands in accordance with traditional laws and customs, and there was no evidence that they continued to acknowledge and observe those laws and customs'.[4]

The *Yorta Yorta* appeal contested Olney's privileging of certain archival material over Indigenous testimony combined with the evidence prepared by an historian, anthropologist and linguist,[5] and notions of what constitutes tradition. In relation to the requirement that 'laws and customs be traditional', and in contrast to five of the judges, Kirby and Gaudron JJ noted their concern that 'In the face of the acknowledged history of dispossession, it must be accepted that laws and customs may properly be described as "traditional" . . . notwithstanding that they do not correspond exactly with the laws and customs acknowledged and observed prior to European settlement'.[6] As the other five judges disagreed, the High Court upheld Olney's earlier judgment that native title had been extinguished.

For Indigenous claimants everywhere, the 2002 High Court decisions will make native title harder to document, easier to extinguish. The principles of what had been promised ten years earlier in the *Mabo* decision and in the 1993 Native Title Act will not now materialise. So much of the huge effort during past decades and especially since 1992 will seem to have been wasted or misdirected, in particular for Indigenous communities who have been continually disappointed and often simply worn down by the struggle required to have their rights in land restored. At the very least and within the confines of a post-colonial discourse, the *Mabo* decision and native title have (or certainly had) the potential symbolically and actually to engender recognition of Indigenous land tenure laws by the Australian legal system and, perhaps less directly, by members of the broader society.

When the dust settles on the most recent decisions in native title history, Miriuwung and Gajerrong and Yorta Yorta families and communities, and other claimant groups, are likely to look to new ways of safeguarding and advancing their interests. Arguments put by applicant groups before the National Native Title Tribunal and the Federal and High courts clearly convey Indigenous beliefs and practices, exemplified in most cases by supporting expert witness accounts. Yet the Miriuwung and Gajerrong, Yorta Yorta and others bruised in the process also know what has been obscured: that their customary law rights and interests in the cultural landscape will continue to exist and have meaning however inadequately they are reflected in and acknowledged by the Australian legal system. The testimony of Yorta Yorta claimant Rochelle Patten captures this ethos:

> My name is Rochelle Patten and I am a Yorta Yorta woman from Ulupna through my grandmother. My totem and that of the Yorta Yorta people is the long necked turtle. My personal totem is the crow. The crow guides me. I was born at Mooroopna Base Hospital which is on the Goulburn River in Yorta Yorta territory. I have seen a copy of the map which shows the Yorta Yorta land claimed in this native title claim and I say that this is the traditional Yorta Yorta land. I know this because my mother told me. Her father told her and his father told him. My relationship with the land goes back to my grandfather and further. The land is part of me. My responsibility to the land is to look after the land like a mother in the way the elders looked after it. This is the responsibility of all Yorta Yorta people.[7]

Anthropologists, linguists, historians and lawyers will also continue to engage with and practise in the native title process. While there is an emerging disquiet among some professionals concerned about their effectiveness in the field of native title,[8] most remain encouraged by the Gramscian notion that in order to bring about change, there will always be a need to maintain a pessimism of intellect and an optimism of will.[9]

Sandy Toussaint and Will Christensen

Notes

Contextualising Native Title, and this Volume

[1] *Mabo v Queensland (No 2)* (1992) 175 CLR 1.
[2] *Milirrpum v Nabalco Pty Ltd* (1970) 17 FLR 141.
[3] *Wik Peoples v Queensland* (1996) 187 CLR 1.
[4] *Ward v Western Australia* (1998) 159 ALR 483.
[5] *Yorta Yorta Aboriginal Community v Victoria* (1998) FCA 1606: (1999) 4 (1) AILR 91. The Yorta Yorta won an application to appeal the decision but this was unsuccessful: (2002) HCA 58. See French, chapter 8 this volume, for discussion.
[6] *Hayes v Northern Territory* (1999) 97 FCR 32: (1999) FCA 1248.
[7] *Clarrie Smith v Western Australia* (2000) FCA 526.
[8] The 1998 *Ward* judgment was appealed in 2002. See French, chapter 8 this volume, for discussion.

1 Raising the Dead

I thank the people in Kowanyama, most particularly Alma Wason, Colin Lawrence and the rest of the Kunjen mob, who for many years now have invited me to stay in their community, shown endless patience in teaching me about their lives, and have been unfailingly kind and hospitable. I am grateful for the help of the Land Office folk—Vol Norris, Gary Drewien and John Clark—who provided support for cultural mapping trips and a friendly administrative base. I would also like to thank Barry Alpher for his enthusiastic language teaching and tolerance of my linguistic ineptitude; Naomi Smith and Gary Clarke for providing research assistance, camp cooking and enforced Sunday afternoons at the beach; and Viv Sinnamon, whose knowledge and generosity has always been an invaluable support to my work in Kowanyama. I also appreciated the comments of colleagues at the original Crossing Boundaries conference, particularly the subsequent helpful discussions with Marcia Langton and Peter Whalley.

[1] Colin Lawrence, in V. Sinnamon and the Kunjen Elders, Kowanyama, *Towards Aboriginal Management*, p. 34.
[2] Though the word 'traditional' is problematic in anthropological terms, it is commonly used in Kowanyama to denote customary practices. Similarly, the term 'traditional owners' has been adopted to define those people regarded as having title to land under Aboriginal law.
[3] These indicators have been described in detail in a number of recent inquiries, including the 1987–90 Royal Commission into Aboriginal Deaths in Custody (Royal Commission into Aboriginal Deaths in Custody, *Final Report*); the 1988 report on the problems and needs of Aborigines living on the New South Wales-Queensland border (Human Rights and Equal

Opportunity Commission, *Toomelah Report*); the 1996 National Inquiry into the Separation of Aboriginal and Torres Strait Islander Children from their Families (*Bringing Them Home*).

4 S. Bennett, *White Politics and Black Australians*, p. 6.

5 R. Brunt, 'The Politics of Identity', p. 151, emphasis in the original.

6 B. Attwood and J. Arnold (eds), *Power, Knowledge and Aborigines*, pp. i, xi.

7 Ibid., p. iv.

8 S. Muecke, 'Available Discourses on Aborigines', pp. 98–111.

9 Bennett, *White Politics and Black Australians*, p. 10.

10 B. Elder, *Blood on the Wattle*, p. 2.

11 See P. Berger, *Facing Up To Modernity*; P. Berger, B. Berger and H. Kellner, *The Homeless Mind*.

12 A. Lattas, *Primitivism, Nationalism and Individualism in Australian Popular Culture*, p. 45.

13 Ibid., p. 56.

14 J. Kapferer, *Being All Equal*, p. 87.

15 See Attwood and Arnold (eds), *Power, Knowledge and Aborigines*; E. Povinelli, 'Settler Modernity and the Quest for an Indigenous Tradition'.

16 S. Sheridan, 'Wives and Mothers Like Ourselves, Poor Remnants of a Dying Race'.

17 D. Martin, The Design of Indigenous Institutions in the 'Recognition Space' of Native Title.

18 M. Langton, The Sacred and Legitimacy, p. 9; E. Povinelli, 'Settler Modernity and the Quest for an Indigenous Tradition', p. 21.

19 D. Ritchie, 'Constructions of Aboriginal Tradition for Public Purpose', p. 255, citing J. Stewart, p. 177.

20 E. Povinelli, 'Settler Modernity and the Quest for an Indigenous Tradition', p. 23.

21 Ibid., p. 28.

22 Sinnamon and the Kunjen Elders, Kowanyama, *Towards Aboriginal Management*.

23 Ibid., p. 32.

24 Ibid., p. 40.

25 Ibid., pp. 30, 39, 41.

26 'Poison places' is a term commonly used to denote sacred sites in North Queensland, referring to the power of the ancestral forces to be either benevolent or malevolent.

27 'Black-armband history' is a phrase employed—usually by right-wing politicians—to suggest that Aboriginal narratives of the colonial past are unnecessarily focused on the negative aspects, and should be rejected or 'left behind', rather than used to induce guilt in the contemporary population.

28 P. Antze and M. Lambek (eds), *Tense Past*, p. vii.

29 A. Feldman, *Formations of Violence*, p. 13.

30 V. Turner, *From Ritual to Theatre*, p. 14; see also R. Schechner, 'Magnitudes of Performance', and B. Myerhoff, *Number Our Days*.

31 Feldman, *Formations of Violence*, Antze and Lambek (eds), *Tense Past*, and Bondi, 'Locating Identity Politics', p. 85.

32 Marcia Langton raised the question of whether it is appropriate for non-Aboriginal people to comment upon the construction of Aboriginal identity. This is a complex ethical question that deserves more space than is available here. I have since attempted to address it elsewhere (see Strang, 'An Appropriate Question?').

2 Anthropology in Native Title Court Cases

Michael Robinson and Robert Blowes kindly provided useful comments on the draft of this chapter.

1 *Yarmirr v Northern Territory* (1998) 156 ALR 370, paragraph 64.

2 A decision as to the admissibility of Robinson's evidence was deferred, to be decided after further argument was heard; meanwhile the anthropologist's evidence was taken *voir dire*. In a later decision (*Daniel v Western Australia* (2000) FCA 1334), Nicholson J subsequently excluded some aspects of the anthropologist's evidence, in application of section 135 of the Evidence Act; the judge thereby exercised discretion to refuse to admit evidence when he considers its probative value is outweighed by its potentially being unfairly prejudicial to a

party. In this case, it appears the judge was persuaded to exclude anthropological evidence on an issue of central importance to the case, so as to ultimately decide certain issues solely by reference to evidence from the Aboriginal claimants.

[3] K. Maddock, 'Bearing Witness', p. 25; K. Maddock, 'Anthropologists in Native Title Claims', p. 90.

[4] R. Brunton, 'Hindmarsh Island and the Hoaxing of Australian Anthropology'; R. Brunton, 'Covering up a Multitude of Social, Ethical Sins'.

[5] N. Peterson, 'Foreword', p. viii; M. Edmunds, 'The Importance of Absolute Accuracy', pp. 13–17; D. Trigger, 'Towards a Cultural Resolution', p. 27.

[6] G. Morgan, 'Advocacy as a Form of Social Science'.

[7] However, there can obviously be a close working relationship between an anthropologist and those with whom lengthy cultural mapping of land is carried out. When it comes to a court trial Aboriginal people may be surprised, baffled or insulted when the anthropologist seemingly suspends the relationship and takes the role of an independent, non-aligned expert. It has probably been less necessary to do this in land claim hearings than it has in the formal setting of Federal Court native title cases. Though in one Northern Territory land claim, my own familiarity with claimants and role in facilitating evidence from them (with permission from my barrister colleague) drew criticism from the Northern Territory land commissioner. His complaint was similar to what we will experience in the courts, namely that it was 'contrary to usual practice for a person who himself is an important witness [in this case I was an anthropologist engaged by the Northern Land Council] . . . to also perform the role of advocate' (H. Olney, *Garawa/Mugularrangu (Robinson River) Land Claim*, p. 9.) Yet I would argue that the judge mistook communicative intimacy for 'advocacy', and this raises the question of how partisanship or bias might be measured or recognised when a researcher cannot ignore the fact of a close relationship with claimants.

[8] G. Neate, 'Proof of Native Title', p. 307.

[9] See also *Northern Territory v Maurice* (1986) 161 CLR 475, at 483.

[10] I leave aside here the further issue that arises in anthropology about whether the most knowledgeable or senior informants among research subjects are appropriately regarded as experts on the subject of their own culture. There has been for some years now an energetic debate in anthropology about the politics of representation and interpretation in areas such as Australian Aboriginal Studies and the label 'expert' is unlikely to be one embraced among researchers other than when required in legal settings. The issue presumably is the appropriateness of recognising claimants' 'expert' standing in relation to valued knowledge and skills arising from Aboriginal traditions, while acknowledging that this differs from the sort of 'expert' standing derived from a formal process of training and education in a social science discipline such as anthropology. The distinction between knowledgeable 'insiders' in any society and analytical models developed by 'outsider' researchers is commonplace in anthropology. In the context of native title claims, the matter of 'insider experts' having a vital personal interest in the proceedings is also clearly relevant. See also G. Neate, 'Proof of Native Title', pp. 282–3.

[11] *Milirrpum v Nabalco Pty Ltd* (1970) 17 FLR 141; see also Paul, chapter 13 in this volume.

[12] G. Neate, *Aboriginal Land Rights Law in the N.T.*, p. 240ff.

[13] *Milirrpum v Nabalco Pty Ltd* (1970) 17 FLR 141.

[14] G. Neate, *Aboriginal Land Rights Law in the N.T*, p. 241.

[15] Cited in G. Neate, *Aboriginal Land Rights Law in the N.T*, p. 242.

[16] Transcript, Daniel & Others v State of Western Australia, WAG6017/1996 22.06.00, p.5081.

[17] Transcript, Daniel & Others v State of Western Australia, WAG6017/1996 22.06.00, p.5021.

[18] G. Neate, *Aboriginal Land Rights Law in the N.T.*, p. 243.

[19] *Yarmirr v Northern Territory* (1998) 156 ALR 370, paragraph 63, iii.

[20] *Ward v Western Australia* (1998) 159 ALR 483.

[21] Ibid., at 531. The parallel notion in anthropology, to the legal view suggesting such genealogical data may represent 'hearsay', is possibly that the data represent a 'social construction' of biological relationships, not necessarily 'the truth'. Bruce Rigsby ('Genealogies, Kinship & Local Group Organisation', pp. 108, 117–18) has discussed the distinction between

genealogies constructed by anthropologists and recorded statements made among research subjects about their relationships with kin. Among other differences, he points out that the analytical documents prepared by anthropologists will consider significant facts such as competing accounts of upper-generation links and divergences between archival records and current memories among research subjects. Living claimants may well discount these versions of their genealogies that do not agree with contemporary oral traditions.

22 *Daniel v Western Australia* (2000) FCA 858, paragraph 30.

23 For a full discussion, see R. Blowes and D. Trigger, 'Experts, Documents and Lawyers in Native Title Claims'.

24 R. Keesing, *Cultural Anthropology*, p. 7.

3 A Short Ride on a Time Machine

1 See P. McConvell, 'Born is Nothing'; for ethnonyms P. McConvell, 'A Linguistic Stratigraphy and Native Title: The Case of Ethnonyms'; for place-names see P. McConvell, 'Changing Places'.

2 For instance, Lumholtz's vocabulary of the group he lived with on the Herbert River in North Queensland consisting of 140 words and a few phrases is more than enough to identify the language as Wargamay (C. Lumholtz, *Among Cannibals*; R. Dixon, 'Wargamay') even though Lumholtz never names either the group or their language, and his spelling is not altogether decipherable. Earlier wordlists of three to ten items taken at Rockingham Bay in the 1840s, however, pose more difficulties since a number of the words are shared between more than one language so that distinctive items are insufficient in the very small samples to indicate unambiguously which languages they are from.

3 The terms 'applicants' and 'claimants' are used interchangably. Both terms refer to persons or groups who are native title claimants and/or named applicants in a native title claim.

4 P. Sutton, *Aboriginal Country Groups and the Community of Native Title Holders*, p. 14.

5 Ibid., p. 14.

6 Since multilingualism was the standard pattern in most parts of Aboriginal Australia before contact, X people would often have spoken a variety of languages other than X. Some X people might have spent so much time in the company of non-X people (in-laws, for instance) that they did not in fact speak X much or perhaps even did not know the language very much.

7 A. Rumsey, 'Language and Territoriality in Aboriginal Australia'.

8 N. Williams, *The Yolngu and Their Land*.

9 E. Hutchins, *Culture and Inference*; L. Goldman, *Talk Never Dies*.

10 It is possible that these two words are cognate—that is that they both go back to a single ancestor language. Both Gurindji and the Yolngu languages are members of the massive Pama-Nyungan language family, which occupies seven-eighths of the continent. If they are cognate this might indicate that the concept of 'law' in the Aboriginal sense and words for it go back several thousand years at least, to that distant common ancestor. The Yolngu word *rumaru* and the word in Western Pama-Nyungan languages *yumari*, both meaning 'avoidance relation', might also be cognate and built from the *rom/yumi* root, meaning something like 'no law; prohibited'. Gurindji *yumi* is probably also more immediately cognate with Warlpiri *yimi* meaning 'talk, speech', but this does not negate the possibility of wider connections in the sense of 'law'. The semantic connection is similar to that of English expressions such as 'You should have a say in that'.

11 P. McConvell and M. Laughren, 'Down Under in Central Australia'.

12 See McConvell, 'Born is Nothing', for more details.

13 Only one team of anthropologists did extensive work in the region, the Berndts, in 1946–47, and their field notes are not publicly available, for many years to come, to check such matters.

14 Sutton, *Aboriginal Country Groups and the Community of Native Title Holders*, pp. 8–9.

15 McConvell, 'A Linguistic Stratigraphy and Native Title: The Case of Ethnonyms'.

[16] B. Sansom, 'Aborigines, Anthropologists and Leviathan'.
[17] Cf. D. McKnight, *People, Land and the Rainbow Serpent.*
[18] K. Hale, 'Linguistic Evidence for Long-term Residence of the Wik-speaking Peoples in their Present Location in Cape York Peninsula'.
[19] M. Harvey, 'Place Names and Land-Language Associations in the Western Top End'.
[20] Ibid., p. 173.
[21] The form *warrij* for 'crocodile' is found in Ngarinyman, Gurindji's northern neighbour, and in the Non-Pama-Nyungan neighbouring languages Jaminjung and Ngaliwurru further north from where the form was undoubtedly borrowed into the Pama-Nyungan Ngumpin languages. Riverine vocabulary was borrowed wholesale from NPN languages into Ngumpin languages in the Victoria River District because Ngumpin languages originated in the semi-desert to the south, where few of these flora and fauna existed (certainly not crocodiles), and moved into the Victoria River District in the last few thousand years; see McConvell, 'Long-lost Relations'.
[22] W. H. Willshire, *The Land of the Dawning.*
[23] P. McConvell, ONLY and Related Concepts in Gurindji.
[24] P. McConvell, 'A Linguistic Stratigraphy and Native Title: The Case of Ethnonyms'.
[25] There is a type of non-finite clause marker –rla-rni in Warlpiri (-LOC-rni). Perhaps this is an ancient construction in the Ngumpin-Yapa subgroup that has been lost except in place-names. Another interesting fact is that Ngaliwurru place-names just north of Ngarinyman have a suffix –ni-wung that is entirely parallel to the Gurindji/Ngarinyman suffix : -LOC-STILL/ONLY.
[26] Kriol is the name of a creole which has developed among Australian Indigenous communities. Creoles are a 'class of languages which are born out of the contact of two different societies and languages, often in the context of colonisation', Kimberley Language Resource Centre, *Moola Bulla: In the Shadow of the Mountain*, p. xii.

4 Method, Mechanism and Mindset

I thank Jeff Stead, Ben Scambary and Samantha Wells for their comments and encouragement on the draft of this chapter.
[1] Quoted in W. R. Wilson, Sillitoe's Tartan in Northern Australia.
[2] Proofing is a legal term used to describe how lawyers confer with clients on the evidence that will be presented in court.
[3] D. Eades, 'A Case of Communicative Clash', pp. 238, 224.
[4] T. G. Strehlow, 'Notes on Native Evidence and its Value', p. 334; A. Elkin, 'Aboriginal Evidence and Justice in North Australia', p. 176; K. Liberman, 'Understanding Aborigines in Australian Courts of Law', p. 248.
[5] *R v Anunga* (1976) 11 ALR 412.
[6] Royal Commission into Aboriginal Deaths in Custody, *Final Report.*
[7] *Ward v Western Australia* (1998) 159 ALR 483.
[8] See A. Thomson, 'Fifty Years On'; B. Attwood, *A History of Relations Between Europeans and Aborigines.*
[9] A. Roberts, 'The Development of Australian Oral History, 1798–1984', p. 15.
[10] B. Shaw, 'Aboriginal Australian Life Histories as Personal Documents and Historical Artefacts', p. 82.
[11] Quoted in E. Furniss, 'Indians, Odysseys and Vast, Empty Lands'.
[12] P. Watson, 'This Precious Foliage'.
[13] M. Paul, The Role of History in Native Title Litigation.
[14] *Ward v Western Australia* (1998) 159 ALR 483.

5 Beyond Traditional Law

[1] B. Rigsby, 'Anthropologists, Land Claims and Objectivity'.
[2] K. Palmer, G. Macdonald and G. McIntyre, 'Engagement for Services by Contract', p. 19.

3 Australian Anthropological Society, 'Code of Ethics', p. 23, emphasis added.
4 R. Tonkinson, 'Anthropology and Aboriginal Tradition', pp. 20, 7.
5 Palmer, Macdonald and McIntyre, 'Engagement for Services by Contract', p. 19.
6 B. Fegan, 'Report from the AAS Ethics Sub-Committee', p. 25.
7 Palmer, Macdonald and McIntyre, 'Engagement for Services by Contract', p. 17.
8 Secret sacred material, for example, does not appear in modern published academic ethnography, unless clearly defined permission has been given by the Indigenous people concerned, and/or unless strict limits have been placed on the ethnography's readership and distribution. There are enforceable academic codes of ethics governing these restrictions (for example, Australian Institute of Aboriginal and Torres Strait Islander Studies, *Guidelines for Ethical Research in Indigenous Studies*).
9 D. Trigger, M. Robinson and L. Gladstone, 'Anthropology and Consultancy Contracts in the 1990s', pp. 7–8.
10 R. Blowes and D. Trigger, 'Experts, Documents and Lawyers in Native Title Claims', pp. 6–8.
11 Blowes and Trigger, 'Experts, Documents and Lawyers in Native Title Claims'.
12 Personal communication with Peter Sutton.
13 Blowes and Trigger, 'Experts, Documents and Lawyers in Native Title Claims', p. 6.
14 See Barker, chapter 15 in this volume.
15 Trigger, Robinson and Gladstone, 'Anthropology and Consultancy Contracts in the 1990s', p. 10.
16 Rigsby, 'Anthropologists, Land Claims and Objectivity', p. 35.
17 Tonkinson, 'Anthropology and Aboriginal Tradition', p. 7.
18 Following further discussion at the Australian Anthropological Society's annual conference, a subsection focused on professional issues was established in 2001.
19 J. Beckett, 'Report from the AAS Ethics Sub-Committee', pp. 20, 23; Fegan, 'Report from the AAS Sub-Committee', pp. 25, 26.
20 Fegan, 'Report from the AAS Sub-Committee', p. 26.
21 S. Toussaint, 'AAS Professionalisation Committee', p. 5.
22 D. Ritter and M. Garnett, 'Building the Perfect Beast'.

6 Designing Institutions in the 'Recognition Space of Native Title

1 See also French, in chapter 8 in this volume, who explains how the High Court's 2002 *Ward* and *Yorta Yorta* decisions displaced legal emphasis on common law.
2 The genesis for this concept lies with the Aboriginal leader and activist, Noel Pearson, although he has subsequently come to an alternative view of native title. See N. Pearson, 'The Concept of Native Title at Common Law'; C. Mantziaris and D. F. Martin, *Native Title Corporations*, p. 24.
3 Mantziaris and Martin, *Native Title Corporations*, p. 9.
4 F. R. Myers, *Pintupi Country, Pintupi Self.*
5 However, see acknowledgment of this issue in the recent majority decision in *Western Australia v Ward* (2002) HCA 28 at [14].
6 Mantziaris and Martin, *Native Title Corporations*, pp. 16–18.
7 Ibid., pp. 123–6.
8 For extended discussions of the problems for native title management arising from the mandatory use of this Act, see P. Sullivan, *A Sacred Land, a Sovereign People, an Aboriginal Corporation*; Mantziaris and Martin, *Native Title Corporations*, ch. 6.
9 See P. Sutton, *Native Title and the Descent of Rights*, chapter 2, 'Families of Polity: Post-classical Aboriginal Society and Native Title', for a discussion of 'families'; and see Mantziaris and Martin, *Native Title Corporations*, pp. 271–81, for a discussion of Indigenous 'organisational culture'.
10 Mantziaris and Martin, *Native Title Corporations*, pp. 126–8.
11 See R. Levitus, D. F. Martin and D. Pollack, *Regionalisation of Northern Territory Land Councils.*

7 Outsourced Professionals in Native Title Claim Research

[1] A connection report, showing how a claimant group is connected to the area being claimed, is prepared in the early stages of a group's claim.
[2] R. Blowes and D. Trigger, 'Experts, Documents and Lawyers in Native Title Claims', p. 7.
[3] Ibid., p. 8.
[4] K. Palmer, G. Macdonald and G. McIntyre, 'Engagement for Services by Contract'.
[5] D. Bell, *Ngarrindjeri Wurruwarrin*, provides details on the Hindmarsh Island case recorded as *Kartinyeri v Commonwealth* (1998) HCA 22: 152 ALR 540: 195 CLR 337.
[6] Native Title Act, Section 6(11).
[7] *Daniel v Western Australia* (1999) FCA 1541; *Esso Australia Resources Ltd v Federal Commissioner of Taxation* (1998) 159 ALR 664.
[8] See also Trigger, chapter 2 in this volume, on the Warrumungu land claim.

8 The Evolving Law of Native Title

[1] *Wik Peoples v Queensland* (1996) 187 CLR 1, at 182.
[2] *North Ganalanja Aboriginal Corporation v Queensland* (1995) 132 ALR 565, at 592.
[3] *Mabo v Queensland (No 2)* (1992) 175 CLR 1, Brennan J, at 59–60, 70; per Deane and Gaudron JJ, at 86, 110; per Toohey J, at 188.
[4] Ibid., Brennan J, at 59; per Deane and Gaudron JJ, at 110.
[5] *Coe v Commonwealth* (1993) 118 ALR 193.
[6] *Mabo v Queensland (No 2)* (1992) 175 CLR 1, at 70.
[7] *Western Australia v Ward* (2000) 170 ALR 159.
[8] Ibid., at 188.
[9] *Western Australia v Ward* (2002) 191 ALR 1, at 17.
[10] Ibid., at 32.
[11] *Western Australia v Ward* (2000) 170 ALR 159, at 218.
[12] Ibid., at 218.
[13] Ibid., at 220.
[14] The Miriuwung Gajerrong claim (*Ward*) and Lee J's 1998 decision are discussed by Barker, Christensen and Choo in chapters 15, 16 and 17 in this volume.
[15] *Western Australia v Ward* (2002) 191 ALR 1, at 31.
[16] *North Ganalanja Aboriginal Corporation v Queensland* (1995) 129 ALR 118, at 133.
[17] *Commonwealth v Yarmirr* (1999) 168 ALR 426.
[18] Ibid., at 443.
[19] *Commonwealth v Yarmirr* (2001) 184 ALR 113.
[20] *Yanner v Eaton* (1996) 175 CLR 1 at 70.
[21] *Commonwealth v Yarmirr* (2001) 184 ALR 113, at 444.
[22] *Yorta Yorta Aboriginal Community v Victoria* (2002) 194 ALR 538.
[23] *Mabo v Queensland (No 2)* (1992) 175 CLR, 1 at 70.
[24] *Wik Peoples v Queensland* (1996) 187 CLR 1, at 184.
[25] *Fejo v Northern Territory* (1998) 195 CRL 96, at 128.
[26] Ibid., at 131.
[27] *Western Australia v Ward* (2002) 191 ALR 1, at 37.

9 The Rules for Engagement

[1] As discussed by French in chapter 8 in this volume, following the High Court's 2002 decisions in *Ward* and *Yorta Yorta*, native title is no longer confined to common law only.
[2] *Mabo v Queensland (No 2)* (1992) 175 CLR, at 15.
[3] *Native Title Act 1993* (Cwlth), ss. 108(1A), 86B, 61.
[4] Ibid., ss. 86E, 136A–G.
[5] Ibid., ss. 109(1); 109(2) (similar provision is made for the Federal Court's way of operating: section 82(2)); 109(3) (by comparison, the Federal Court is bound by the rules of evidence,

except to the extent that the Court otherwise orders: section 82(1)); 127 (the Act extends to each external Territory, to the coastal sea of Australia and of each external Territory, and to any waters over which Australia asserts sovereign rights under the 1973 Seas and Submerged Lands Act).

[6] Ibid., s. 86B(1).

[7] *General Guidelines for Native Title Determinations and Agreements, Western Australian Government,* 2000.

[8] *State of Queensland, Guide to Compiling a Connection Report,* 1999.

[9] Ibid., p. 6.

[10] Ibid., p. 9.

[11] Ibid., p. 8.

[12] *Yorta Yorta Aboriginal Community v Victoria* (1998) FCA 1606; (1999) 4 (1) AILR 91; (2002) 194 ALR 538; *Yarmirr v Northern Territory* (1998) 771 FCA: 156 ALR 370, also known as the Croker Sea Claim; *Ward v Western Australia* (1998) 159 ALR 483; *Western Australia v Ward* (2000) 170 ALR 159; (2002) 191 ALR 1, also known as *Ward.*

[13] *State of Queensland, Guide to Compiling a Connection Report,* p. 10.

10 Confidentiality and Privilege

[1] Anthropological Society of Western Australia, *The Constitution and the Code of Ethics,* Clauses 3.1, 3.2.

[2] Ibid., Clause 3.3.

[3] Ibid., Clause 3.8.

[4] *Foster v Mountford* (1976) 14 ALR 71.

[5] See *Esso Australia Resources Ltd v Federal Commissioner of Taxation* (1999) HCA 67.

[6] See the case of journalist Tony Barrass, *DPP v. Luders,* unreported, District Court of WA No. 177 of 1990.

[7] *Attorney-General v Maurice* (1986) 161 CLR 475.

[8] *Towney v Minister for Land and Water Conservation* (1997) 147 ALR 402.

[9] Ibid., at 414.

[10] *Daniel v Western Australia* (1999) FCA 1541.

[11] See also Trigger in chapter 2 in this volume for discussion on this case.

[12] *Clarrie Smith v Western Australia* (2000) FCA 526.

[13] *Aboriginal Sacred Sites Protection Authority v Maurice* (1987) 65 ALR 247.

[14] Ibid., at 256.

[15] *Clarrie Smith v Western Australia* (2000) FCA 526.

11 The Nharnuwangga, Wajarri and Ngarlawangga Claim

[1] *Clarrie Smith v Western Australia* (2000) FCA 526.

[2] Ibid., at 18.

[3] Ibid., at 20.

[4] Ibid., at 15.

[5] Ibid., at 27.

[6] *Western Australia v Ward* (2000) 99 FCR 316.

[7] *Clarrie Smith v Western Australia* (2000) FCA 526, at 16. See also Barker, Christensen and Choo, chapters 15, 16 and 17 in this volume, for discussion on the *Ward* case, and French for discussion on the 2002 High Court decisions on *Ward* and *Yorta Yorta.*

[8] See French, chapter 8 in this volume.

12 Lawyers and Rats

[1] C. Dickens, *Bleak House,* Mandarin, London, 1991 (reprint), p. 4.

[2] A. Hutchinson (ed.), *Critical Legal Studies,* p. 292.

[3] S. Ross, *Ethics in Law*, p. 31. ABA Model Rule 1.2 states that 'lawyers are agents of their clients and are under contractual obligations to them. Therefore they are required to do what their clients instruct them to do within the terms of the contract'.

[4] Such a view is ostensibly supported when one considers the number of political leaders who ceased to be lawyers before they became political advocates, including Lenin, Gandhi, Lloyd-George, Whitlam and so on. This observation has led one commentator to conclude that 'lawyers cannot be revolutionaries and at the same time uphold the legal system they seek to overthrow. If lawyers remain in the system they act as a moderating force that compromises revolutionary or radical goals', Ross, *Ethics in Law*, p. 20.

[5] The Native Title Act states that the applicants have the power to deal with not only the application but also all matters arising in relation to it: section 62(1)(a)(iv).

[6] This criticism is made of lawyers generally. See H. Astor and C. Chinkin, *Dispute Resolution in Australia*, pp. 185–212.

[7] J. Altman, 'Economic Development of the Indigenous Economy and the Potential Leverage of Native Title'.

[8] Ross states that 'objectivity' is a dominant ethical requirement of the profession. 'A detached approach to the client's problem is the proper approach and rarely should they be friends', Ross, *Ethics of Law*, p. 35.

[9] Even allowing for the usual fiduciary duties owed by a solicitor to his or her client.

[10] Equally though, there are numerous lawyers who work in the field of native title because it is profitable.

[11] This statement requires some qualification, as the Aboriginal and Torres Strait Islander Commission and the Commonwealth Minister's office described receiving numerous complaints. It is our perception, however, that such complaints are most often an expression of intra-Indigenous political struggle, rarely directed towards any professional shortcomings of native title lawyers.

[12] Regrettably, there is no simple 'solution' to the issue of conflict. Representative bodies must endeavour to set up decision-making processes that are as transparent and fair as possible, notwithstanding the (arguable) conflict of interest that is entrenched within any Native Title Representative Body incorporated under the Aboriginal Councils and Associations Act. See *Hicks v Aboriginal Legal Service of Western Australia (Inc)* (2000) FCA 544.

[13] See D. Ritter, *The Mediation Process and the Parties to It*.

[14] P. Sullivan, ' Problems of Mediation in the National Native Title Tribunal', p. 97.

[15] D. Miller, 'Knowing Your Rights', p. 54.

[16] Ritter, *The Mediation Process and the Parties to It*, pp. 1814–15.

[17] It is, in any event, also arguably the appropriate jurisprudential basis of the doctrine of native title. See R. Bartlett, An Overview of Native Title.

[18] The origins of the movement are discussed at length in Hutchinson, *Critical Legal Studies*, pp. 1–11; K. Crenshaw, 'Race, Reform and Retrenchment', p. 1331; and Miller, 'Knowing Your Rights', p. 53. In general terms, critical legal studies scholarship has been influenced by a variety of currents in contemporary radical social theory; however, it does not reflect any agreed upon set of political tenets or methodological approaches.

[19] K. Upston Hooper, 'Slaying the Leviathan'.

[20] G. Leane, 'Testing Some Theories About Law'.

[21] Crenshaw., 'Race, Reform and Retrenchment', p. 1334.

[22] It should be emphasised that there is no coherence on this point within the critical legal studies movement. Many theorists have argued that the value of critical legal studies rests entirely in its 'deconstructive' phase. See, for example, Crenshaw, 'Race, Reform and Retrenchment', p. 1334.

[23] Gordon in K. Crenshaw, 'Race, Reform and Retrenchment', p. 1334.

[24] A. Hutchinson, personal communication, 1990.

[25] Gramsci defined hegemony as 'the means by which a system of attitudes and beliefs, permeating both popular consciousness and the ideology of elites, reinforces existing social

arrangements and convinces the dominated classes that the existing order is inevitable', A. Gramsci, *Selections from the Prison Notebooks*, pp. 169–70.

26 Upston Hooper, 'Slaying the Leviathan', p. 700.

27 Freeman, quoted in Upston Hooper, 'Slaying the Leviathan', p. 712.

28 Upston Hooper, 'Slaying the Leviathan', p. 687.

29 Freeman, in Upston Hooper, 'Slaying the Leviathan', p. 712.

30 As distinct from rights themselves, which are exercised as real, lived and enjoyed freedoms.

31 Crenshaw, 'Race, Reform and Retrenchment', p. 1334.

32 M. Tushnet, 'An Essay on Rights', pp. 1363, 1384.

33 See W. Simon, 'Visions of Practice in Legal Thought'; P. Gabel and P. Harris, 'Building Power and Breaking Images'.

34 A diverse compilation of critical race theory can be found in R. Delgado (ed.), *Critical Race Theory*.

35 For example, Delgado writes, 'White critical legal theory members see rights as oppressive, alienating and mystifying. For minorities, they are invigorating cloaks of safety that unite us in a common bond. Instead of coming to grips with the different function of rights for the two groups, critics insist that minorities adopt their viewpoint, labelling disagreement on our part false consciousness or a lack of political sophistication' (quoted in K. Upston Hooper, p. 705). See also Miller, 'Knowing Your Rights', p. 55.

36 These theories also suggest different forms that critical analysis of law may take. Critical race theory makes extensive use of 'narrative, story-telling and allegory' in conveying 'the Word', an articulation and validation of common experience: Upston Hooper, 'Slaying the Leviathan', p. 707.

37 *Mabo v Queensland (No 2)* (1992) 175 CLR 1.

38 Section 61(1) of the Native Title Act states that an application for a determination of native title may be made by a person or persons ('the applicant') authorised by all the persons who, according to their traditional laws and custom, hold the common or group rights and interest.

39 An application for determination of native title must be referred by the Federal Court to the National Native Title Tribunal for mediation as soon as practicable after three months subsequent to the notification day of the application: ss. 66, 86B(1), Native Title Act.

40 An order in which the Federal Court makes a determination of native title must set out whether native title exists and, if it does exist, the persons or groups holding the common or group rights, the nature and extent of any other interests, the relationship between the rights and interests, and whether the native title rights and interests confer possession, occupation, use and enjoyment to the exclusion of all others: ss. 94A, 225, Native Title Act.

41 Section 190 of the Native Title Act states that copies of claimant applications must be given by the Federal Court to the Native Title Registrar, who must then consider if the application and any amended application should be registered. If notice is given under section 29 of an act affecting the area claimed, the Registrar must give the claim expedited consideration and finish considering the claim by four months after the notification day: section 190A(2), Native Title Act. A claim that meets all of the application requirements must be registered: section 190A(6), Native Title Act.

42 All negotiation parties must negotiate in good faith with a view to obtaining the agreement of each of the native title parties to the doing of the act, with or without conditions: section 31(1), Native Title Act.

43 J. Tully, *Strange Multiplicity*, p. 38.

44 The preamble to the Native Title Act states (inter alia) that 'a special procedure needs to be available for the just and proper ascertainment of native title rights and interests which will ensure that, if possible, this is done by conciliation and, if not, in a manner that has due regard to their unique character'.

45 *Mabo* indicates that the following elements must be proved in order for there to be a finding of native title: connection, occupation, use or presence under the laws or customs of an identifiable community, society or group. These elements have been applied differently in

the cases following *Mabo*. An example of the standard of proof required of applicants being apparently 'raised' can be found in the issue of proof of membership of the relevant community. Brennan J referred to the membership of an identifiable community entailing identification 'by one another as members of that community living under its laws and customs': *Mabo v Queensland (No 2)* (1992) 175 CLR 1, at 44. There was no declaration that every member of the applicant group must necessarily be a biological descendant of the community in occupation at the time of the acquisition of sovereignty. However, in *Yorta Yorta Aboriginal Community v Victoria* (1998) FCA 1606, Olney J rejected the claim in part because the claimants failed to establish sufficient ancestral connection with the Indigenous inhabitants who occupied the claim area at the acquisition of sovereignty. See also French in chapter 8 in this volume.

46 In *Western Australia v Ward* (2000) 170 ALR 159, the majority considered native title to comprise of a bundle of individual rights that may be extinguished individually, and that, contrary to the view of the trial judge, Lee J, there is a common-law concept of 'partial extinguishment' based on *Delgamuukw v British Columbia* (1998) 1 CNLR 14, which states, at 111, 'Aboriginal title is a right in land and, as such, is more than the right to engage in specific activities'.

47 In *Mabo v Queensland (No 2)* (1992) 175 CLR 1, the High Court articulated the 'clear and plain intention' test for extinguishment. In *Western Australia v Ward* (2000) 170 ALR 159, the majority took the view that statutory reservations that qualified the enjoyment of native title on pastoral leases partially extinguished native title. The justices applied this reasoning to the statutory reservations in place in Western Australia since the Land Act 1933 that permitted Aboriginal persons to seek their traditional sustenance on 'unenclosed and unimproved' parts of a pastoral lease, and found that native title was totally extinguished in the 'enclosed' or 'improved' portions of the lease. See also French, chapter 8 in this volume.

48 Miller, 'Knowing Your Rights', p. 62.

49 There are some references to 'fairness' in the Native Title Act, but they are limited to specific matters concerning the administration of native title. For example, section 109 requires the National Native Title Tribunal to carry out its functions in 'a fair, just, economical, informal and prompt way'.

50 'So long as the people remain an identifiable community, the members of whom are identified by one another as members of that community living under its laws and customs, the communal native title survives': *Mabo v Queensland (No 2)* (1992) 175 CLR 1, at 44, per Brennan J.

51 'Native title . . . is extinguished if the clan or group, by ceasing to acknowledge those laws . . . and (so far as practicable) observe those customs, loses its connection with the land or on the death of the last of the members of the group or clan': ibid., at 70, per Brennan J.

52 '[I]t is immaterial that the laws and customs have undergone some change since the Crown acquired sovereignty provided the general nature of the connection between Indigenous people and the land remains': ibid., at 70, per Brennan J.

53 If there is no traditional connection at the acquisition of sovereignty, the beneficial interest of the Crown will vest upon the acquisition of sovereignty unburdened by native title: ibid., at 48.

54 *Mabo* explains extinguishment thus: 'Where an executive act is relied upon to extinguish traditional title, the intention of the legislature that executive power should extend this far must likewise appear plainly and with clarity': (ibid.), at 153, per Toohey J.

55 'If the tide of history had washed away any real acknowledgement of traditional law and real observance of traditional customs, the foundation for native title has disappeared': ibid., at 60 per Brennan J). Applied in *Yorta Yorta Aboriginal Community v Victoria* (1998) FCA 1606 (unreported, BC 9806799).

56 'In discharging its duty to declare the common law of Australia, this court is not free to adopt rules that accord with contemporary notions of justice and human rights if their adoption would fracture the skeleton of principle which gives the body of our law its shape and internal consistency' (*Mabo v Queensland (No 2)* (1992) 175 CLR 1, at 9, per Brennan J).

[57] Leane, 'Testing Some Theories About Law', p. 937.
[58] *Yorta Yorta Aboriginal Community v Victoria* (1998) FCA 1606 (unreported, BC 9806799).
[59] *Clarrie Smith v Western Australia* (2000) FCA 526.
[60] For an excellent critical analysis of the *Yorta Yorta* judgment, see V. Kerruish and C. Perrin, 'Awash in Colonialism'.
[61] *Yorta Yorta Aboriginal Community v Victoria* (1998) FCA 1606 (unreported, BC 9806799) at 21.
[62] Ibid., pp. 17, 21.
[63] Kerruish and Perrin, 'Awash in Colonialism', p. 4.
[64] This is because 'native title ... is given its content by the traditional laws and customs observed by the Indigenous inhabitants of a territory. The nature and incidents of native title must be ascertained as a matter of fact by reference to those laws and customs': (*Mabo v Queensland (No 2)* (1992) 175 CLR 1, at 58, per Brennan J.
[65] Altman, 'Economic Development of the Indigenous Economy and the Potential Leverage of Native Title'.
[66] Miller, 'Knowing Your Rights', p. 64.
[67] V. Kerruish and J. Purdy, 'He "Look" Honest—Big White Thief', p. 163; see also Tan and Vincent, chapters 10 and 11 in this volume, for discussion of the decision in *Clarrie Smith v Western Australia* (2000) FCA 526.
[68] See the Native Title Act, ss. 61(1)(2), 190C(3) and 190B(2).
[69] George Irving, native title lawyer, personal communication.
[70] Aboriginal Land Rights Commission, Northern Territory, *Final Report*, p. 138.
[71] Miller, 'Knowing Your Rights', p. 69.
[72] Gabel and Harris, 'Building Power and Breaking Images', pp. 303, 304.
[73] W. Simon, 'Visions of Practice in Legal Thought', p. 301.
[74] Ibid., p. 302.
[75] J. Tully, *Strange Multiplicity*, pp. 133–4.
[76] Simon, 'Visions of Practice in Legal Thought', p. 299.
[77] Gabel and Harris, 'Building Power and Breaking Images', p. 304.
[78] Pearson, 'Our Right to Take Responsibility'.
[79] Bartlett, 'An Overview of Native Title'.
[80] Native Title Act, section 53.
[81] For instance, in response to *Mabo*, several state governments enacted legislation that attempted to extinguish native title in the form of, respectively, the *Queensland Coast Islands Declaratory Act 1985*) and the Victorian *Land (Titles and Traditional Usage) Act 1993*. Both Acts were held to be inconsistent with the *Racial Discrimination Act 1975* (Cwlth) and therefore inoperative by reason of section 109 of the Commonwealth Constitution.
[82] *Re Waanyi People's Native Title Application* (1995) 129 ALR 100 at 167–8.
[83] Miller, 'Knowing Your Rights', p. 59.
[84] Altman, 'Economic Development of the Indigenous Economy and the Potential Leverage of Native Title', p. 5.
[85] Ibid., p. 6.
[86] Miller, 'Knowing Your Rights', p. 51.
[87] Crenshaw, 'Race, Reform and Retrenchment', p. 1367.
[88] D. Ritter, 'The Rejection of *Terra Nullius* in *Mabo*', p. 5.
[89] Aboriginal and Torres Strait Islander Social Justice Commission (M. Dodson), *Second Report*, p. 7.
[90] A. Gleeson, 'Individualised Justice—The Holy Grail', p. 421.

13 Reflecting on Past Practice

[1] W. E. H. Stanner, *After the Dreaming*, p. 18.
[2] For some significant works in a rich field, see C. D. Rowley's trilogy, *The Destruction of Aboriginal Society, The Remote Aborigines*, and *Outcasts in White Australia*; Henry Reynolds, *The Other Side of the Frontier* and *The Law of the Land*; Richard Broome's *Aboriginal Australians*; and the journal *Aboriginal History*, published since 1978.

[3] *Mabo v Queensland (No 2)* (1992) 175 CLR 1; *Milirrpum v Nabalco Pty Ltd* (1970) 17 FLR 141.
[4] *Australian*, 28 April 2000.
[5] *Hayes v Northern Territory* (1999) 97 FCR 32: (1999) FCA 1248.
[6] *Wik Peoples v Queensland* (1996) 187 CLR 1.
[7] *Hayes v Northern Territory* (1999) FCA 1248 at 52.
[8] J. Dalziel, 'Pastoral leases in the Northern Territory and the reservation of Aboriginal rights', pp. 462–505.
[9] H. Goodall, ' "The Whole Truth and Nothing But . . ." ', p. 108.
[10] *Bellevue Crescent v Marland Holdings* (1998) 43 NSWLR 364.
[11] Ann McGrath, in 'Contested Ground', has provided a useful survey of these developments.
[12] See, for example, D. B. Rose, 'Histories and Rituals'; Goodall, ' "The Whole Truth and Nothing But . . ." '.
[13] D. B. Rose, 'The Treatment of Historical Evidence in the Yorta Yorta case'.
[14] *Cubillo v Commonwealth* (2000) FCA 1084.
[15] On the former, see, for example, K. Darian-Smith and P. Hamilton (eds), *Memory and History in Twentieth Century Australia*; on the latter see, for example, A. McGrath, 'Stories for Country'; A. Curthoys, 'The Proof of Continuity of Native Title'; and many contributions to the field by Bruce Shaw.
[16] See, for example, *Daniel v Western Australia* (1999) 194 FCR 537: (1999) FCA 1541; (2000) 178 ALR 542.
[17] J. Finlayson, 'Sustaining Memories', p. 95.
[18] *Hayes v Northern Territory* (1999) 97 FCR 32: (1999) FCA 1248.
[19] R. Hunter, 'Aboriginal Histories, Australian Histories, and the Law', p. 1.

14 Three-legged Elephants

[1] Federal Court of Australia, *Guidelines for Expert Witnesses*.
[2] Ibid.
[3] *Daniel v Western Australia* (1999) 97 FCR 537: (1999) FCA 1541; (2000) 178 ALR 542.
[4] G. R. Elton, *The Practice of History*, p. 34.
[5] *Ward v Western Australia* (1998) 159 ALR 483.
[6] *Clarrie Smith v Western Australia* (2000) FCA 526. (See also Vincent, in chapter 11 in this volume.)
[7] Elton, *The Practice of History*, p. 28.
[8] Ibid., p. 21.

15 Working as a Barrister on the Miriuwung Gajerrong Native Title Claim

[1] Law Reform Commission of Western Australia, *Review of the Criminal and Civil Justice System in Western Australia*, p. 187.
[2] *Ward v Western Australia (1998)* 159 ALR 483.
[3] *Western Australia v Ward* (2000) FCA 191: (2000) 107 ALR 159.
[4] See French, in chapter 8 in this volume, for analysis of the 2002 appeal.
[5] *Ward v Western Australia* (1998) 159 ALR 483, at 514–23.
[6] Ibid., at 523–5.
[7] Ibid., at 526–31.
[8] Ibid., at 531–5.
[9] Ibid., at 525–6.
[10] Ibid., at 535–9.
[11] Ibid., at 544–50.
[12] *Mabo v Queensland (No 2)* (1992) 175 CLR 1.
[13] Ibid., at 61.
[14] *Ward v Western Australia* (1998) 159 ALR 483, at 517.
[15] Ibid., at 532.

[16] *Western Australia v Ward* (2000) FCA 191, para 269.
[17] *Ward v Western Australia* (1998) 159 ALR 483, at 524.
[18] Ibid., at 523.
[19] Ibid., at 523.
[20] Ibid., at 542.
[21] Ibid., at 542.
[22] *Western Australia v Ward* (2000) FCA 191, paras 192, 193.

16 Working as an Anthropologist on the Miriuwung Gajerrong Native Title Claim

[1] *Ward v Western Australia* (1998) 159 ALR 483; *Western Australia v Ward* (2000) 99 FCR 316: (2000) 170 ALR 159: (2000) FCA 191; (2002) 191 ALR 1.
[2] French, in chapter 8 in this volume, discusses the 2002 appeal; see also Afterword.
[3] K. Maddock, *East Kimberley Anthropological Report*; K. Barber and K. Palmer, *Native Title Claim to the Keep River National Park.*
[4] P. Kaberry, *Aboriginal Woman Sacred and Profane*, and her Field Notes; J. Birdsell, Unpublished Field Journal; N. B. Tindale, Unpublished Field Journal, and *Aboriginal Tribes of Australia.*

17 Working as a Historian on the Miriuwung Gajerrong Native Title Claim

[1] D. B. Rose, *Hidden Histories*, p. 8.
[2] A. Curthoys, 'The Proof of Continuity of Native Title'.
[3] C. Choo and M. O'Connell, 'Historical Narrative and Proof of Native Title'.
[4] Federal Court of Australia, *Guidelines for Expert Witnesses in Proceedings in the Federal Court of Australia.*
[5] P. Duara, *Rescuing History from the Nation*, p. 6.
[6] J. C. Scott, *Seeing Like a State*, p. 6.
[7] I. Clendinnen, *Reading the Holocaust*, p. 202; Clendinnen, *True Stories.*
[8] See R. Poole, *Nation and Identity.*

Afterword

[1] *Western Australia v Ward* (2002) 191 ALR 1.
[2] With regard to pastoral leases and the nature of extinguishment, the *Miriuwung Gajerrong* 2002 appeal judgment represents a narrower interpretation than that found in the 1996 *Wik* decision.
[3] Olney J 1998 Determination of Native Title Pursuant the Native Title Act re Claim No VG6001 of 1995 between *Yorta Yorta Aboriginal Community v State of Victoria.*
[4] *Yorta Yorta Aboriginal Community v Victoria* (2002) HCA 58, at 92–6.
[5] See Bowe, 'Linguistics and the Yorta Yorta Native Title Claim', pp. 101–59.
[6] *Yorta Yorta Aboriginal Community v Victoria* (2002) HCA 58, at 113.
[7] *Yorta Yorta Aboriginal Community v Victoria* (1998), quote from claim transcript cited in K. Auty and R. Patten, 'Turning Country into Clay', p. 6.
[8] Toussaint, 'Unfinished Business': Plural Anthropologies in Australia?
[9] A. Gramsci, *Selections from the Prison Notebooks.*

Bibliography

Cases cited

Aboriginal Sacred Sites Protection Authority v Maurice (1987) 65 ALR 247.
Attorney-General v Maurice (1986) 161 CLR 475.
Bellevue Crescent v Marland Holdings (1998) 43 NSWLR 364.
Clarrie Smith v Western Australia (2000) FCA 526.
Coe v Commonwealth (1993) 118 ALR 193.
Commonwealth v Yarmirr (1999) 168 ALR 426; (2001) 184 ALR 113.
Cubillo v Commonwealth (2000) 103 FCR 1: (2000) 174 ALR 97: (2000) FCA 1084.
Daniel v Western Australia (1999) 94 FCR 537: (1999) FCA 1541; (2000) 178 ALR 542.
Delgamuukw v British Columbia (1998) 1 CNLR 14.
Esso Australia Resources Ltd v Federal Commissioner of Taxation (1998) 159 ALR 664; (1999) HCA 67.
Fejo v Northern Territory (1998) 195 CLR 96.
Foster v Mountford (1976) 14 ALR 71.
Hayes v Northern Territory (1999) 97 FCR 32: (1999) FCA 1248.
Mabo v Queensland (No 2) (1992) 175 CLR 1.
Milirrpum v Nabalco Pty Ltd (1970) 17 FLR 141.
Northern Territory v Maurice (1986) 161 CLR 475.
North Ganalanja Aboriginal Corporation v Queensland (1995) 61 FCR 1: (1995) 132 ALR 565; (1996) 185 CLR 595.
R v Anunga (1976) 11 ALR 412.
Re Waanyi People's Native Title Application (1995) 129 ALR 100; (1995) 129 ALR 118.
Towney v Minister for Land and Water Conservation (1997) 147 ALR 402.
Ward v Western Australia (1998) 159 ALR 483.
Western Australia v Ward (2000) 99 FCR 316: (2000) 170 ALR 159: (2000) FCA 191; (2002) 191 ALR 1: (2002) HCA 28.
Wik Peoples v Queensland (1996) 187 CLR 1.
Yanner v Eaton (1996) 175 CLR 1; (1999) 201 CLR 351.
Yarmirr v Northern Territory (1998) 82 FCR 533: (1998) 156 ALR 370.
Yorta Yorta Aboriginal Community v Victoria (1998) FCA 1606: (1999) 4 (1) AILR 91 (unreported, BC 9806799); (2002) 194 ALR 538: (2002) HCA 58.

Reports to the Court

Akerman, K. *Report of Anthropologist,* filed pursuant to Order 11.2 of Lee J (for Miriuwung Gajerrong Claim), 1995/1996.

Barber, K. and Palmer, K. *Native Title Claim to the Keep River National Park: Anthropologists' Report on Behalf of the Native Title Claimants* (for Miriuwung Gajerrong Claim), 1996.

Choo, C. *Report No 1 of Historian,* filed pursuant to Order 11.2 of Lee J (for Miriuwung Gajerrong Claim), 1996.

——. *Report No 2 of Historian,* filed pursuant to Order 11.2 of Lee J (for Miriuwung Gajerrong Claim), 1996.

——. *Report No 3 of Historian,* filed pursuant to Order 11.2 of Lee J (for Miriuwung Gajerrong Claim), 1996.

Christensen, W. J. K. *Anthropological Report: Miriuwung and Gajerrong Native Title Claim,* filed in the Federal Court of Australia pursuant to Order 11.2 of Lee J, 1996.

——. *Final Anthropological Report: Miriuwung and Gajerrong Native Title Claim,* filed in the Federal Court of Australia on behalf of the First Applicants, 1997.

Doohan, K. *The Balangarra Group and their Connection to Land and Waters,* filed pursuant to Order 11.2 of Lee J (for Miriuwung Gajerrong Claim), 1995/1997.

Fullager, R. *Report of Archaeologist,* filed pursuant to Order 11.2 of Lee J (for Miriuwung Gajerrong Claim), 1996.

Kofod, F. *Report of Linguist,* filed pursuant to Order of 11.2 of Lee J (for Miriuwung Gajerrong Claim), 1995/1996.

Maddock, K. *East Kimberley Anthropological Report,* filed pursuant to Order 11.2 of Lee J (for Miriuwung Gajerrong Claim), 1995/1996.

——. *East Kimberley Supplementary Anthropological Report,* filed in the Federal Court of Australia (for Miriuwung Gajerrong Claim), 1997.

Olney, J. H. *Garawa/Mugularrang: Robinson River Land Claim,* report no. 33, Canberra, Australian Government Publishing Service (for Robinson River Claim), 1991.

Shaw, B. *Report of Oral Historian,* filed pursuant to Order 11.2 of Lee J (for Miriuwung Gajerrong Claim), 1996.

Books, articles, papers and theses

Aboriginal Land Rights Commission, Northern Territory. *Final Report: Aboriginal Land Rights Commission,* Australian Government Publishing Service, Canberra, 1974.

Aboriginal and Torres Strait Islander Social Justice Commission (M. Dodson). *Second Report,* Australian Government Publishing Service, Canberra, 1995.

Altman, J. Economic Development of the Indigenous Economy and the Potential Leverage of Native Title, paper presented at the Native Title in the New Millennium Representative Bodies Legal Conference, 16–20 April 2000.

Anthropological Society of Western Australia, *The Constitution and the Code of Ethics,* Perth, n.d.

Antze, P. and Lambek, M. (eds). *Tense Past: Cultural Essays in Trauma and Memory,* Routledge, New York/London, 1996.

Asche, W. Commonalities and Tensions in the Roles of Anthropologists, Linguists, Historians and Lawyers, paper presented at the conference on Crossing Boundaries: Anthropology, Linguistics, History and Law in Native Title, Perth, 2000.

Astor, H and Chinkin, C. *Dispute Resolution in Australia,* Butterworths, Sydney, 1992.

Attwood, B. *A History of Relations Between Europeans and Aborigines,* Melbourne University Press, Carlton, 1994.

Attwood, B. and Arnold, J. (eds). *Power, Knowledge and Aborigines,* special edition of the *Journal of Australian Studies,* La Trobe University Press in association with the National Centre for Australian Studies, Monash University, Clayton, 1992.

Australian Anthropological Society. 'Code of Ethics', *Australian Anthropological Society Newsletter,* no. 74, 1998, pp. 22–4.

Australian Institute of Aboriginal and Torres Strait Islander Studies, *Guidelines for Ethical Research in Indigenous Studies,* Canberra, Aboriginal Studies Press, n.d.

Auty, K. and R. Patten. Turning 'Country' into Clay—Native Title in Australia, unpublished paper, Australian Indigenous Studies, Deakin University, 2001, pp. 1–15.

Bartlett, R. An Overview of Native Title: Pragmatism or Equality, paper given at the International Bar Association 25th Biennial Conference, Melbourne, October, 1994.

Beckett, J. 'Report from the AAS Ethics Sub-Committee: Introduction'. *Australian Anthropological Society Newsletter,* no. 79/80, 2000, pp. 21–3.

Bell, D. *Ngarrindjeri Wurruwarrin: A World that Was and Will Be,* Spinifex Press, North Melbourne, 1998.

Bennett, S. *White Politics and Black Australians,* Allen & Unwin, St Leonards, 1999.

Berger, P. *Facing Up To Modernity,* Basic Books, New York, 1977.

Berger, P., Berger, B. and Kellner, H. *The Homeless Mind,* Vintage, New York, 1973.

Birdsell, J. Unpublished Field Journal, 1954, held by the South Australian Museum.

Blowes, R. and Trigger D. 'Experts, Documents and Lawyers in Native Title Claims: The Implications of *Daniel v State of Western Australia*', *Indigenous Law Bulletin,* vol. 4, no. 28, March 2000, pp. 4–9.

Bolt, J., Hoddinott, W. and Kofod, F. An Elementary Grammar of the Ngaliwurru Language, unpublished manuscript, 1971.

Botsman, P. (ed.). *Theoretical Strategies,* Local Consumptions, Sydney, 1982.

Bondi, L. 'Locating Identity Politics', in M. Keith and S. Pile (eds), *Place and the Politics of Identity,* Routledge, London/New York, 1993, pp. 84–101.

Broome, R. *Aboriginal Australians: Black Response to White Dominance 1788–1980,* Allen & Unwin, Sydney, 1982.

Brunt, R. 'The Politics of Identity', in S. Hall and M. Jacques (eds), *New Times: The Changing Face of Politics in the 1990s,* Lawrence & Wishart, London, 1989, pp. 150–9.

Bowe, H. 'Linguistics and the Yorta Yorta Native Title Claim', in J. Henderson and D. Nash (eds), *Language in Native Title,* Aboriginal Studies Press, Canberra, 2002, pp. 101–60.

Brunton, R. 'Covering up a Multitude of Social, Ethical Sins', *Courier Mail,* 10 July 1999, p. 23.

——. 'Hindmarsh Island and the Hoaxing of Australian Anthropology', *Quadrant,* May 1999, pp. 11–17.

Choo, C. 'History, Native Title and Reconciliation: History in Practice', *Limina: A Journal of Historical and Cultural Studies,* vol. 5, 1999, pp. 138–42.

Choo, C. and O'Connell, M. 'Historical Narrative and Proof of Native Title', in *Land, Rights, Laws: Issues in Native Title,* Issues Paper vol. 3, no. 2, March, Native Title

Research Unit, Australian Institute of Aboriginal and Torres Strait Islander Studies, 2000.

Choo, C. and Hallback, S. (eds). 'History and Native Title', *Studies in Western Australian History* (Special Issue), vol. 23, 2003.

Clendinnen, I. *Reading the Holocaust*, Text Publishing, Melbourne, 1998.

Clendinnen, I. *True Stories*, The Boyer Lectures, Australian Broadcasting Corporation, Sydney, 1999.

Crenshaw, K. 'Race, Reform and Retrenchment: Transformation and Legitimation in Anti-Discrimination Law', *Harvard Law Review*, vol. 101, no. 7, 1998, pp. 1331–68.

Curthoys, A. 'The Proof of Continuity of Native Title: An Historian's Perspective', *Land, Rights, Law: Issues of Native Title*, Issues Paper vol. 1, no. 18, Native Title Research Unit, Australian Institute of Aboriginal and Torres Strait Islander Studies, 1998.

Dalziel, J. 'Pastoral Leases in the Northern Territory and the Reservation of Aboriginal Rights, 1863–1931', *University of New South Wales Law Journal*, vol. 22, no. 2, 1999, pp. 462–505.

Darian-Smith, K. and Hamilton, P. (eds). *Memory and History in Twentieth Century Australia*, Oxford University Press, South Melbourne, 1994.

Delgado, R. (ed.). *Critical Race Theory: The Cutting Edge*, Temple University Press, Philadelphia, 1995.

Dixon, R. M. W. 'Wargamay', in R. Dixon and B. Blake (eds), *Handbook of Australian Languages*, Australian National University Press, Canberra, 1982, pp. 1–146.

Duara, P. *Rescuing History from the Nation: Questioning the Narratives of Modern China*, University of Chicago Press, Chicago, 1995.

Eades, D. 'A Case of Communicative Clash: Aboriginal English and the Legal System', in J. Gibbons (ed.), *Language and the Law*, Longman, London, 1994, pp. 234–64.

Edmunds, M. 'The Importance of Absolute Accuracy: Anthropology and Native Title', *Academy of the Social Sciences Newsletter*, vol. 17, no. 3, 1998, pp. 13–17.

Ekman, P. 'Universal and Cultural Differences in Facial Expression of Emotion'. *Nebraska Symposium*, no. 197, University of Nebraska Press, Omaha, 1972, pp. 207–83.

Elder, B. *Blood on the Wattle: Massacres and Maltreatment of Aboriginal Australians since 1788*, New Holland Publishers, French's Forest, 1998.

Elkin, A. 'Aboriginal Evidence and Justice in North Australia', *Oceania*, vol. 17, no. 3, 1947, pp. 173–210.

——. *The Australian Aborigines*, Angus & Robertson, Sydney, [1954] 1974.

Elton, G. R. *The Practice of History*, Collins, Fontana Library, London, 1970.

Federal Court of Australia. *Guidelines for Expert Witnesses in Proceedings in the Federal Court of Australia*, 15 September 1998, http://www.fedcourt.gov.au/practice.htm/

Fegan, B. 'Report from the AAS Ethics Sub-Committee: Ethics and Professional or Consultant Anthropologists', *Australian Anthropological Society Newsletter*, no. 79/80, 2000, pp. 25–6.

Feldman, A. *Formations of Violence: The Narrative of the Body and Political Terror in Northern Ireland*. University of Chicago Press, Chicago/London, 1991.

Finlayson, J. 'Sustaining Memories: The Status of Oral and Written Evidence in Native Title Claims', in J. D. Finlayson, B. Rigsby and H. J. Beck (eds), *Connections in Native Title: Genealogies, Kinship and Groups*, Centre for Aboriginal Economic Policy Research, Australian National University, Research Monograph no. 13, 1999, pp. 85–98.

——. 'Comment on Professionalisation and the Possible Establishment of a Separate AAS Section for Applied Anthropologists', *Australian Anthropological Society Newsletter*, no. 79/80, 2000, pp. 27–8.

Freud, S. 'Mourning and Melancholia', in his *Collected Papers*, vol. 4, Basic Books, New York, 1959.

Furniss, E. 'Indians, Odysseys and Vast, Empty Lands: The Myth of the Frontier in the Canadian Justice System', *Anthropologica* (forthcoming).

Gabel, P. and Harris, P. 'Building Power and Breaking Images: Critical Legal Theory and the Practice of Law', in A. Hutchinson (ed.), *Critical Legal Studies*, Rowman & Littlefield, Toronto, 1989.

Gleeson, A. 'Individualised Justice—The Holy Grail', *Australian Law Journal*, no. 69, 1995.

Goldman, L. *Talk Never Dies: The Language of Huli Disputes*, Clarendon Press, Oxford, 1983.

Goodall, H. '"The Whole Truth and Nothing But . . .": Some Intersections of Western Law, Aboriginal History and Community Memory', in B. Attwood and J. Arnold (eds), *Power, Knowledge and Aborigines*, special edition of the *Journal of Australian Studies*, La Trobe University Press in association with the National Centre for Australian Studies, Monash University, Clayton, 1992.

Gramsci, A. *Selections from the Prison Notebooks*, Lawrence & Wishart, London, 1971.

Hale, K. 'Linguistic Evidence for Long-term Residence of the Wik-speaking Peoples in their present Location in Cape York Peninsula', in Sutton, P. and K. Hale (eds), *Language, Time and Native Title: The Wik Case of North Australia* (forthcoming).

Harvey, M. 'Place Names and Land-Language Associations in the Western Top End', *Australian Journal of Linguistics*, vol. 19, no. 2, 1999, pp. 161–96.

Human Rights and Equal Opportunity Commission (J. Killen, M. Einfield, K. Mundine). *Toomelah Report: Report on the Problems and Needs of Aborigines Living on the New South Wales–Queensland Border*, Human Rights and Equal Opportunity Commission, Sydney, 1988.

Hunter, R. 'Aboriginal Histories, Australian Histories, and the Law', in B. Attwood (ed.), *In the Age of Mabo: History, Aborigines and Australia*, Allen & Unwin, Sydney, 1996, pp. 1–16.

Hutchins, E. *Culture and Inference: A Trobriand Case Study*, Harvard University Press, Cambridge, Mass., 1980.

Hutchinson, A. (ed.). *Critical Legal Studies*, Rowman & Littlefield, Toronto, 1989.

Kaberry, P. M. *Aboriginal Woman Sacred and Profane*, George Routledge & Son, London, 1939.

——. Field Notes (Ivanhoe, Argyle, Newry Stations), 1934–35, held by the Australian Institute of Aboriginal and Torres Strait Islander Studies, Canberra.

Kapferer, J. *Being All Equal: Identity, Difference and Australian Cultural Practice*, Berg, Oxford/Washington, DC, 1996.

Keesing, R. *Cultural Anthropology: A Contemporary Perspective*, Holt, Rinehart & Winston, New York, 1981.

Kerruish, V. and Perrin, C. 'Awash in Colonialism: A Critical Analysis of the Federal Court Decision in the Matter of *The Members of the Yorta Yorta Aboriginal Community v The State of Victoria and Ors*', *Alternative Law Journal*, vol. 24, no. 3, 1999, pp. 4–6.

Kerruish, V. and Purdy, J. 'He "Look" Honest—Big White Thief', *Law, Text, Culture: In the Wake of Terra Nullius*, vol. 4, no. 1, 1998.

Kimberley Language Resource Centre. *Moola Bulla: In the Shadow of the Mountain*, Magabala Books, Broome, 1996.

Langton, M. The Sacred and Legitimacy: Property as an Expression of Temporal and Spatial Dimensions, paper presented at the conference on Crossing Boundaries: Anthropology, Linguistics, History and Law in Native Title, Perth, 2000.

Lattas, A. 'Primitivism, Nationalism and Individualism in Australian Popular Culture', in B. Attwood and J. Arnold (eds), *Power, Knowledge and Aborigines*, special edition of the *Journal of Australian Studies*, La Trobe University Press in association with the National Centre for Australian Studies, Monash University, Clayton, 1992, pp. 45–58.

Law Reform Commission of Western Australia. *Review of Criminal and Civil Justice System in Western Australia*, Government Printers, Perth, 1999.

Leane, G. 'Testing Some Theories About Law: Can We Find Substantive Justice Within Law's Rules?', *Melbourne University Law Review*, no. 19, 1994.

Levitus, R., Martin D. F. and Pollack, D. *Regionalisation of Northern Territory Land Councils*, Discussion Paper no. 192, Centre for Aboriginal Economic Policy Research, Australian National University, Canberra, 1999.

Liberman, K. 'Understanding Aborigines in Australian Courts of Law', *Human Organisation*, vol. 1, 1981, pp. 247–55.

Lumholtz, C. *Among Cannibals: Account of Four Years Travels in Australia, and of Camp Life with Aborigines of Queensland*, Facsimile reprint, Australian National University Press, Canberra, [1889] 1980.

McConvell, P. ONLY and related concepts in Gurindji, unpublished manuscript, 1986.

——. 'Long-lost Relations: Pama-Nyungan and Northern Kinship', in P. McConvell and N. Evans (eds), *Archaeology and Linguistics: Aboriginal Australia in Global Perspective*, Oxford University Press, Melbourne, 1997, pp. 207–35.

——. ' "Born is Nothing": Roots, Family Trees and Other Attachments to Land in the Victoria River District and Kimberleys', *Aboriginal History*, vol. 22, 1998/2000, p. 202.

——. 'Language Shift and Language Spread among Hunter-Gatherers', in C. Panter-Brick, P. Rowley-Conway and R. Layton (eds), *Hunter-Gatherers: Social and Biological Perspectives*, Cambridge University Press, Cambridge, 2000.

——. 'A Linguistic Stratigraphy and Native Title: The Case of Ethnonyms', in J. Henderson and D. Nash (eds), *Linguistics and Native Title*, Aboriginal Studies Press, Canberra, 2002, pp. 259–90.

——. 'Changing Places: Indigenous and Settler Styles', in L. Hercus, F. Hodges, and J. Simpson (eds), *The Land is a Map: Indigenous Place Names in Australia*, Canberra, Pandanus Press, 2002, pp. 50–61.

McConvell, P. and M. Laughren. Down Under in Central Australia: Spatial Metaphors in Ngumpin-Yapa, paper given to meeting of the American Anthropological Association, Chicago, 1999.

McGrath, A. '"Stories from Country": Oral History and Aboriginal Land Claims', *Oral History Association of Australia Journal,* no. 9, 1987.

——. 'Contested Ground: What is Aboriginal History?', in A. McGrath (ed.), *Contested Ground: Australian Aborigines under the British Crown,* Allen & Unwin, St Leonards, 1995.

McKnight, David, *People, Land and the Rainbow Serpent,* Oxford University Press, Melbourne, 1999.

Maddock, K. 'Anthropologists in Native Title Claims', *Anthropological Forum,* vol. 1, no. 2, 1998, pp. 85–90.

——. 'Bearing Witness', *Australian Anthropological Society Newsletter,* vol. 75, 1998, pp. 23–5.

Mantziaris, C. and Martin, D. F. *Guide to the Design of Native Title Corporations,* National Native Title Tribunal, Perth, 1999.

——. *Native Title Corporations: A Legal and Anthropological Analysis,* Federation Press, Sydney, 2000.

Martin, D. The Design of Indigenous Institutions in the 'Recognition Space' of Native Title, paper presented at the conference on Crossing Boundaries: Anthropology, Linguistics, History and Law in Native Title, Perth, 2000.

Maurice, J. *Warrumungu Land Claim,* Australian Government Publishing Service, Canberra, 1998.

Miller, D. 'Knowing Your Rights: Implications of the Critical Legal Studies Critique of Rights for Indigenous Australians', *Australian Journal of Human Rights,* vol. 5, no. 1, 1998.

Morgan, G. 'Advocacy as a Form of Social Science', in, P. Harries-Jones (ed.), *Making Knowledge Count,* McGill-Queens University Press, Montreal, 1991, pp. 223–31.

Muecke, S. 'Available Discourses on Aborigines', in P. Botsman (ed.), *Theoretical Strategies,* Local Consumptions, Sydney, 1982, pp. 98–111.

——. 'Lonely Representations: Aboriginality and Cultural Studies', in B. Attwood and J. Arnold (eds), *Power, Knowledge and Aborigines,* special edition of the *Journal of Australian Studies,* La Trobe University Press in association with the National Centre for Australian Studies, Monash University, Clayton, 1992, pp. 32–44.

Myerhoff, B. *Number Our Days,* Dutton, New York, 1978.

Myers, F. R. *Pintupi Country, Pintupi Self: Sentiment, Place and Politics among Western Desert Aborigines,* Australian Institute of Aboriginal Studies and Smithsonian Institution Press, Canberra/Washington, DC, 1986.

National Inquiry into the Separation of Aboriginal and Torres Strait Islander Children from their Families (Australia). *Bringing Them Home: Final Report,* Human Rights and Equal Opportunity Commission, Sydney, 1997.

Neate, G. *Aboriginal Land Rights Law in the N.T.,* Alternative Publishing Co. Chippendale, 1989.

——. 'Proof of Native Title', in B. Horrigan and S. Young (eds), *Commercial Implications of Native Title,* Federation Press, Annandale, 1997, pp. 240–319.

Osborn, P. G. *Concise Law Dictionary,* Sweet & Maxwell, London, 1993.

Palmer, K., Macdonald, G. and McIntyre, G. 'Engagement for Services by Contract', *Australian Anthropological Society Newsletter,* no. 79/80, 2000, pp. 16–21.

Paul, M. The Role of History in Native Title Litigation, paper given at The Use of History in Native Title Processes workshop organised by the Australian Institute of Aboriginal and Torres Strait Islander Studies, Native Title Research Unit, 1999.

Pearson, N. 'The Concept of Native Title at Common Law', in G. Yunupingu (ed.), *Our Land is Our Life: Land Rights Past, Present and Future,* University of Queensland Press, St Lucia, 1997.

——. 'Our Right to Take Responsibility', discussion paper prepared for the Aboriginal leaders and community members of Cape York Peninsula, June 1999.

Peterson, N. 'Foreword', in P. Sutton, *Country: Aboriginal Boundaries and Land Ownership in Australia,* Aboriginal History Monograph no. 3, 1995, pp. vii–viii.

Poole, R. *Nation and Identity,* Routledge, London, 1999.

Povinelli, E. 'Settler Modernity and the Quest for an Indigenous Tradition', in D. Gaonkar (ed.), *Alternative Modernities,* Duke University Press, Durham, NC, 2001, pp. 19–48.

Reynolds, H. *The Other Side of the Frontier,* Penguin, Ringwood, 1982.

——. *The Law of the Land, Penguin,* Ringwood, 1987.

Rigsby, B. 'Anthropologists, Land Claims and Objectivity: Some Canadian and Australian Cases', in J. Finlayson and D. E. Smith (eds), *Native Title: Emerging Issues for Research, Policy and Practice*, Research Monograph no. 10, Centre for Aboriginal Economic Policy Research, Australian National University, Canberra, 1995, pp. 23–38.

——. 'Genealogies, Kinship and Local Group Organisation: Old Yintjingga (Port Stewart) in the late 1920s', in J. Finlayson, B. Rigsby and H. Beck (eds), *Connections in Native Title: Genealogies, Kinship & Groups,* Centre for Aboriginal Economic Policy Research, Australian National University, Canberra 1999, pp. 107–24.

Ritchie, D. 'Constructions of Aboriginal Tradition for Public Purpose', in S. Toussaint and J. Taylor (eds), *Applied Anthropology in Australasia,* University of Western Australia Press, Nedlands, 1999, pp. 255–81.

Ritter, D. *The Mediation Process and the Parties to It,* Native Title Loose Leaf Service, Butterworths, Sydney, 1996.

——. 'The Rejection of Terra Nullius in *Mabo*: A Critical Analysis', *Sydney Law Review,* vol. 18, no. 1, 1996.

Ritter, D. and Garnett, M. 'Building the Perfect Beast: Native Title Lawyers and the Practice of Native Title Lawyering', in L. Strelein (ed.), *Land, Rights, Laws: Issues of Native Title,* Issues paper no. 30, Australian Institute of Aboriginal and Torres Strait Islander Studies, Canberra, 1999.

Roberts, A. 'The Development of Australian Oral History, 1798–1984', *Oral History Association of Australia Journal,* no. 7, 1985.

Rose, D. B. *Hidden Histories: Black Stories from Victoria River Downs, Humbert River and Wave Hill Stations,* Canberra, Aboriginal Studies Press, 1991.

——. 'The Treatment of Historical Evidence in the Yorta Yorta Case', in M. Paul and G. Gray (eds), *Through a Smoky Mirror: History and Native Title,* Native Title Research Series, Aboriginal Studies Press, Canberra, 2002, pp. 35–48.

Ross, S. *Ethics in Law: Lawyers' Responsibility and Accountability in Australia,* 2nd edn, Butterworths, Sydney, 1998.

Rowley, C. D. *The Destruction of Aboriginal Society,* Australian National University Press, Canberra, 1970.

——. *The Remote Aborigines,* Australian National University Press, Canberra, 1971.

——. *Outcasts in White Australia,* Australian National University Press, Canberra, 1971.

Royal Commission into Aboriginal Deaths in Custody. *Final Report of the Royal Commission into Aboriginal Deaths in Custody*, vols 1–5, Australian Government Publishing Service, Canberra, 1991.

Rumsey, Alan. 'Language and Territoriality in Aboriginal Australia', in M. Walsh and C. Yallop (eds), *Language and Culture in Aboriginal Australia*, Aboriginal Studies Press, Canberra, 1996, pp. 191–206.

Sansom, B. 'Aborigines, Anthropologists and Leviathan', in N. Dyck (ed.), *Indigenous People and the Nation-state*, Institute of Social and Economic Relations, Memorial University of Newfoundland, St Johns, 1985, pp. 67–94.

Schechner, R. 'Magnitudes of Performance', in R. Schechner and W. Appel (eds), *By Means of Performance: Intercultural Studies of Theatre and Ritual*, Cambridge University Press, Cambridge, 1990.

Schultze-Berndt, E. Simple and Complex Verbs in Jaminjung, PhD thesis, Nijmegen, Netherlands, 2000.

Scott, J. C. *Seeing Like a State: How Certain Schemes to Improve the Human Condition Have Failed*, Yale University Press, New Haven/London, 1998.

Shaw, B. 'Aboriginal Australian Life Histories as Personal Documents and Historical Artefacts', *Oral History Association of Australia Journal*, no. 7, 1985.

Sheridan, S. 'Wives and Mothers Like Ourselves, Poor Remnants of a Dying Race: Aborigines in Colonial Women's Writing', in A. Rutherford (ed.), *Aboriginal Culture Today*, Kangaroo Press, Sydney, 1988.

Simon, W. 'Visions of Practice in Legal Thought', in A. Hutchinson (ed.), *Critical Legal Studies*, Rowman & Littlefield, Toronto, 1989.

Sinnamon, V. and the Kunjen Elders, Kowanyama. *Towards Aboriginal Management: Alice-Mitchell River National Park*, Kowanyama Aboriginal Land and Natural Resources Management Office, Cape York, 2000.

Stanner, W. E. H. *After the Dreaming: Black and White Australians—an Anthropologist's View*, The Boyer Lectures, Australian Broadcasting Commission, Sydney, 1968.

Stewart, J. *Report to the Minister for Aboriginal Affairs Under Section 10(4) of the Aboriginal and Torres Strait Islander Heritage Protection Act 1984 on the Kakadu Conservation Zone*, Australian Government Publishing Service, Canberra, 1991.

Strang, V. 'An Appropriate Question? The Propriety of Anthropological Analysis in the Australian Political Arena', in P. Caplan (ed.), *The Ethics of Anthropology: Debates and Dilemmas*, Routledge, London, 2003.

Strehlow, T. G. 'Notes on Native Evidence and its Value', *Oceania*, vol. 6, no. 3, 1936, pp. 323–35.

Sullivan, P. *A Sacred Land, a Sovereign People, an Aboriginal Corporation: Prescribed Bodies and the Native Title Act*, North Australia Research Unit Report Series, Report no. 3, North Australia Research Unit, Australian National University, Canberra, 1997.

——. 'Problems of Mediation in the National Native Title Tribunal', *Anthropology in the Native Title Era*, Australian Institute of Aboriginal and Torres Strait Islander Studies, Canberra, 1995.

Sutton, P. 'Forensic Anthropology in Australia: Does it Have a Case to Answer?', in J. Finlayson and D. E. Smith (eds), *Native Title: Emerging Issues for Research, Policy and Practice*, Research Monograph no. 10, Centre for Aboriginal Economic Policy Research, Australian National University, Canberra, 1995, pp. 83–100.

——. *Native Title and the Descent of Rights*, National Native Title Tribunal, Perth, 1998.
——. *Aboriginal Country Groups and the Community of Native Title Holders*, Occasional Papers, National Native Title Tribunal, Perth, 2000.
Thomson, A. 'Fifty Years On: An International Perspective on Oral History', in 'Tales of the Century', *Oral History Association of Australia Journal*, no. 21, 1999.
Tindale, N. B. Unpublished Field Journal, 1953–54, held by the South Australian Museum.
——. *Aboriginal Tribes of Australia*, University of California Press, Berkeley, 1974.
Tonkinson, R. 'Anthropology and Aboriginal Tradition: The Hindmarsh Island Bridge Affair and the Politics of Interpretation', *Oceania*, vol. 68, no. 1, 1997, pp. 1–26.
Toussaint, S. 'AAS Professionalisation Committee: Report on "Contemporary Issues" for Annual Conference, University of New South Wales, 10–12 July 1999', *Australian Anthropological Society Newsletter*, no. 77/78, 1999, pp. 5–6.
——. 'Unfinished Business': Plural Anthropologies in Australia?, paper presented at the World Anthropologies Symposium, Wenner-Gren Foundation, Venice, March 2003.
Trigger, D. 'Towards a Cultural Resolution', *Australian*, January, 2000, p. 27.
Trigger, D., Robinson, M. and Gladstone, L. 'Anthropology and Consultancy Contracts in the 1990s: Who Owns Your Brain? A discussion paper commissioned by and prepared for the Professional Committee of the Anthropological Society of Western Australia (ASWA)', *Australian Anthropological Society Newsletter*, no. 74, 1998, pp. 5–10.
Tully, J. *Strange Multiplicity: Constitutionalism in an Age of Diversity*, Cambridge University Press, Cambridge, 1995.
Tushnet, M. 'An Essay on Rights', *Texas Law Review*, vol. 6, 1984.
Turner, V. *From Ritual to Theatre: The Human Seriousness of Play*, Performing Arts Journal Publications, New York, 1982.
Upston Hooper, K. 'Slaying the Leviathan: Critical Jurisprudence and the Treaty of Waitangi', *Victoria University of Wellington Law Review*, no. 28, 1998.
Watson, P. 'This Precious Foliage: A Study of the Aboriginal Psycho-active Drug Pituri', *Oceania* Monograph no. 26, University of Sydney, 1983.
Williams, N. *The Yolgnu and Their Land*, Stanford University Press, Stanford, California, 1986.
Willshire, William Henry. *The Land of the Dawning : Being Facts Gleaned from Cannibals in the Australian Stone Age*, Thomas, Adelaide, 1896.
Wilson, W. R. Sillitoe's Tartan in Northern Australia, Honours thesis, History, Northern Territory University, 1996.

Index

Aboriginal Councils and Associations Act, 66–7 *passim*; 81
Aboriginal and Torres Strait Islander Commission, 83, 215 (fn.11)
Aboriginal Land Rights (Northern Territory) Act 1976, 1, 54, 61, 70, 75, 79, 169
Aboriginal Legal Service, 6, 121, 178, 180, 182–3, 185–6, 189
advocacy, 25, 153, 159–60, 209 (fn.7)
Alice Springs, 142–151 *passim*; *see also* Arrernte claim, *Hayes v. Northern Territory*
Anunga Rules, 53
arbitration, 125, 127
archaeology, 18, 34, 41, 49, 162, 167
Arrernte, claim, 142–151 *passim*; *see also* Alice Springs, *Hayes v. Northern Territory*
Australian Anthropological Society, 65–6, 105

Balangarra people, 160, 171, 173, 179
Beckett, Jeremy, 64–5
Bellevue Crescent v. Morland Holdings, 145
Berndt, R. M., 162–3
black armband history, 19, 142, 154, 208 (fn. 27)
Brennan, J., 88–91, 133; on extinguishment, 91; *see also Mabo*

Carpentaria Land Council, 77–8
Central Land Council, 143–44, 148
Coe v. Commonwealth, 88
colonisation, 22, 34, 49, 97, 135, 137, 140, 148, 153, 166, 195, 200; prior to, 137, 179, 188
common law, 67, 86–8, 97, 134, 159, 166; limits of 94–5; rules, 169
compensation, 86, 126–7, 136, 140
confidentiality issues, 32–3, 60–2, 102, 183; 105–20 *passim*
connection reports, 79, 80, 101–3, 149, 213 (fn. 1)
consent determination, 101, 121–4, 136; *see also* Nharnuwangga, Wajarri Ngarlawangga
critical legal theory, 128, 130–2, 138, 140
Croker Island claim, 24, 30, 103; *see also Yarmirr v. Northern Territory*
cross-disciplinary research, 66, 84–85, 103, 150–1, 175, 191, 196; problems associated with absence of, 33, 66, 189–91, 202–3
cross-examination, 32, 61, 105, 111, 113–4, 166, 197
cultural continuities, 93, 123, 186, 188, 190; *see also* language and linguistics
customary law, 35, 38–9, 42, 68, 72, 88–9, 91–2, 102, 104, 123–33, 164, 166–7, 173, 179, 186, 203, 210 (fn. 10)

Daniel v. Western Australia, *see* Ngarluma/Yindjibarndi claim
Delgamuukw v. British Columbia, 55, 217 (fn. 46)
disclosure, 106–7, 111, 113, 115; protection from, 116, 129
dispossession, 15, 19, 123, 135, 137, 143, 153, 157, 204; *see also* colonisation
Dodson, Michael, 141
Dreaming associations, 20, 84–5, 173

economics, communities, 204; development, 104; purposes, 98
Edmunds, Mary, 26

estate groups, 170, 173, 185
ethics, anthropologists, 59, 65, 105–6, 119, 129; journalists, 109; lawyers, 129; practice issues, 202; restricted material, 212 (fn. 8)
ethnography, ethnographic research, 23, 29–30, 33, 51, 62–3, 79, 82, 113, 118, 145, 149, 167, 168, 171–2, 212 (fn. 8)
evidence, Aboriginal claimants 52–3, 57, 169, 175; absence of, 89; anthropological 82, 89, 123, 168, 173–4; claim books, 109, 114; complementary, 175; Commonwealth Evidence Act, 27, 109–11, 149; contamination of, 158; email 80; exclusion of, 208–9 (fn. 2); genealogies, 54; hearsay, 166, 168; historical, 57, 145, 147, 157, 165–6, 174, 195; land claims, 25, 31, 79, 123; linguistic, 42, 44, 47, 49, 53; on oath, 116; oral history, 148, 170; peer review, 81; rules of, 5, 99; Queensland government requirements, 103; reports, 186, 187; video, 112, Western Australian government requirements, 101; women's restricted, 54; *see also* Arrernte, Miriuwung Gajerrong, Ngarluma/Yindjibarndi, Yorta Yorta
expert witness accounts, 24, 27, 31, 80, 107, 110, 116, 152–3, 156, 159–60, 162, 167, 169–70, 180–1, 185, 197, 209 (fn. 10); *see also* guidelines for expert witnesses
extinguishment of native title, 2, 88, 91, 93–4, 126, 134, 137, 140, 143, 149, 162, 217 (fn. 47, 51, 54) definition of, 94; in relation to mining leases, 124, 203–4; in relation to pastoral leases, 95, 203–4; partial extinguishment, 161, 204; *see also* Native Title Act, native title

factionalism, politicking, conflicts, 76, 78, 83, 129, 179, 183–4
Fejo v. Northern Territory, 94
fiduciary duties, 71, 139
Foster v. Mountford, 106
future acts, 78, 98, 114, 118, 129

genealogies, 79, 102, 112, 210 (fn. 21); as evidence, 54, 163, 170–1, 182
Goodall, Heather, 145
governance, 71, 74–5
Gramsci, Antonio, 206, 215 (fn. 25)
guidelines, for expert witnesses, 152–3, 156, 160, 197; *see also* expert witness accounts

hearsay, 24–8, 32, 166–8, 209 (fn. 21)
hegemony, 131, 215 (fn. 25)
Hayes v. Northern Territory, 142–151 *passim; see also* Arrernte claim and Alice Springs
heritage surveys, 109, 112, 114, 117, 126
Hindmarsh Island Dispute, 81
Holocaust, 22, 198
hunting, gathering and fishing activities, 14, 17, 37, 173, 200, 203–4; rights 92, 124, 136

identity, 4, 10–11, 15, 20–3, 36, 71, 82, 153, 173, 176, 190
Indigenous Land Corporation, 122
Indigenous Land Use Agreements, 121, 125–7, 143
inequalities, health, 10, 23; in negotiations, 14; legal, 130, 135; racial, 132; social and economic, 129, 134, 138; social injustice, 141; structural, 131–3, 138, 199
informed consent, 70, 76, 147
intellectual property rights, 78, 81, 120

Kaberry, Phyllis, 162–3, 170, 188–9
Keep River National Park, 160, 168, 173, 180
Kimber, Dick, 148
Kimberley Land Council, 178, 181
Kofod, Frances, 162, 172, 187
kinship, 71, 82, 170

Langton, M. 22, 208 (fn. 32)
language, 25–49 *passim*; borrowing, 42, 44–6; change, 43; of rights, 132, 134, 172; of history; *see also* linguistics
Lee, J. *see* Miriuwung Gajerrong, *Ward*
legal privilege, 61–3, 84; waiver of, 109; 105–20 *passim*
linguistics, 25–49 *passim*; continuity, 34, 36, 48–9; glottochronology, 43; prehistory, 41; stratigraphy 37, 49; *see also* language

Mabo decision, 1–2, 4, 58, 64, 67, 69, 87–8, 92, 97–8, 133–134, 142, 163, 205; *see also* Brennan, J.
Macdonald, Gaynor, 110–11
Maddock, Kenneth, 26, 162
Madgwick, J. *see* Nharnuwangga, Wajarri Ngarlawangga, *Clarrie Smith v. Western Australia*
massacres, 17, 19, 38, 157
Maurice, J., *see* Warrumungu claim
mediation, 79, 83, 98, 100, 102–4, 117, 123, 127, 130, 135, 139, 143
memory, 21–2, 33, 38, 110, 147, 157–8, 198

methodological issues, 26, 32–3, 62, 81–2, 84, 118, 141, 145–8, 155, 166, 170, 185, 197
Milirrpum v. Nabalco, 1, 28, 42, 89, 142
mining, 77–8, 122–3, 126–7, 136–7; agreements, 140; leases 95, 203–4
Miriuwung Gajerrong claim, 2, 6–7, 31, 53, 57, 89–90, 195–201; 1998 claim, 173–4, 181; claim area, 178–90; 2000 appeal, 161, 171, 174; 2002 appeal, 194, 203; archaeology, 190–1; composite claim, 180, 193; cultural continuities, 186, 190; customary land tenure, 179; estate groups, 185–6; evidence, 31, 163, 166, 168, 184, 189; expert witnesses, 180–1, 186–9, 201; history on trial, 199–201; genealogies, 170–1, 187–8, 190, 192; landowning units, 193; language, linguistics, 171–2, 191; mining leases, 203–4; oral history, 166; pastoral leases, 94–5, 180, 203–4; sovereignty, 174; Western Australian government opposition, 181, 183

national parks, Queensland, 9–23 *passim;* Western Australia, 95
National Native Title Tribunal, 54, 91, 98–9, 103, 122, 125–6, 140, 143, 180, 205
Native Title Act, 3, 67, 70, 75–7, 86–7, 96, 127, 130, 133, 136, 160, 205; 1998 amendments, 4, 73, 79, 83, 149; preamble to, 98, 216 (fn. 44); specific sections in, 89, 91–2, 94, 124–6, 137
native title, definition of, 93; as right, 133; as 'bundle of rights', 161; determined as 'fact', 160, 169; group membership, 82, 86, 98, 134, 164; off-shore, 91, 213–4 (fn. 5); recognition of, 2, 87–8, 216 (fn. 45); revival of, 94; survival of, 164, 182; *see also* extinguishment, evidence
Native Title Representative Bodies, 52, 59, 63, 64, 77, 80–1, 83, 129, 178
Native Welfare Department, 153
negotiated agreements, Queensland, 102
Ngarluma/Yindjibarndi claim, 24, 27, 31, 61, 113–4, 116, 118, 153
Nharnuwangga, Wajarri Ngarlawangga, 5, 113, 116, 118, 122, 121–7, 135–7, 156
Nicholson, J. *see* Ngarluma/Yindjibarndi
Northern Land Council, 50–7 *passim;* 178, 181

Olney, J. *see* Arrernte, Croker Island, Yorta Yorta
oral history, 54, 57, 148
Ord River Irrigation Project, 95, 161, 176–7
overlapping interests, 78, 101, 185

pastoralists, 122–3, 153; pastoral leases, 2, 95, 121, 124–5, 143, 161, 180, 203–4; pastoral stations, 177; *see also Wik*
patrilineal, 40, 51, 89–90
Pearson, Noel, 139, 212 (fn. 2)
peer review, 79–80, 119
Prescribed Bodies Corporate, 67–76 *passim*
proof, burden of, 134, 162–3, 175, 216 (fn. 45)
property law, 68–9, 137
public interest immunity, 108, 115, 120

Queensland government, guidelines, 102; team approach, 104

Racial Discrimination Act, 2, 124, 218 (fn. 81)
rations, 146–7
reconciliation, 3, 22, 199
registration test, 78, 99–100
removal of children, 17, 147, 153, 207–8 (fn. 3), 219 (fn. 13); *see also* stolen generations
reconciliation, 3, 8, 22
referendum (1967), 145
representations, politics of, 10–11, 19–21, 71–2, 86, 185; of history, 198; of law, 139
Reynolds, Henry, 142, 154–5
rights discourse, 131–2
Ritchie, David, 12, 208 (fn. 19)
Robinson, Michael, 24–5, 111–3, 116, 208 (fn. 2); *see also* Ngarluma/Yindjibarndi claim
Royal Commission into Aboriginal Deaths in Custody, 53, 207 (fn. 3)
Rose, Deborah Bird, 147
Rumsey, Alan, 38, 42, 162

Said, Edward, 10
self-determination, 23, 67, 72–5, 137
Shaw, Bruce, 166, 187
silence, in historical record, 142, 151, 154, 157, 165, 196, 198, 202
site protection, 107, 114–5, 126–7
Smith v. Western Australia, see Nharnuwangga, Wajarri Ngarlawangga
social justice, 132–3
songlines, 41
sovereignty, 90, 92–4, 134, 137, 197, 162–3, 167, 171, 174
Stanner, W. E. H., 142, 145, 154
statute law, 86, 95

stolen generations, 17, 147, 153, 207–8 (fn. 3), 219 (fn. 13); *see also* removal of children
state agreements, 101
subjectivity in research, 26–7, 54, 197
subpoenas, 105–7, 110–11, 113, 117
succession, 91, 93, 179
Sutton, Peter, 37, 41, 62, 110–11, 119

terra nullius, 1, 97
Tonkinson, Robert, 65
Toohey, J., 28, 89, 94
Towney v Minister for Lands and Water Conservation, 110–11, 119
trade, trading routes, 56–7
traditional laws and customs, *see* customary law
traditions, problematic definitions of, 10, 12, 15, 39, 92, 135, 147, 204–5, 207 (fn. 2)
treaties, 74

Waanyi case, 87, 91, 93
Ward decision, 94–6, 103, 124–5; *see also* Miriuwung Gajerrong and Lee, J.
Warrumungu claim, 29–30, 84, 109–10, 114–15
Western Australian government, guidelines, 101
Wik decision, 87, 94–5, 143–44, 220 (fn. 2); *see also* pastoral leases
witness statements, 113, 150

Yanner v. Eaton, 92
Yarmirr v. Northern Territory, 24, 30, 92; *see also* Croker Island
Yorta Yorta, 3, 92, 96, 103, 135, 147; Rochelle Patten's testimony, 205; constructions of tradition, 135, 204; issues of connection, 103; selective use of history, 135, 147, 204–5; 2002 appeal, 204–5

Printed and bound by CPI Group (UK) Ltd, Croydon, CR0 4YY

16/09/2026

14963438-0001